Education, Industrialization, and Selection

George Timmons

To what extent does secondary education contribute to the process of selection in industrialized societies? The relationship between education and selection can be seen as a tenuous one, implying that something like market forces are in operation. Or, this relationship might even be described as covert and part of a conspiracy hatched by an élite to maintain existing inequalities.

In the light of such diametrically opposing views, George Timmons has set out to compare the education systems of four advanced industrial nations – Britain, France, the United States, and the Soviet Union. He exposes great similarities in their response to the social, economic, and political pressures which accompany the later stages of industrialization. Adopting an historical as well as a sociological approach, he shows how the development of modern education systems since the Second World War has legitimated the process of selection, especially with regard to recent emphasis on vocationalism.

Education, Industrialization, and Selection will have much to offer students of comparative education as well as sociologists and historians.

George Timmons is Lecturer in Education, University of Warwick.

Education, Industrialization, and Selection

George Timmons

ROUTLEDGE
London and New York

First published in 1988 by
Routledge
11 New Fetter Lane, London EC4P 4EE

Published in the USA by
Routledge
in association with Routledge, Chapman & Hall, Inc.
29 West 35th Street, New York NY 10001

Typeset by Times Graphics, Singapore
Printed in Great Britain by T.J. Press (Padstow) Ltd, Cornwall

British Library Cataloguing in Publication Data
Timmons, George
Education, industrialization, and selection.
1. Education, Secondary — 1965–
I. Title
373'.09172'2 LB1607

ISBN 0-415-00702-X

Library of Congress Cataloging in Publication Data
Timmons, George, 1936–
Education, industrialization, and selection/George Timmons.
p. cm.
Bibliography: p.
Includes index.
ISBN 0-415-00702-x
1. Comparative education. 2. Education, Secondary.
3. Industrialization. 4. Labor supply — Effect of education on.
5. Education — Social aspects. I. Title.
LB43. T56 1988 87-30789
370. 19--dc19 CIP

Contents

Introduction 1

Part 1 Early indications of the relationship between industrialization and education 5

1 Industrialization and social change 7

2 Education and society in the first half of the nineteenth century 24

3 Developments in education in the second phase of industrialization: the beginning of selection 30

Part 2 Education becomes the most important agent of selection in industrial societies 59

4 Industry and education in the first half of the twentieth century: selection by differentiation 61

5 Britain, France, the USA, and the USSR as advanced industrial societies 98

6 Education for advanced industrial countries 122

Part 3 Selection now 155

7 Selection: educational or social? 157

8 The legitimation of selection 169

Epilogue 206

Name index 227

Subject index 232

Introduction

There is much confusion in our thinking about the ways in which secondary education contributes to the process of selection in industrialized societies and this confusion has increased in recent years because the relationship between education and selection has become much subtler. Indeed, from certain political standpoints the relationship can be seen as tenuous or diffuse, suggesting that something like market forces are in operation. On the other hand, looked at from a different political angle, the relationship could be described as more obscure or covert than formerly and part of a conspiracy hatched by an élite to keep 'the lower orders' in subjection.

That two such diametrically opposed views can be held of the same education system suggests that our understanding of how education works is not very clear. Yet there was a time, not so very long ago, when the secondary schools of countries like the USA, the USSR, Britain, and France were quite clearly meant to educate only the few who would enter into the superior positions in society. Admittedly, universal secondary education was introduced into the USA rather earlier than into the other countries, but the origins of secondary education in America are nevertheless very similar to theirs. Furthermore, the stages of development through which all these systems have passed are also remarkably similar, even though the overall time scales and even the length of particular periods within those scales may differ from country to country. This suggests that whatever has happened to their education systems is somehow linked with their progress as industrial nations, and that as their forms of industrial organization have become more sophisticated so have their education systems, particularly at the secondary and higher levels. Moreover, with such increasing complexity, the purposes of education proliferate and become less easy to separate one from another. Hence the confusion in our thinking especially when we try to understand a problem such as selection.

However, what makes the problem even more difficult is that changes in the means of production, increases in the variety of things produced, and greater concentration on services, depend also on the structure of society: they are affected by it and also bring about changes in it. In fact, education is only one, though a very important one, among a number of social forces which both help to shape and are in their turn shaped by the process of industrialization.

The final part of this book is concerned with selection mechanisms in the education systems of four countries, the United States, France, the Soviet Union, and Britain (England and Wales), all of which can be described as advanced industrial nations. It also draws attention to the growing importance in all these countries of vocational education and vocational guidance to the process of selection and shows how they help to legitimate the selection which undoubtedly takes place even in supposedly egalitarian societies. However, how the mechanisms function and are made acceptable can be better understood if they are set against a background of how industrial societies have developed particularly during this century and most especially since the Second World War, and it is for this reason that the first chapter tries to unravel the way in which industrialization, social change, and developments in education are related to each other, because that very interplay forms the substance of selection (which is meaningless unless described in terms of the structure of society in which it exists). It is also hoped that some of the confusion which surrounds education in all the countries concerned can be dispelled. With this in mind an historical as well as a sociological line is argued because it seems that only from these two perspectives can the increasing demands made on education be delineated with any clarity, especially as those demands are not always compatible with each other, at least not at first sight. The importance of making comparisons between countries should also be seen: they all exhibit certain characteristics which seem to be due to their industrial progress and even their contrasting political ideologies cannot prevent them from changing their education systems in response to the economic requirements of advanced industrialization, especially as they are in competition with each other, to some extent at least.

The period since the Second World War is the most important one to be dealt with because it has been during that time that the pressures exerted on education systems have been most clearly recognized by the governments of the countries concerned. The contradictions within the systems they inherited from the past have forced them all not only to expand secondary and higher education but also to change the structure of both. Such developments have obscured selection. However, it continues to exist – as it must – but it has to take on more sophisticated forms: the fundamental principle remains but the mechanisms change. This situation has arisen partly because of the increase in the number and the variety of occupations which accompany advanced industrialization, but it is made more problematical because such occupational possibilities increase the likelihood of social mobility. Moreover, it has been politically expedient in all four countries to expand educational opportunities, even though at first sight, such developments may seem to be incompatible with selection and especially the cruder forms of it which operated before the war and in modified form after the war. Patterns of secondary and higher education have to be adopted through which selection can continue to operate in a less drastic and therefore less obvious way, and through which the raised aspirations of quite large numbers of people can be catered for, because even covert selection will lead to discontent and unrest unless it is accompanied by some sort of process which makes it more palatable generally to most people. The acceptance of educational qualifications by the majority of people in a society will go some way towards alleviating tension of this kind, provided that the routes to those qualifications are not too restricted. What has happened in all four countries is that the number of possible qualifications has increased (though certain of them retain their crucial importance) making education a maze through which the pupil (and his parents) need the help of an expert guide. However, the guidance itself can play a part in the process and indeed, in all the countries described here, it has become one of the ways of making selection more acceptable.

Even though the main theme of this book – how selection operates in industrial societies – can be seen emerging clearly only in the second half of the nineteenth century, it is quite instructive to look at the earlier period because some of the confusion about the meaning (and therefore the social consequences of) industrialization derives from what occurred before 1850 – and particularly in England and Wales. Most models of industrial society, even now, are influenced by theories – such as those of Marx – which attempted, soon after the early events of industrialization, to explain what happened during that early period.

Part 1

Early indications of the relationship between industrialization and education

1

Industrialization and social change

It is obvious now, in the second half of the twentieth century, that a healthy education system is important to the working and further development of the economy. No government, whether of an advanced or a developing country, would leave education to chance or even to market forces. This was recognized in the nineteenth century. Two countries in particular, Germany and Japan, deliberately set about organizing their education systems in order to speed up the modernization of their economies through industrialization. And yet the country in which extensive industrialization first occurred, i.e. Britain, seemed largely unconcerned about educational provision until after 1850. This has led some historians to play down the importance of education to early industrial development. However, as Musson and Robinson show[1] there were all sorts of links between early industrial growth in Britain and a whole host of educational influences, many of which, though short-lived and only partly institutionalized, were effective. Nicholas Hans also claims[2] that the eighteenth century was not a period, as once supposed, of educational stagnation and decline, and that even the nine great schools with their obscurantist attitudes, made a contribution to economic development. However, for a number of reasons which included the growing distinction between science and technology, the undoubted success of seemingly uneducated entrepreneurs like Richard Arkwright and the political and social turmoil of the late eighteenth and early nineteenth centuries, the relevance of education to industrial development was obscured[3] even though it was the intention of some educational initiatives (such as those of the Lunar Society) to influence the economy.

On the other hand, the social significance of education was not ignored during the same period: academies (whether dissenting or otherwise), many of the endowed schools in the eighteenth century and the proprietary and reformed public schools in the early nineteenth century stressed the importance of moral development. Indeed, the advice not to use the nine great schools (as far back as the late seventeenth century) was given on the grounds that they were bad influences. Locke recommended the private tutor instead. However, much more significant were the efforts, no matter how puny at first, made to educate the poor. These ran from the period after the Restoration when support for charity schools became popular (particularly with the 'middling sort'), through the eighteenth century when schools of industry and then Sunday schools were introduced, and into the nineteenth century when the denominational elementary schools were established in increasingly significant numbers. These schools, important though they could be to economic developments, were primarily organs of social control, as their founding statutes (where they still exist) and their curricula clearly indicate.

What is also significant is that both these functions of education were occurring together and during a period of what is recognized as being one of momentous change. Moreover, though in some absolute sense the two ought to be compatible with each other, usually they are not: there has always been tension between them, so much so that they have often run counter to each other in all the four countries here under consideration. Indeed, the relationship, that tension between them, has been a very important factor in the way the systems of educational institutions have developed in Britain, Russia, France and the United States. The relationship may have varied over time, with the economic function predominating at one stage and that of social control at another, but they have always been there. For example, the establishment of the Science and Art Department was motivated by the economic needs of Britain in the 1850s, whereas the regularization of the control of elementary education through the creation of the Education Department in the same decade grew out of the desire to 'gentle the masses'. Similarly, the rapid expansion of education in the USA at the turn of the last century was caused as much by the need to Americanize immigrants as to cater for the requirements of the rapidly expanding economy. If we look at these two examples a little more closely, we find that the interplay between these two factors is considerable. They do not merely occur together, they influence each other. The possibility of science and art qualifications encouraged the extended use of the elementary schools which in turn helped to deepen their curriculum. In the same way, the American city systems were enlarged to deal with the social problems perceived as attendant on mass immigration and encouraged the view amongst the wider population that education could be a vehicle of social mobility which in turn meant that the new occupations created by the rapidly developing economy could be filled.

However, what is more interesting is that these two basic causes of the expansion of education, for that is what they are, hardly appear before the modern period. They are indicators of modernization, hallmarks of industrialization. Accordingly, it is necessary to look at industrialization and the social consequences which flowed from it, in order to understand why education systems developed in the way that they did from the eighteenth century onwards. Firstly, let us consider industrialization. An extended quotation from Hobsbawm would be useful here:

> What does the phrase 'the Industrial Revolution broke out' mean? It means that some time in the 1780s, for the first time in human history, the shackles were taken off the productive power of human societies, which henceforth became capable of the constant, rapid and up to the present, limitless multiplication of men, goods, and services. This is now technically known to the economists as the 'take off into self-sustained growth'. No previous society had been able to break through the ceiling which a pre-industrial social structure, defective science and technology, and consequently periodic breakdown, famine and death, imposed on production. . . . If the sudden, qualitative and fundamental transformation . . . was not a revolution then the word has no commonsense meaning. The Industrial Revolution was not an episode with a beginning and an end. To ask when it was 'complete' is senseless, for its

> essence was that henceforth revolutionary change became the norm. It is still going on; at most we can ask when the economic transformation had gone far enough to establish a substantially industrialized economy, capable of producing, broadly speaking, anything it wanted within the range of the available techniques, a 'mature economy' to use the technical term.[4]

Spelt out further, what this meant was that first the British economy, and then others, a little later, but in some cases even more rapidly, went from being concerned primarily with agriculture to being concerned largely with manufacture. Furthermore, this transformation was based on changes in technology which took a good deal of production into factories where new sources of power could be used to drive machinery more efficiently than before. It usually also meant that industrial towns grew in size and number, especially when factors such as fuel and raw materials could be brought together easily, often because of improvements in transport – as seen in the development of the cotton towns of Lancashire. Moreover, because the factories were in private, and usually few hands, this meant that industry was organized for profit, i.e. it was a capitalist form of production and this had serious consequences for the structure of the developing industrial society. Bilton *et al.* say:

> Industrialism involves basic changes in the structure of a society. A fundamental change is that, in industrial societies, most people become employees. This is in marked contrast to non-industrial societies, where three-quarters or more of the occupied population are employers, self-employed, or family workers. The change to a society dominated by wage-labour is a relatively recent one which is associated with the factory system of production . . . (which) . . . developed alongside craft and domestic systems of production and took some time to supersede them – never replacing them entirely. . . . The craft system operated within a society marked by poverty, deprivation and brutal exploitation. There was, nevertheless, a difference in the nature of the relationship which existed between craft employers and employees, in that it was a *personal* relationship in which both . . . had mutual

> obligations much broader than anything expected today. . . . (Factory) . . . workers . . . (on the other hand) . . . were subject to the discipline of employers who required that they worked regular hours with regular intensity. Although legally free, they were subordinate and dependent both economically and socially.[5]

In most factories, the way the work was organized also had a depressing effect on the workers as they repeated simple tasks over and over again. Adam Smith, who described how the making of pins could be hugely profitable when each stage in the process was performed by a different worker, also said that this would tend to deprave them. And Karl Marx later wrote that though the division of labour might make the initial gaining of profits easy, competition between the capitalists, especially when most of them had adopted the new technologies, would lead them to reduce both employment levels and wages thus depressing the conditions of the operatives still further. To an extent this did happen – indeed, Marx's analysis of the iniquitous social relationships of nineteenth-century capitalism was based on descriptions of actual conditions in the north of England provided for him by Friedrich Engels. However, these descriptions were probably out of date even when Engels sent them. While the conditions of workers remained bad for many years to come (and still are, even now, in some instances), the 'dark satanic mills' picture of industrialization *at its worst* was valid only for a relatively brief period, though its horrors were repeated over again in the countries of this study (and others) as they industrialized. But there are two meanings to the term division of labour and this can lead to difficulties. Krishan Kumar writes:

> It was this, the *detailed* division of labour, rather than simply the division of labour in society at large, that Adam Smith in a famous passage in *The Wealth of Nations* has described and advocated. . . . It was this aspect of the division of labour that Marx took as central to the process of capitalist industrialization. . . . The social division of labour implied no more than that independent producers bought and exchanged commodities among themselves, subject to no other authority than market forces and free

competition. The division of labour in the workshop, on the contrary, implied the absolute and despotic authority of the capitalist over the workers.[6]

Let us take first this latter sort of division of labour. It had far-reaching effects on societies and it dominated the early changes in them as it widened the gap between the classes, depressing members of one to degradation, as Adam Smith said it would, and amassing for members of another, wealth the like of which had never been seen before. It also encouraged political conditions of conflict between those classes. Now, whether the class structure described by Marx was a product solely of this workshop division of labour is arguable: what is important at this point is that it certainly appeared to be a factor, especially in the decades either side of the year 1800 in Britain because, in certain sections of the economy, change was very rapid, the rate of industrialization being accelerated by the wars with France. The numbers of people subjected to the workshop division of labour certainly increased and its ill-effects became all too apparent in the uncontrolled mushrooming of industrial towns especially in the Midlands and North. This was what Marx seized upon. His analysis of capitalist society was not without justification because the working classes *were* exploited by the bourgeoisie. Perhaps the all-important socio-economic relationship of the nineteenth century, and maybe the twentieth too, was the exploitation by those who owned the means of production of those who had nothing to sell but their labour or their intelligence or their skill, of whatever variety. This is what made it appear that the workshop division of labour was the crucial factor – and for a time it may have been, especially as it did appear that the landed gentry and aristocracy might cease to be important, leaving the future struggle to take place between the proletariat and the bourgeoisie, which Marx saw as the crucial consequence of the industrial mode of production.

Furthermore, the dark satanic mills picture, short-lived though it might have been, was no mere image for those who suffered from it. Its mesmerizing effect is understandable, but it gave rise to other oversimplifications which were to have quite serious consequences for Britain as the first industrial country. This was because it led early factory owners and the like not to understand the implications of the technologies they were using. For example, the changes in textile production did not appear to be brought about by research and development as we understand them: they seemed to be the result of piecemeal changes made by craftsmen. And yet would Arkwright have succeeded without Crompton, a man of considerable education, whom he exploited? Cartwright also is worth a mention here because, though he failed as an entrepreneur, he saw the construction of a powerloom as an *intellectual* challenge, because he had had an education. Furthermore, Arkwright was more dependent on scientists, if we can give such a title to James Watt, than he was prepared to admit. There is extant a letter from Watt to his father-in-law, in which he wrote:

> as to Mr Arkwright, he is to say no more, one of the most self-sufficient ignorant men I have ever met with. Yet . . . whosoever invented the Spinning Machine, Arkwright certainly had the merit of performing the most difficult part, which was making it useful. . . . Some years ago he applied to us at two different times for our advice which we took the trouble to give him in one or more big letters, which he never had the manners to answer.[7]

As the textile industry grew to be the most important in Britain, and probably the world, such factors were forgotten or ignored by the entrepreneurs: everything seemed to depend instead on the exploitation of the machine operatives. The same was true in the mines which provided fuel for these factories, and drove the trains and later the steamships by means of which they obtained their raw materials and distributed their finished products. Technology (and behind that, science) had made possible mining on a large scale – not only in the form of the steam engine which pumped out the floods and hauled up the coal but also because of Buddle's exhaust fan and Davy's safety-lamp. Yet the actual digging of the coal remained crude and miners little more than savages, which again made the relationship between mineowner and miner appear to be the only one which mattered. The production of iron, using the Cort process, can be interpreted in the same way. But from the very beginning, the new technologies which lay behind these developments were having an impact on the social structure – and not simply through the creation of the capitalist class on the one hand and the proletariat on the other – though this is significant. This refers rather to how the work which people engage in helps to give them their identity – the technology they use affects their consciousness of themselves and their position in society, i.e. their sense of who they are in relation to everybody else. And even early industrialization created a greater variety of roles, or occupations, than merely those of the unskilled operative and the entrepreneur. If we refer back to the Kumar quotation we can look at the other meaning of the phrase, division of labour, what he calls 'the social division of labour' which at its simplest means the variety of occupations. That variety increased and can be detected increasing even in the very early modern period. Its social consequences can also be observed.

This has presented writers on social change with something of a problem. Was it due to industrialization or to something else? It was certainly evident before the point of industrial take-off described by Hobsbawm (above). However, Hobsbawm does point out that the process of industrialization was under way long before the 1780s – that decade simply marks what historians consider to be the point of no return. Moreover, a number of factors contributed to the creation of conditions which permitted take-off – commercial expansion, changes in agriculture, the development of new and very necessary financial mechanisms, the existence already of capital-intensive industries such as coal, and so on – all had gone some way towards effecting the dismantling of feudal relationships which had characterized earlier social structures. Moreover, earlier forms of industrial organization, such as the domestic system of textiles, were not without sophistication. More importantly perceptions of social relationships were changing long before take-off point was reached. P. J. Corfield says that this can be seen from the changes which were taking place in the terms used to describe the structure of Georgian society. She refers to the falling into disuse of the custom of doffing one's hat to social superiors and then continues:

> As well as the intricacies of body language, eighteenth-century England was also innovative in its use of words and

> concepts to describe society. Notably, it brought into currency one new collective noun, eventually of great and controversial resonance. But 'class' in the eighteenth century glided into the language. It was then a new, modernizing term. The impulsion of social change had the effect of making the old terminology of 'rank and order' seem at first partisan, then archaic and finally obsolescent.[8]

She also says that this new expression of relationships referred to socio-economic status and not to birth and parentage. The implication of this was that the new relationship was more dynamic because ' "Classes" could adapt, emulate, co-operate, compete, or conflict, whereas "ranks" were serried not to say regimented'.[9] Furthermore they refer to broader, looser social categories which led to the use of a three-fold classification. This was a gradual process – at first through the use of the terms 'higher', 'middling', and 'lower' ranks. However, these were transformed into 'upper classes', for which Corfield maintains idleness was not necessarily a criterial factor; 'the middle classes', a term less open to 'satirical representation'; and 'the working classes', which gave the toiling masses more dignity than their earlier nomenclature, this last being an interesting point, in the light of Adam Smith's comment on the effects of the workshop division of labour on the same people!

This complicates matters for us because we can see that Marx's interpretation of society has some force behind it – the means of production and the technologies which go with them have important consequences for the social structure and, as we saw earlier, the workshop division of labour went a long way towards creating the proletariat and the bourgeoisie. But his writings taken in toto show that he saw industrial development as much more complex. Braverman says that:

> Marx shows how the processes of production are, in a capitalist society incessantly transformed under the impetus of the principal driving force of that society, the accumulation of capital. In the working population this transformation manifests itself first as the continuous change in the labour process of each branch of industry and second as the redistribution of labour among occupations and industries.[10]

However, Marx isolated what he saw as the crucial factors and ignored others in order to stress their importance. To some extent his arguments are justified by the early events – but not only by them. The essential features of capitalist society could have continued to have an underlying significance in the second half of the nineteenth century (Braverman says even now). However, we are not helped in trying to unravel all of this by the ambiguity of the terms 'division of labour' and 'class'. Moreover, the situation became even more confusing as industrialization proceeded because not only did the technologies become more highly developed and in some cases obviously science-based, but also the increasing scale of production led to innovation in administration and marketing which in turn affected the social structure. The number and variety of occupations increased even more rapidly. With occupations in mind it is worth considering what Max Weber has to say about social stratification – to dispel some of the confusion.

In part, he is in agreement with Marx that the economic structure is important especially in terms of social class, but he does not agree completely on how that relationship works. Moreover he also thought other factors, such as prestige, could be involved. Bilton *et al.* say that:

> Weber certainly did regard capitalism as a class society – economic relations form the basis of inequality. We might suppose from this that Weber is merely echoing Marx's theories but in fact Weber emphasizes the importance of the *market* as the economic basis for class much more than *property*. For him, the primary cause of inequality in capitalism is *market capacity* – this is the skills brought to the labour market by the employee. Differences in reward between occupations result from the scarce skill held by the occupational group. If the skill is in demand, the reward will be high.[11]

Weber is not denying that property is important, but he is saying that patterns of occupation have also to be considered, and one thing we know is that in the long run those patterns became more intricate as industrialization progressed. Weber also saw status as related to class, not only through occupations but also through the life styles which accompanied them: he is worth quoting at some length, despite the density of his language.

> we may speak of a class when (a) a number of people have in common a specific causal component of their life chances, in so far as (b) this component is represented exclusively by economic interests in the possession of goods and the opportunities for income and (c) is represented under the conditions of the commodity or labour market. In contrast to classes, status groups are normally communities. They are however often of an amorphous kind. In contrast to the purely economically determined 'class situation', we wish to designate as 'status situation' every typical component of life fate of men that is determined by a specific positive or negative social estimation of *honour*. This honour may be connected with any quality shared by the plurality and, of course, it can be knit to a class situation: class distinctions are linked in the most varied ways with status distinctions. Property as such is not always recognized as a status qualification, but in the long run it is, and with extraordinary regularity . . . with some oversimplification one might say that classes are stratified according to their relation with the *production and acquisition of goods*; whereas 'status groups' are stratified according to the principles of their *consumption of goods* as presented by special 'styles of life'.[12]

We need to look at this question of status a little more closely, but firstly we should note that what Weber is saying was meant to complement Marx's view of class, and not contradict it, even though one implication of it is that societies are stratified in a more complex way than in Marx's essential division into bourgeoisie and proletariat. In fact Marx was aware of that complexity in industrial societies. Goldthorpe says that though Marx did not find the notion congenial,

> this is the case of his discussion of the 'intermediate strata' within capitalist society – that is the strata made up of occupational groupings whose class situation was neither that of the bourgeoisie nor of the proletariat but in some sense lies between the two. . . . For Marx, the 'third

> parties' – *dritte personen* – which existed along with the two great classes of capitalist society could be said to be of two clearly different kinds. On the one hand, there were those groupings which . . . were destined . . . to decline. . . . On the other hand, however, there were third-party groupings which were clearly in expansion: either new groupings, largely created by the development of capitalism itself, or groupings . . . which had found it possible to survive, and to flourish, within capitalist society.[13]

And this would fit with what Braverman says (above).

If we accept this view of the structure of nineteenth-century society, we can see that it dovetails with that of Weber, where occupations and the skills required to engage in them are criterial factors in describing the gradations of that society. Furthermore, it does not preclude the continued acceptance of Marx's notion that the owners of the means of production are of paramount importance: it also describes more faithfully what we know historically of the divisions in society after 1850. Moreover, this combination of the ideas of Marx and Weber, because it stresses the importance of occupations of the *dritte personen*, can go some way towards explaining what happened to a changing society undergoing the *second* stage of industrialization when advancing technology and increasing complexity in organization created a greater variety of occupations not only in industry and commerce but also throughout the whole of society. Goldthorpe commenting on a view of this expressed by Sorokin in the 1920s says that,

> he seeks to show that the results of the available statistical studies of mobility in such societies all point to the same general conclusion: namely, that a considerable volume of both intergenerational and intragenerational mobility occurs, at least in occupational terms, and that in the recent past the trend appears, if anything, to have been towards an increase in mobility, notably in the movement of men from manual into the expanding forms of non-manual employment.[14]

Not that people always recognized this immediately at the time. Perhaps the factory owners, and Marx, had a vested interest in seeing the divisions in society as simpler than they really were – the former because it helped them to justify their continued exploitation of their employees and he because it suited his vision of future political developments. Even so, people in general are loath to drop their traditional perceptions of each other.

For this reason we need to think again of status and what Weber has to say about it, because as we saw, though he described it as linked with class, it is different. It is concerned with prestige, which may be attached to how a person acquires, or is endowed with, the wherewithal to live, but is not necessarily so. What can happen is that status can hide true economic relationships, especially where people continue to think of themselves and others in traditional ways. In fact, there is usually a lag between changes in economic relationships and changes in status. In Britain in the second half of the nineteenth century this is why, though the occupational structure was changing, many people persisted in thinking of themselves and others in outmoded ways. As we shall see in Chapter 3, this had important consequences for education. Indeed it was one of the causes of the failure to realize just how important education was to economic development (which is where this chapter began) and helps to explain why many of those with high status, when they did supply education to those with low status, saw this in moral terms so that elementary education's most important purpose – for them – was social control.

However, much more important is the other aspect of status to be taken from Weber's definition of it because this provides us with part of an explanation for the countervailing force in society, i.e. one which ran *with* changing economic relationships and against traditional notions of social relationships. He says that prestige is attached to life style and that this is strongly linked with consumption of goods. What industrialization did was to provide goods – and in the second half of the nineteenth century, a far greater variety of goods – for all classes. This meant that, though large numbers of poor people continued to fare badly, there was an increasingly important section of society (*dritte personen*?), which, able to take advantage of the increase in the number of occupations, began to consume, in some small degree at least, like their supposed betters. Because this affected their status, it also altered their perceptions of themselves, and, even more important, their aspirations. This process has gathered momentum in all advanced societies right up to the present day. There may be a submerged tenth (at times of depression, more than this) of the population but life styles have become more alike, and if what Weber has to say carries any weight, this means that statuses have also been changing. However, status is a vague notion and so, though social class and social status remain closely linked, that very relationship often masks the fact that class is the more important of the two. The reason for this is that, though status alone might give a temporary or tenuous access to power, class gives a stronger and more enduring access because it gives control over resources. Such control might be wrested from the grip of powerful groups in time of very rapid social change, e.g. during a revolution, but even then, if a group can actually gain or retain control over resources, it will have power. Different classes have different levels of power. Parkin says that 'to speak of the distribution of power could be understood as another way of describing the flow of rewards; the very fact that the dominant class successfully claims a disproportionate share of rewards vis-à-vis the subordinate class, is in a sense a *measure* of the former's power over the latter'.[15]

In the early stages of industrialization where power lay was more easily perceived than has been the case since. Again, Marx's notion of the distribution of power according to control over the means of production seemed to fit the social facts of the initial stages of technological development, but the elaboration of the social structure which occurred when the intermediate strata expanded and became more differentiated internally, obscured the patterns of power which underlay social relationships. It could be that the difficulty we now have of locating where real power lies stems from what Giddens refers to as power's two different facets. He says:

> that power has two aspects: a 'collective' aspect, in the sense that the 'parameters' of any concrete set of power relationships are contingent upon the overall system of organization of a society; and a 'distinctive' aspect in the sense that certain groups are able to exert their will at the

> expense of others. The mediation of control is thus expressed in terms of 'effective' power, manifest in terms of the capacity either to take, or to influence the taking, of decisions which affect the interests of two or more parties differentially.[16]

These two are present at one and the same time: 'effective' power is there – in one sense made manifest in how decisions are actually taken, and yet in another sense not manifest because it *appears* to work within the 'parameters' of collective power which arise out of the total social structure, i.e. the conventions, such as the political institutions of that society, which can give the outward appearance of a wider spread of power than actually exists. The real distribution is hidden and this is not surprising. We should remember that the social structure itself is not always clear to the individuals who make it up, concerned as they are, more often than not, with status rather than class, i.e. with life style rather than occupation, though it is the latter with its measure (no matter how weak) of control over resources which decides where they are placed in the power structure.

What is important, and as we will see later, very important for education, is how people understand the social milieu in which they exist, their perceptions of reality. With further industrialization it became more difficult to understand that reality as the interrelationships became more complex. The two forms of the division of labour were both at work. The number of gradations in society increased as the primary sector of the economy (largely farming) became less important and, to begin with, the secondary sector (for the most part, manufacturing), and then the tertiary or service sector grew in importance, making the terms 'working class' and 'middle class' less easy to define as each one covered ever-wider sets of occupational categories. Knowing where one ended and the next began became problematical. Now, Braverman maintains that though this process might have stimulated new craft skills (e.g. boiler making) in the nineteenth century, in the present century further developments (e.g. Taylorism) in the workshop division of labour have led to the deskilling not only of blue-collar workers but white-collar too: Marx is still relevant.[17] But people misinterpret their own positions because even the status of the de-skilled occupations gives access to goods. Many Americans, for instance, believe that they live in conditions of fluidity where social mobility is easy. (Even Marx thought that the USA was exceptional in this respect. Whether this 'exceptionalism' is justified does not matter: all advanced industrial countries have relatively high rates of social mobility.)[18] Blau and Duncan[19] say that the sort of stratification which has developed in modern America means that classes have very little socio-political significance, i.e. they hardly exist, so that where an individual might be situated in relation to others depends upon either a Samuel Smiles type of personal effort or even on good luck. Davies and Moore put forward similar notions.[20] If people believe this, and there is evidence to show that many do, then the chances are that they accept the status quo because they believe their aspirations can be met and that where inequality of condition exists it is somehow legitimate. On the other hand, other commentators on advanced societies, such as Mosca or Pareto,[21] maintain that democracy itself is a myth and that real power is held by certain ruling élites. Yet others, such as Dahl[22] claim that there are several élites and that entry into them is easy, almost a matter of choice. He also says that, though large-scale participation in decision making by the mass of people is only occasional, it occurs often enough to legitimate the power of the élites. What is certain is that in all the countries under discussion here the political ideologies usually proclaimed by their governments are democratic in tone so that their political institutions must have at least the appearance of democracy, and most people in France, Britain, the USA and even the Soviet Union, despite their often expressed cynicism, seem to accept this.

That there should be several different paradigms of the structure of modern societies should not be surprising because not only are these societies integrated in very complicated ways, but also the relationships between the basic ingredients of social stratification, i.e. class, status, and power, are very difficult to define and people are never quite sure what they mean by these: the three are no longer as congruent as they were in the past. Nevertheless, this confusion is a very important factor in understanding how education developed in each of these countries because it is not only the relevance of education to the development of the skills required in an industrialized country which matters, but also how people aspire to schooling. Had the lower orders remained merely the bottom rungs of the serried ranks (i.e. been fixed as in some caste systems), they would never have aspired to education. People's perceptions of themselves are important – indeed, Barnett maintains that the British working class retained some element of 'lower rank' identity and he uses this to explain the lower level of educational ambition which they displayed in comparison with their counterparts in the USA even in the twentieth century.[23] Nevertheless, many of them did desire more education because they recognized the possibilities offered by extension of occupations – whether skilled, semi-skilled or even de-skilled.

Now, we could be in danger of jumping the gun because even in the second half of the nineteenth century class divisions were still clearly drawn in all countries. Furthermore, status coincided very directly with class and so did the distribution of power. The intermediate stratum, there from the beginning, was about to expand rapidly, but as yet not sufficiently to throw doubt on traditional notions of social relationships – except perhaps in the USA where traditions were a little different anyway because of the frontier and because the aristocratic class as it existed in Europe, hardly figured at all. But even in America the sort of education available followed class lines.

Before we leave this section, the point should be made now, because it will be important to the rest of what has to be said, that education as a means of selection can only be understood when put in the social setting in which it works. All societies are stratified – and, according to how class, status and power are related to each other in each case. Put at its simplest, this means that occupations are important and so are life styles and their patterns of consumption – as industrialization progressed towards greater technological and organizational sophistication, this became more apparent, especially as education was recognized as a means of improving both of these.

Therefore, we need to consider how the economies of each of these countries changed after 1850, but before we look at the effects of these changes, especially on education, perhaps we should briefly discuss the kind of education available in each of them and how it fitted their individual economic structures.

2

Education and society in the first half of the nineteenth century

Though the three great reports on education in Britain occur in the 1860s, they describe the systems of an earlier period. The Newscastle Commission of 1861 enquired into elementary education, i.e. the education of the lower orders. The word 'elementary' is important because education thus described provided little more than basic literacy and numeracy: it was not primary, and therefore to be followed by something else, but was whole and entire in itself and considered all that was needed by the hewers of wood and the drawers of water. Its architect was Sir James Kay-Shuttleworth, who, when secretary to the Committee for Education, a sub-committee of the Privy Council, had introduced inspectors into those denominational schools which depended on government grants. He had used the influence which this gave him to dismantle the monitorial system and had advocated class teaching. He had also improved teacher training but he saw elementary education as a form of social control – as an innoculation against Chartism – 'to rear the population in obedience to the laws, in submission to their superiors'.[1] The Clarendon Report of 1864 enquired into the state of the education of the ruling classes (whom everyone recognized as such) to be had in the nine great schools, which had become distinct from the other endowed schools. Only later were they to become the core of what we now call the public schools. There were several proprietary schools which even then could be considered as being in this category also. The clientele of these superior schools was made up from the sons of the aristocracy and gentry, the upper echelons of the professions and some of the new capitalists. Sitting between these two sections came the schools looked at by the Taunton Commission of 1868, i.e. the endowed schools, though this report like Clarendon also considered the new proprietary schools. Taunton graded the schools by saying that:

> Education, as distinct from preparation for employment can at present be classified as that which is to stop at 14, that which is to stop at about 16, and that which is to continue till 18 or 19; and for convenience we shall call these the Third, the Second and the First Grade of education respectively . . . . It is obvious that these distinctions correspond roughly, but by no means exactly, to the gradations of society.[2]

The clients of the first grade were hardly distinguishable from those who attended the Clarendon Schools, but the pupils of the second and third grade institutions came from the new middle class which, as we saw in Chapter 1, was emerging from the eighteenth century onwards, though it was not until after 1870 that its great expansion and increase in complexity came. The point to be stressed here is that those divisions in education followed the pattern of social stratification found in British society at the time. The educational echelons were distinct and there were virtually no links between them – just as there were few social links between the groups which attended each set of schools. Furthermore, those with the highest status, whether measured according to their possession of property or according to their life-styles, sent their children to the nine great schools, or had private tutors. The status of those using the Taunton schools was lower, but though graded according to his three categories, was still much higher than that of those attending the schools reported on by Newcastle. All of this was quite obvious at the time and so was the fact that power was distributed in the same way: it fitted the class structure of the time, and any exceptions were rare.

What has been said about British education could be shown to be true for American education, at least as far as the basic structure is concerned. Of the period immediately after the Civil War, Bowles says:

> A system of class stratification developed within this rapidly expanding educational system. Children of the social élite normally attended private schools. Because working-class children tended to leave school early, the class composition of the public high schools was distinctly more élite than the public primary schools. And as a university education ceased to be merely training for teaching or the divinity and became important in gaining access to the pinnacles of the business world, upper class families used their money and influence to get their children into the best universities, often at the expense of the children of less élite families.[3]

What is important here is not only that the same tripartite classification of education as in England and Wales can be discerned but also that status and power are distributed according to social class in a much more obvious way than is to be the case later, and that the configuration of the education system follows class lines without causing any vociferous outbursts against inequality of educational opportunity.

In nineteenth-century France the situation was the same, even though the struggle between the Church and State over the control of education often distracted attention away from the basic divisions within the system. The lycée was established by Napoleon in 1802 in order to train the new élite and by 1833, Guizot could insist that every commune should maintain its own primary school:

> The rudiments of education were to be given not to ensure greater equality but to acquaint future citizens with their duties. . . . To Guizot must also be attributed the doubtful honour of having formalized primary and secondary education into two separate educational channels rather than into two consecutive levels: a state of affairs that lasted until 1859.[4]

The backwardness of nineteenth-century Russia meant that education developed more slowly there than in any of the other countries under discussion. Nevertheless, education did exist but followed the social divisions in the same way as in Britain, France and the United States. Furthermore, because the certainties of those social divisions were so much stronger in Czarist Russia, the appropriateness of the educational divisions were seldom questioned by the majority of people, even after the abolition of serfdom in 1861, though this did result necessarily in the expansion of elementary education and even to a low-level form of social mobility.[5]

So then, the circumstances which prevailed in each of the countries, about the middle of the nineteenth century, were such that a selective function for education was hardly discernible. Though the English examination system was beginning to take shape about this time, and the crucial building block of the French system, i.e. the baccalaureat, already existed, selection was not really undertaken by the schools, but by parents when they decided to which schools they would send their children, or whether they would send them at all. Selection was much more obviously social rather than educational and it operated according to the class divisions which prevailed in each country, and because class coincided, as we have seen, with status and both of these with the division of power, then no real articulation between the various parts of the education systems was deemed necessary.

The great educational reports of the 1860s in Britain illustrate the relationship between class, status, power, and education in a country undergoing industrialization because the links between them at that time can be so graphically illustrated. However what is significant here is that this was probably the last period of British, French, or American social history when these factors fitted together so neatly. From that time onwards the pressures of continued industrialization were made more readily recognizable and led to changes in education, because the ways in which large numbers of people earned their livings changed. Moreover, the occupational changes which occurred after 1860 were much subtler than the earlier ones and had much more serious consequences for education. Indeed, the kind of occupational differentiation which occurred in Britain, France, and the United States in the second half of the nineteenth century (later in the case of Russia) is what made articulation between the parts of their education systems necessary and also obliged them to become, in a more thoroughgoing way, agents of selection. Though the occupational structures of all four countries show variations, this is understandable as the timing and rate of industrialization is different in each case – at first, at least. However, they do become more similar as time goes on. Even so perhaps a word should be said about this, at this point, in order to justify the kind of comparisons made later in the book.

Because industrialization occurred in Britain first, it sometimes seems as if it was of an order different from that which took place in other countries later. However, it can be argued that industrialization is all of a piece no matter where it occurs. Habakkuk says of the first half of the nineteenth century:

> There was no significant difference in the stock of fundamental ideas available to technologists. In this period, Britain and the USA, along with Germany and France and some of the smaller European countries, shared a common stock of such ideas, in that there were many people in each country who were intellectual masters of the notions underlying the new developments in technology. From this point of view, these countries form a group clearly distinguished from most of the rest of the world.[6]

Admittedly, this leaves out Russia, but with so many examples of industrialization before her, she was able to catch up quickly later and did so from a firmer base than is sometimes imagined (see below). This is not to deny that there were differences. Britain's experiences were bound to be affected by the fact that there were no precedents for her to follow, whereas France, the United States, and Russia were all affected by what happened in Britain.

French industrial progress was slowed down by the political turmoil of the revolution of 1789, by the rule of Napoleon, and then by the effects of his overthrow. Moreover, the peasantry, left in an entrenched position, proved to be one of the most conservative forces in Europe. In America, the seemingly ever-expanding frontier, the aspirations of the emigrants, and the very size of the United States were such as to make the McCormick reaper *appear* at first as the most important of the American exhibits at the Great Exhibition (1851), important, that is, to the economic future of the Unites States. Russia was hardly in the race.

Nevertheless the differences can be exaggerated: industrialization was already underway in all of these countries and its nature in each case was not so different from what had occurred in Britain. The mass production of both textiles and leather goods was already to be found in France before 1860, and the first spate of French railway building had already happened. The signs of the United States' industrial greatness were already to be seen: the Singer sewing machine and the Colt revolver were also exhibited at the Crystal Palace and the methods used to make these are now recognized as being crucial influences on the way in which not only American industrialization was to proceed, but industrialization everywhere. Even Russia was beginning to stir: British spinning machinery had been introduced in the 1840s and ten years later there were a million spindles in operation there, which made the Russian textile industry the fourth largest in Europe (after Britain, Germany, and France).[7] Furthermore, Russia was producing a quarter of a million tons of pig iron by the middle of the century.[8] Lastly, it must also be remembered that, according to the census of 1851, Britain was not yet an industrialized country. What is more, Britain's early lead was (ultimately) to work to her disadvantage because the changes which had taken place, though not as thoroughgoing as often imagined, were dramatic and created that stereotyped image of industrialization, the mesmerizing effect of which was to make further change painful, especially as the divisions of labour which had already occurred made further divisions or newer sorts of division difficult.[9]

If we next consider the changes which did take place in the industrial structures of these countries in the second half of the nineteenth century, we then might have a clearer notion of why their education systems changed as they did, and also why they became more important to the economic futures of those countries.

3

Developments in education in the second phase of industrialization: the beginning of selection

Making comparisons between the economic developments which took place in these four countries is easier for the second half of the nineteenth century than it is for the first: Britain's lead is less and less important and America's real supremacy becomes clear only late in the century. Russia, being so backward, does present problems, even though the bases of her modern industrialization were laid in this period, particularly during Sergei Witte's term of office as minister of finance from 1892 to 1903. Moreover most of the changes which took place in the USA, France, and Britain between about 1850 and 1914 simply occurred later in Russia. Also Russia cannot be discounted as many undeveloped countries could now: her per capita income might have been low, but Russian agriculture was actually in a position, as a result of Stolypin's laws, where it could have produced a surplus with which to feed an urban population and also to buy raw materials, and there already existed the necessary infrastructure of investment.[1] It is not so much Russia's economic backwardness as the autocratic and repressive Czarist rule which has such a distorting effect on developments in Russia. With this in mind, Russia will be dealt with separately at the end of this chapter because weaving into the main body of the text her economic and educational developments does not always ring true. Nevertheless, the relevance of Russian experiences will be shown. The strands can be brought together again in Chapter 4 because this will deal with a period when the similarities between Russia and the other three countries become more obvious.

As for Britain, France, and the United States, there are great similarities in the underlying forces which were at work, even if the details are different in each case. Though it is still a matter of debate, it can be argued that industrialization is likely to proceed according to a particular pattern, once it has got off the ground, no matter where it might occur, as Habakkuk suggests (see above, p. 28). E. Etzioni-Halévy[2] points out that whereas production of textiles, iron, and coal dominated the economic developments of the first half of the nineteenth century, in the second half there was a much greater variety of goods produced by industrial methods and even the older crafts drew on such products. Shipman says that, 'only after 1851 did the organization of large numbers of men mass producing standardized parts through power-driven machinery become profitable'.[3] So Britain was not so far ahead of her rivals, and hence not so different.

Moreover the forms of organization and administration which were developed in this later period were much more complex than earlier ones. If we take an industry such as steel where production leapt astonishingly, we find that technological know-how and scientific knowledge were much more important than they had been when the iron industry underwent its initial expansion: Cort's innovations appear crude when set against those of Bessemer, Siemens, or Gilchrist-Thomas. Moreover the uses to which steel could be put were far greater than those for iron and the size of concerns involved in making steel were far larger: in the USA the average number of employees increased four-fold between 1870 and 1900.[4] British and French expansion was not as rapid as that of the United States but output increased tremendously in both countries: 334,000 tons of crude steel were produced in Britain in 1861; 7,787,000 in 1913. The figures for France are 84,000 and 4,687,000 tons.

One of the reasons for the increased demand for steel was the building of railways. Obviously the great age of railway building in Britain had passed but the network was not completed until after 1850, and it was only then that the revenue from freight came into its own.[5] The demands made by railways on steel production continued to increase and what can be described as a railway industry developed. In France there had been a pause in railway construction after the 1848 Revolution, but the greater stability felt during the early years of the reign of Napoleon III resulted in another spate of building. It was also during this period that the great lines which opened up the United States and linked the various states even more closely together were laid down. But railways were not the only form of transport which contributed to the continuing transformation of the economies of these countries. The steamship also had a considerable impact not only because it was to lead to greater integration of their economies with each other (e.g., of agriculture) but also because it extended their markets for manufactured goods and added another dimension to their industrial development, i.e. the large-scale construction of steel ships which again demanded more steel and also advanced and intermediate technical skills.

However what was really important in this period was the very large increase in the mass production of consumer goods. In America the shortage of labour led to the widespread adoption of Whitney's system of producing interchangeable parts which in turn led to the growth of what was known as the American system of manufacturing (ASM). Though mass production implied the splitting up of work into small tasks to be repeated over and over again, this did not necessarily mean that the majority of workers would become depraved as Adam Smith had suggested they would. This was because these newer kinds of industry (e.g. the production of rayon or of bicycles) required a considerable technical or scientific input and were not so labour-intensive as earlier industrial forms. They also tended to be organized differently. Daniel Nelson has said that the ASM, 'dictated cleaner and healthier work environments, employed more highly skilled and hence highly paid workers, encouraged a decentralized pattern of production management and promoted inside contracting, which preserved personal relationships between labour and management and offered greater opportunities for economic and social mobility'.[6] The ASM was introduced into the Singer Sewing Machine Factory in the 1870s and then spread to other firms. Similarly in Britain, it was a combination of the techniques of Whitworth and those of Bessemer which allowed the precision mass production of goods of all kinds.[7] The same developments occurred in France, though a little later. Dupeux says that the periods, 1895 to 1904, and 1905 to 1913, showed very rapid growth, and modern industries appeared.[8] In fact industrial production tripled between 1895 and 1914.[9]

Just what was happening to the economies of industrialized countries in the late nineteenth century can be seen from the financial columns of *The Times*, if Britain can be taken as typical. Singer, Holmyard, Hall, and Williams say that, 'in the 1860's a growing number of large firms in coalmining, iron making and engineering took advantage of the new laws to raise from the public the capital required by the new technology and expanding output'.[10] They then show how the increasing number of quotations in the stocks and shares index demonstrates that new enterprises of all kinds were developing, for besides gilt-edged securities and the like, the list included railways, telegraph companies, fourteen large brewers, seven large coal and iron and steel firms, and fifty miscellaneous companies which covered the chemical industry and cotton but also great stores such as Liptons, producers of soap (e.g. Sunlight), margarine, jam and Bovril. Here we see the real beginnings of the modern mass market because all classes of people took advantage of what such companies made available to them. Moreover, the channels through which the products were distributed were also important. The wholesale and retail trades began to take on a modern shape at this time and it was not always Britain or America which led the field: the French could be just as adventurous in merchandising – the departmental store being introduced originally in France as far back as the Second Empire. More and more people were involved in distribution, transport and warehousing.

Technical expertise, especially in engineering, but also in chemistry, was becoming more important. Indeed Habakkuk claims that Britain's falling behind the United States in the late nineteenth century was due in part to inadequate fostering of technical skills:

> in iron and steel for example, the founders of the older British firms succeeded by the operation of qualities which were not those required in the 1880s and 1890s. The ability most evidently absent was technical expertise. The later innovations embodied more technical knowledge than the earlier ones, that is, there were fewer within the scope of the ingenious artisan.[11]

Engineering was specially important because the new machines which were to produce masses of identical goods had to do so in a precise way, otherwise interchangeability was not possible. The making of such machines and their maintenance meant that all sorts of levels of skill in metal working had to become more widespread. Veblen referred to engineers and engineering technicians as the general staff of the industrial system saying that without them the mechanical appliances of industry were so much junk.[12]

The greater variety of products created by the advancing industrialization was accompanied by greater complexity of organization. Not only were there more companies, as we saw earlier, but there were also institutions of greater complexity than their predecessors. One reason for this was that so many more of them were large concerns. This was only to be expected in industries such as steel or shipbuilding where new processes made large-scale production possible, not to say imperative, but it occurred in other spheres too. Textile firms in Britain, for example, grew larger between 1800 and 1910: they employed more workers and increased their capacity.[13] Similar changes took place in the United States – even more extensively. Of France, Kemp says that 'in heavy industry there were a number of giant enterprises which had few equals even in Britain. Industrial structure was extremely variegated and included firms of many sizes and very unequal levels of efficiency'.[14] Old and new may have continued to exist cheek by jowl but the new were part of profound changes.

Paradoxically, just when the workshop division of labour was becoming more refined, the social division of labour became more important as a trend in the development of industrial societies. In fact, most of the expansion in industry was not amongst those directly concerned with production, i.e. the actual assembling of goods: the number of low-grade operatives rose only very slowly. The really rapid expansion was in technical and clerical staff: the former because the processes involved required their expert knowledge and the latter firstly because organizations were larger and more complex in structure and secondly because the wider industrial society in which they were situated had become more sophisticated. On the one hand, more and more people were concerned with the day-today administration of the companies within which they worked and on the other more were also required to engage in activities such as buying, selling, and transportation. But it was not only in industry and commerce that the numbers involved in administration increased: the British Civil Service grew from 50,000 in 1880 to 250,000 in 1914;[15] the United States' government service from 7,000 in 1821 to 239,000 in 1901;[16] and the French from 130,000 in 1839 to 500,000 in 1914.[17] Though the initial figure is large for France, this is because of the tradition of centralized government which was strengthened rather than weakened by the Revolution and by what happened afterwards. The increase is enormous just the same. Nevertheless, in their way, the figures for the United States and Britain are equally remarkable especially when their traditional laissez-faire posture is taken into account. However, what the figures show is that, no matter how reluctantly, the governments of all three countries were obliged to regulate more and more the commercial, industrial, and social activities of their populations, because of the increasing complexity of all interrelationships.

Kumar, quoted in Chapter 1 to illustrate the difference between the workshop division of labour and the social division of labour, goes on to say that the latter, 'the spectacular growth in roles and tasks',[18] came as a surprise to Herbert Spencer and was greater mobility, the traditional attitudes displayed by directly in manufacturing were increasing less rapidly than ization. Those roles could not be filled, those tasks could not be completed by a society stratified on the oversimplified lines described by Marx as consequent upon the first phase of industrialization. However, as we know, the proletariat was never homogeneous anyway: there always had been a working-class aristocracy, and many of the new roles were not so inappropriate to this section of the lower orders. Furthermore, there had always been, as even Marx admitted, a set of intermediate strata, no matter how shadowy, between the working class and the proprietors, even in the earliest stages of industrialization when the degradation of the factory operatives was at its worst. This is where the social expansion and proliferation occurred in response to the technological and managerial elaboration taking place: the sort of clear distinctions which had marked society gradually became less easy to discern. Nevertheless, before the turn of the century the broad divisions described by Corfield were still there. It was at the edges that the blurring was taking place, so that though there was greater mobility, the traditional attitudes displayed by classes towards each other were still strong. This was truer of France and Britain than it was of the USA, because this mobility was almost completely structural, i.e. it grew out of the occupational rearrangements suggested above. There was, as yet, very little political leverage behind it. Nevertheless, incomes, particularly of wage-earners, were rising in America and Britain. Kemp says that in France,

> by the end of the nineteenth century the wage-earners were also beginning to aspire to a petty bourgeois mode of existence. In the factory and mining areas higher wage levels and greater stability of employment enabled many workers to rise out of the depths of brutalized poverty characteristic of the first stages of industrialization.[19]

Life-styles, then, were beginning to alter; aspirations to stir. The service sector of each economy was steadily becoming more important as the numbers engaged in agriculture continued to decline even in France (though slowly) and those working directly in manufacturing were increasing less rapidly than formerly and more of them could be classed as skilled. A larger proportion worked in transport (of various kinds and in numerous capacities) or as clerks, or in shops.

Though the relationship between class, status, and power could still be described in the relatively simple terms used earlier, some evidence of dislocation could, therefore, be discerned. The life styles of the moderately rich and the not too poor may have still been quite distinct from each other, but the number of social gradations in each of these societies had increased – hence the aspirations of French wage-earners mentioned by Kemp. Because wages were rising and more ways of earning a living existed, class was less easy to define. Moreover, if we take Weber's notion that status is usually indicated by consumption, then it is as well to remember what was claimed earlier, that the number and variety of goods that were available to *all* classes of people had increased. In this situation status was not so easily assigned as it had been formerly and it coincided less neatly with class. This might explain why, in Britain particularly, lower middle-class snobbery of the kind illustrated by George and Weedon Grossmith's *Diary of a Nobody* was widespread. Furthermore, power was a little more diffuse and expressed in subtler terms. In Britain, 'new model' unionism exerted more influence in the long run than ever had the physical force faction of Chartism led by Fergus O'Connor. Even Robert Lowe, whose views on elementary education made it clear that he was in no doubt about the moral superiority of his own class, recognized that change was afoot. He supported the passage of the Education Act of 1870 largely because the Reform Act of 1867 had given the vote at least to working-class householders in the towns. Expansion of the franchise such as this can be taken as an indication of the new patterns of political relationships which were beginning to take shape. In America, all but four states had universal manhood suffrage by 1870 and blacks had the vote in 1867 though they were actively discouraged from using it. Moreover, 'a series of major strikes – Homestead in 1892, Pullman in 1894, and others – signalled a growing militancy among workers. Labor organizations proliferated; membership in labor unions grew fourfold between 1897 and 1904'.[20] And Dupeux, writing of the period immediately before 1870 in France says that 'the grande bourgeoisie did fear the growing power of the working classes which it had so ruthlessly exploited. The working classes were slowly becoming more conscious of their power as a class.'[21] Universal manhood suffrage was introduced on a permanent basis shortly after this but the first real French equivalent of the British Trade Union Congress, the *Conféderation Generale du Travail*, was not founded until 1895 and even then got off to a very shaky start.

The educational forms which had prevailed in Britain, France and the USA in the first half of the nineteenth century and which had catered for societies where class divisions were obvious and where economic development seemed only tentatively related to scientific knowledge or technical skill were inadequate in the altered circumstances and therefore came under increasing pressure for change. However, the reconstructions which took place in the education systems of these industrialized countries were conditioned by the social climates which prevailed in each of them. Consequently, they were not based on any rational (or even national) plan, mostly because the social forces which had dominated the early phases of industrialization, though they had undergone some change, were still strong, especially in Europe. What happened to education in the second half of the nineteenth century was only the beginning of a modernization process which is still proceeding now. Indeed, the struggle between the forces of conservatism and innovation which occurred at that time resulted in the creation of a set of contradictions, the resolution of which forms one of the main planks in the history of education in the twentieth century. That the contradictions appear to have been resolved rather less painfully across the Atlantic is a mark of the looser social arrangements to be found in the United States in the nineteenth century, and with this in mind, it would be better to deal with education in Britain and France together first.

From reading history backwards, it can be seen that the whole notion of *elementary* education as something separate and complete in itself and only for the lower orders made less sense after 1850. The modern idea of *primary* education for all looks more sensible. However, those who were concerned with the problem of education in 1850 or 1860 had to begin with what they understood, conditioned as they were by preconceived ideas of the relationship between social class and education. Consequently, in spite of the pleadings of reformers such as William Lovett (who advocated comprehensive education as early as 1841[22] as a remedy for the social ills which perplexed Britain at that time) and because of – some might say in spite of – the work of men like Henry Barnard in the United States and Jules Ferry in France, elementary education continued to be the only education available to the working classes for far too long. Nevertheless, it was modified to some extent. Even the notorious revised code in Britain lasted only briefly in its most restricted form because by 1867 the first substantial changes were made in it. From then on it was extended and developed until, with the introduction of a new code in 1890, it appeared quite modern in its scope (though far from it in practice). Nevertheless, social control remained one of its most important functions.

This was also true of French primary education. Prost says that to read, to write, and to count were no longer enough and the elementary schools had to teach '*tout le savoir pratique*' and that included history, geography, and useful sciences.[23] In both countries, these developments occurred in the general body of elementary education and they arose out of the growing realization that the older styles of elementary education were inadequate even as a means of social control, that the lower classes of the second half of the nineteenth century were not those of the first. However, what is even more illuminating is that the elementary systems of Britain and France actually threw up what were, in effect, their own secondary forms. In the case of Britain a distinction became discernible between the lower and upper standards, especially after standard seven was added, and resulted in the establishment of higher tops or even higher-grade schools in separate buildings. These latter schools often developed into serious rivals to local grammar schools because the education they gave was more relevant to the changing occupational structure of the time and they offered marketable qualifications (usually Science and Art Department or Royal Society of Arts examination certificates). In France elementary education was 'for the people' and in no sense '*le vestibule*'[24] to secondary education, but in the second half of the nineteenth century it was reorganized into three sections – elementary, intermediate, and advanced (*supérieur*). This latter course was originally launched in 1833, in a flush of enthusiasm for Prussian methods of education, but failed then because so few children went on beyond the initial stages of elementary education. When the courses did survive (e.g. l'école Turgot in Paris) they provided for the working-class élite. Their revival in the 1880s put them into competition with parts of the secondary system. Like the higher-grade schools they were preferred to certain secondary courses because they offered an education more directly relevant to opportunities for jobs.

Such developments in elementary education were almost inevitable. They formed part of an attempt to give coherence to an area of education which was surrounded by confusion and lack of definition. Elementary education (in the British meaning of the words) was a nonsense. The three Rs have no moral value[25] of their own and this was shown by Tufnell (HMI and friend of Kay-Shuttleworth) who closed the elementary school in the village of Eton for gross immorality, though its 'academic' record was excellent, just at the time when Robert Lowe was claiming in an unacknowledged letter to *The Times* that the three Rs were the essence of moral education.[26] The three Rs make sense as 'primary' education (again the British meaning) because they are the basic tools of education: it is what they make possible which endows them with moral purpose, or any other purpose. Robert Lowe, and so many like him before and since, did not understand this and tried to make what we, with the benefit of hindsight, now call primary education do a job it could not do. What it *could* do was lead to secondary education. Hence the divisions which occurred in the British and French elementary system: they were meant to make the first part primary and the second part secondary, because that would give education a useful meaning in the conditions of the time and in England this division was introduced not by the central government but by school boards concerned to provide for the industrial and commercial needs of their immediate surroundings. Such a development was a true response to the second phase of industrialization which was best served by universal primary education followed by a form of secondary education which firstly would cater for the extension in the variety of occupational roles which was taking place at that time, and secondly reach a larger proportion of the population.

Secondary educaton in both Britain and France, however, remained too narrow and restricted to too few people. Nevertheless, the pressure for change brought about by the developing circumstances was not without effect. Though it was to remain surprisingly resilient for a long time, the classical curriculum began, during this period, its long descent towards obscurity (though it still retains some importance in France). New subjects were introduced on a regular basis – foreign languages, modern subjects (history, geography) and science. Mathematics had already managed to secure a foothold, dating back to the seventeenth century. Moreover the numbers receiving secondary education increased and included more girls than in the past.

Both the Clarendon and Taunton Reports had recommended that the curriculum of secondary schools should be extended and that science should be introduced on something more than the squalid and intermittent basis on which it was to be found in most schools. Yet the Devonshire Commission (1870–75) claimed that the public schools, with the honourable exception of Rugby, had done little about it. The other endowed schools had made progress but it was only in the 1880s and 1890s that science, urged on by men like Huxley and Playfair, made any real headway but by then the challenge (though on a narrow front) was beginning to be felt from the higher grade schools and the realization began to dawn that Science and Art Department grants could help relieve some of the financial embarrassment which many schools felt. This was particularly so if they were willing to become organized science schools and therefore make themselves eligible for special grants. Typical of schools which did this was Bablake school in Coventry which became an organized science school in 1890, but by then its headmaster was Joseph Bates who had, whilst head of St Peter's elementary school, graduated from London University after having obtained Science and Art Department qualifications in evening classes. Bablake had always been more prepared than its rival, Henry VIII School, to provide an education of direct use to the industries and trades of the city.

Such differences between secondary schools were typical. A résumé of Bablake's curriculum appeared in the Bryce Report of 1895 because it was a good example of a particular kind of endowed school. This report does indicate the extent to which many of the grammar schools had improved. It also claimed that secondary education was still inadequate and that the greatest deficiency was lack of coherence in the system, what it called the administrative muddle. The confusion was due partly to the lack of definition of the relationship between elementary and secondary education. Where technical education fitted in seemed to be even more imponderable. Bryce claimed that it fell into the secondary sphere but others, such as Morant, were determined to keep it in the elementary sector. The ad hoc way with which technical education in Britain was dealt helps to explain the problem and also throws light on how education had to respond, willy-nilly, to the changing conditions.

The lack of skilled labour and of technological expertise, the lack of acquaintance with science, and the uninspired nature of British design led to fully justified fears that Britain could not compete on equal terms with her up-and-coming rivals, particularly the United States and Germany, but also France. The establishment of the Science and Art Department was one move in the attempt to solve the problem. Another was the establishment of the City and Guilds of London Institute for the Advancement of Technical Education, which took over and extended the technological examinations formerly administered by the Royal Society of Arts. This also led to the establishment of the polytechnics. However it was not until 1889 that Parliament became involved and passed the Technical Instruction Acts which permitted the newly established local authorities, through technical instruction committees, to support technical education out of the rates. County and County Borough Council response was not too encouraging until Whisky Money[27] became available for the purpose. Technical instruction committees such as that for London (where to add to the confusion it was known as the Technical Education Board) became very active in the encouragement of technical scientific and commercial subjects in all sorts of schools – elementary evening classes, technical schools (which some town corporations had set up or which had evolved out of earlier institutions such as mechanics institutes), art schools and so on. They made grants to endowed schools for almost any subject other than Latin and Greek and they also gave impetus to the practice, already established in some areas, of supporting children from elementary schools so that they could enter grammar schools by means of scholarships. Sidney Webb, when secretary to the London Technical Education Board, maintained that through its activities a ladder was provided from the gutter to the University. All this has been dealt with at some length because it shows how even in a country where so many influential people were complacent about education, the system responded to the new needs. The response might appear haphazard, but two things are obvious and they are the beginning of trends which were to become more important. The first is that there is a proliferation of forms of education whether elementary or secondary in order to deal directly with the demands of further industrial progress. The second is that the parts of the system are no longer separate from each other: they begin to overlap. This is not simply due to the proliferation, because articulation can also be delineated –

particularly with the early form of scholarship system. Even though no one is willing to define either elementary education or secondary education or the relationship between them, they are becoming related to each other, nevertheless, and in a way which both caters for the new industrial needs and attends to the growing aspirations of ever-larger sections of the community.

Central control of education in France meant that the system, and particularly the secondary sphere, had that coherence which British education lacked and this made the whole ethos of French education appear different. Yet because the same sorts of forces were at work in French society, certain underlying trends similar to those in Britain can be observed within secondary education just as they were within elementary education. The classical curriculum retained its primacy in the lycée but attempts were made to reduce its aridity and the instructions from 1890 onwards aimed at making it '*emperique*' mostly by stressing the importance of the explication of texts – in such a way as to make pupils 'reflect on the moral nature of man'.[28] But even this reform was really meant only to deflect the criticism that classics did not cater for the needs of the time, and the point of the criticism appeared sharper because since 1852 a rival had appeared when the science baccalaureat had been introduced. Now science had formed part of secondary education since the Revolution but from 1852 it had more prestige, even though this 'bifurcation' had been condemned by many *agrégés*, and teachers still encouraged the brightest pupils to proceed towards the literary side. Attempts to strengthen the science side were made during the 1880s but even these reforms were gradually dismantled. Then in 1890, bifurcation came to an end and a single baccalaureat was reintroduced: it was in two parts, the first being common to all and the second divided into two sections, one philosophic and the other scientific. However, in practice, entrance to the grandes écoles was more likely through the classical side and so a further elaboration was introduced in 1902. All pupils were to follow a classical cycle for four years with Greek being introduced in the third or fourth year. Then the next two years were divided into three sections: (a) Latin and Greek, (b) Latin-modern languages, (c) Latin-science. Then a fourth, (d) languages-science, was added. However this fourth section had an origin rather different from the others and its history is instructive.

The original advanced primary schools in France had failed when introduced in 1833 because of the stigma of 'elementary' education. But at about the same time a special two-year course was established in the collèges to study 'the sciences and their application to industry, modern languages, and the theory of commerce and design'.[29] This prospered and was firstly extended to three years in 1847 and then in 1863 given its own title of '*l'enseignement secondaire spécial*'. The collèges aimed to educate 'the NCOs of the army of workers' and they proved to be very successful, their intake increasing from 16,882 in 1865 to 22,700 in 1876. Moreover, most of their pupils came from agricultural, commercial, or industrial backgrounds and they returned to these areas of work on the completion of their studies. However, many of them left after two years only of their course, so in 1881, the total course was extended to five years but divided into an intermediate part of three years (after which pupils could leave with a certificate of studies), followed by an advanced part of two years. Though this seemed to be a sensible reform it was ominous because practicals were dropped and a 'special' baccalaureat was introduced which could give access to science and medical faculties, thus bringing this branch of secondary education closer to other forms. Further adjustments were made to the course and the title of the baccalaureat was changed from 'special' to 'modern'. Finally, as we have seen, it was absorbed into secondary education proper as section (d) above. However, it then lost its appeal to its former clientele: there is strong evidence to suggest that such pupils went instead into the revived advanced primary classes.

Here again, then, as in Britain, the struggle between the need to innovate in order to take account of changing patterns of employment, and the desire to conserve a traditional form of education can be seen. The élite groups manage to retain their dominance, but ways and means still have to be found of catering for the middle ranks in order to ensure the economic health of the country. The struggle results in secondary education expanding downwards, so to speak, and elementary education upwards, so that the two overlap. The fact that a group of pupils can desert a section of secondary education, despite its prestige, because it becomes inappropriate to their needs and move towards an area of elementary education because it gives them what they want suggests that fundamental differences between the two systems should not really exist. Yet separation ensured that the advanced primary courses kept their 'useful' bent and were not in danger of being absorbed as special secondary education had been. Even so, the most likely future of these pupils was in commerce or office work. Technical education was still neglected.

Antoine Prost says that in the nineteenth century, and especially after 1870, technical education at the highest level had few problems but in the lower echelons it was badly deficient. Mechanization was one cause of this because it led to a decline in the apprenticeship system which had in the past guaranteed some measure of technical education. Attempts to revive the system during the nineteenth century usually succeeded only briefly. Factory schools were set up but they were not of general value because they were over-specialized. Industrial societies of one kind or another, chambers of commerce and municipal authorities (e.g. Le Havre in 1867) set up their own apprenticeship schools, but there were arguments about the extent of specialization they should aim for. At about the same time a number of primary schools set up manual schools of apprenticeship. However, this meant that there were now two kinds of further primary education – one technical, the apprentice schools, and the other professional (in the French sense), the advanced primary schools proper. To distinguish between the two the former were put under the control of the minister of commerce. However, because in this aspect of his work this minister was dependent for finance on the minister of public instruction, he found it very difficult to encourage any expansion in technical education until in 1892 he was given full control of the schools. Certain former advanced primary schools (of a more technical bent) were also put under his charge and changed their name to 'Practical Schools of Commerce and Industry'. This situation was encouraging, but in 1914 there were still only 25,000 pupils in government professional schools of all kinds and they catered only for the élite of the working class. Evening, and in some cases day, classes such as those run by the Association Polytechnique and various private organizations made training available to workmen but were not very effective. Moves to bring in continuation (or day-release) education were not successful until after the war.

There simply was not sufficient political will to improve technical education extensively because French traditions, acting as a deadweight, slowed down change to the minimum. This was justified at the time by Buisson who contrasted 'the intellectual aptitudes which make a man' with 'the practical aptitudes which make the worker'.[30] Even so, opportunities for technical and commercial education did increase as they were bound to when opportunities in the job market developed. Yet even in this growth of professional education there was a bias towards general courses, or rather courses developed a bias towards the theoretical because of the prestige of the academic tradition and the effect this had on the working class, many of whom wanted to ape their betters. They desired at least a small share in what Gambetta is reported to have called '*la nouvelle couche sociale*' by joining the lower ranks of '*les capacités*'.[31] But, not only did the proliferation of the forms of education follow the proliferation of types of occupation but also those forms did show signs of articulation as technical education overlapped with elementary education just as the latter did with secondary.

Though education in the United States resembled that in Europe to the extent that the elementary schools, the early high schools and the academies were not articulated in any successive way, it is dealt with separately here because it changed faster than did European systems once America entered the second phase of industrialization. It is as though, less encumbered by long and entrenched traditions, with power more diffuse, and a social system less hierarchical than any found in Europe, the United States embraced changes in the means of production and social reorganization more rapidly than did either France or Britain. Added to this was the influence of successive waves of immigrants who contributed to the sense of flux in social relationships. Nevertheless, it was the fact of industrialization that was important: in the long run the similarities were greater than the differences and the solutions to educational problems in the United States laid down patterns which European countries were to adopt later. This is not to say that Britain and

France 'borrowed' from the United States any more than is to be expected of countries with a common cultural heritage, but it does mean that in the long run advanced industrialization obliged them to adopt educational solutions similar to those found in the USA at this time, even though American expansion and elaboration of education began from a narrower and less well defined base, certainly less well defined than the French system.

The number of private day schools in cities such as New York had declined by the middle of the last century[32] because families of moderate means which had used them could no longer afford to pay both tuition fees for their children and taxes for the provision of common schools.[33] This happened in other states too, so much so, that the title 'common' was not so much of a misnomer as it would have been in Europe. Even so, the enthusiasm aroused in Francis Adams for the American common school on his visit from England in 1875 was not fully justified. They were not as comprehensive as he imagined and many were poorly equipped and overcrowded, but there was a greater likelihood that American children of different social backgrounds would find themselves together in school than would British or French children. And though the district in which a school was situated affected (and always has done) its social make up, an ideal was established in the USA in the nineteenth century that elementary schools should be common. It might have been something of a myth, but myths can be powerful. It was influential enough to establish a trend which, despite the shameless segregation of Blacks and all the infighting between wards, boards, states and social groups for control of the schools, was to be a very important factor in the development of education in the twentieth century, once the link between occupational opportunities and education became more widely recognized.

The curriculum of these schools improved as it recovered from the Lancasterianism which had infected it earlier. Teaching also improved once the normal schools understood better the tasks involved in training teachers. However, progress was slow and expansion beyond the three Rs to the point where 'common branches' were included involved sometimes bitter struggles. Freeman Butts says:

> drawing came into the curriculum of some of the common schools of the cities. This seemed to respond to a learner-oriented pedagogy designed to develop the co-ordination of eye, hand, and mind, and at the same time satisfied the achievement-oriented requirements of captains of commerce and industry by developing the practical capabilities of youngsters in mechanical drawing.[34]

However, he then goes on to show how important was William H. McGuffy whose graded readers stressed 'the ideals of hard work, thrift, punctuality, modesty, propriety, contentment and conformity'. Butts comments on how applicable these virtues were to factory workers as part of the modernization process, which was about to throw America into such turmoil.

Though the classical curriculum had dominated secondary education proper in the USA as it had in Europe, it began to lose its hold there at an earlier period. The great age of the private academy in the United States was the period before the Civil War. In 1860 there were about 6,000 of them. They combined the teaching of classics for university entrance with a more 'useful' curriculum by introducing modern languages, science, commercial subjects, and various fine arts. Though the academies were to decline later in the century in the face of the rapid expansion of the public high schools, the grip of Latin had already been broken.

The first public high school appeared in Boston in 1821 and though others followed throughout the century, development was delayed because of the unpopularity of providing for secondary education out of public funds – this had been a problem which the elementary schools had faced earlier – and Katz cites the example of Beverly, Massachusetts, where in 1860, the lower classes of the town outvoted the professional and business interests and closed down a new public high school because they knew that few of their children would ever attend it.[35] But in the 1870s a series of court cases made public funds available for secondary education and this was at a time when certain states were enacting compulsory education laws, sometimes to the age of sixteen. The academies at this point went into decline as their clientele began more and more to make use of the high schools. However, some boarding schools remained in existence and others were refounded: some became very exclusive. There has existed since then an American equivalent of the English top-flight public school.[36] Few children from the working class were likely to be found in the public high school until the very end of the last century when, especially after 1895, the situation changed and the intake of the high schools became more extensive both numerically and socially. By then the effects of the economic developments discussed in the first part of this chapter were being felt – it was the time when the number of non-manual employees began to grow rapidly and children of lowly origin began to recognize the opportunity for social mobility through extended education. Seven per cent of fourteen- to seventeen-year-olds attended public high schools in 1890. By the 1920s this had risen to almost 50 per cent. Furthermore, though there were opportunities for manual training in trade schools or within the higher schools, this was not what the children of workers wanted. What appealed to them was the fact that, besides greater security and higher status, white-collar jobs paid better, e.g. clerks in the railway companies could earn a thousand dollars per year and postal employees nearly that much whilst manual jobs earned only half that.[37] Moreover, such occupations, as well as supervisory occupations in industry, were regarded as fitting for native born Americans. Immigrants could fill the lower ranks. In such a situation it is no wonder that the increase in numbers in the high schools matched the increase in the numbers in office and sales work.

However, it is what happened *inside* the American high school which is most important for the future of education, not only in America but throughout most of the world. It was during this period that an early form of comprehensive education was created within the high school. The way in which this came about is instructive not only because it illustrates how, in the future, education systems in advanced societies would have to allow for the growing aspirations of wider sections of society, whilst at the same time acting as agents for selection within those societies, but also how the protagonists in the struggle over the purposes of education usually acted out of self interest, albeit unconsciously.

The high school kept its academic curriculum (and even Latin for a while) for those pupils who would either enter higher education or proceed to white-collar occupations, but it also developed vocational courses. The movement towards this extension of the schools' work began really in the 1880s with the call for manual training in education generally by men such as J.D. Runkle, the president of Massachusetts Institute of Technology, who maintained that children no longer got this at home and that they needed it because they were entering an industrial society. Prospective employers would obviously be interested in this line of argument, but neither labour unions nor teachers and educationists were certain of the wisdom of it: the former because through it they might lose control over entrance to apprenticeship, the latter because it might weaken education as an intellectual discipline (their monopoly) and also act as a divisive factor in society. W.T. Harris, the St Louis superintendent, on these grounds, opposed the introduction of manual training into the city's schools. Later, however, a manual school was established there and other cities followed suit.[38] This sort of education was also deemed appropriate for Blacks, though one of them, Du Bois, argued against it because 'true education is not to make men carpenters, it is to make carpenters men',[39] which is ironic because it is exactly the same argument as that used by Buisson in France.

The depression of 1893–4 turned the campaign for manual instruction into one for vocational education because organizations such as the National Association of Manufactures (NAM) believed that many of their difficulties were created by competition from Germany, a country where technical schools were highly developed. Hence they supported vocational education, which like manual training, had the additional benefit of breaking union hold over apprenticeship, because this would lose its importance if training took place elsewhere. The NAM even accepted the Platonic tripartite division of human types, later to be so significant in Britain, to justify vocational education. The unions were consequently in a difficult position. They wished to defend their control over apprenticeship as this gave them at least one lever with which to influence what went on in industry, but they also realized that, as it stood, apprenticeship was outmoded. Finally, the unions came in behind groups such as National Society for the Promotion of Industrial

Education which, though supported by industrialists, at least had a reformist humanitarian wing. They therefore pushed for vocational education *within* the high schools:

> Vocational school courses should at all times be under the guidance and control of school authorities having control of the general education of the children. The unit system of administration is best adapted to educating our children properly for their future guidance as citizens and workers.[40]

This combined movement, and the 1914 Report of the Commission on National Aid to Vocational Education, led to the passing of the Smith-Hughes Act of 1917 which gave federal aid to vocational education in the public high schools and to the training of teachers for it. Even the National Education Association came down in favour of vocational education but in its *Cardinal Principles* it insisted that such education should not take place in separate trade schools. However, that battle had to be fought out in each individual state. Nevertheless, with support from men such as Dewey who saw any bifurcation as anti-democratic, the notion of the comprehensive high school took root and differentiated courses were introduced into them. Moreover, as the new century wore on more and more pupils opted for non-academic courses.

What we are seeing here in the developments in education in all three countries is a struggle to cope with the pressures which changing industrial conditions create in society. The old divisions begin – if not to break down – then at least to change their shape, even though many people continue to judge class and status by outmoded criteria. Even so, new needs impose themselves. Two, in particular, are important. First, new and more diverse occupations have to be provided for, otherwise serious economic dislocation might follow. Second, larger numbers are likely to aspire to fill the new roles and to avoid serious social disruption. These aspirations have to be catered for, in part at least. The two needs work in tandem. They stimulate each other, but are dealt with by groups of people or individuals whose own self-interest and preconceived notions do not always permit them to make rational decisions about education.

In such circumstances, the old forms of education have to

change but those changes are modified by tradition. One important development is in elementary education (again in the British sense: that which is appropriate to the lower orders, mostly as a means of social control). It has to become universal and it also has to do more than merely teach the three Rs and religious (or moral) education. But, because any sort of education is cumulative in its effect, elementary education will encourage at least some of its participants to go further, and this is made easier by the changing circumstances.

At the same time, secondary education has to become more relevant to the world of work whilst retaining its academic purpose, which continues to be buttressed by its link with higher education. Forms of secondary education (and with them increasingly complex curricula) will proliferate. Elementary and secondary education begin to overlap. However, much more than mere overlap is occurring: the two (or even three) once separate systems show signs of becoming articulated and, in America in particular, elementary education begins to suggest it might become primary education and thus lead to secondary education which itself might even become universal. The links in France also begin to take shape, and in England too when the Educational Provisions Act of 1907 reserved 25 per cent of places in government-supported secondary schools for children from the elementary schools.

Another important development begins to crystallize at this stage and particularly in the United States. Education, besides establishing channels through which aspirations towards the new jobs can work, also becomes one of the agents of selection. Selection – as it operated in the past, in that it was carried out largely by parents themselves when they chose the type of education their children should have – was becoming less appropriate. Parents are still very important up to 1900, and especially in Britain and in France, but with higher numbers going through a more complicated education system, there is little guarantee that the needs of an industrial society will be thus catered for. Education's role as a sorting house, which has always been there, becomes more pronounced. This is why examination systems were developed in all three countries, though obviously different levels of importance were attached to them in each of the three. The baccalaureat, significantly enough, was introduced by Napolean to *select* those worthy of '*une carrière ouverte aux talents*'. What is interesting is how elaborate it has become by 1902.

The British system grew out of the middle-class desire to establish something of a meritocracy in order to challenge aristocratic control of the establishment, to satisfy new economic and social needs by giving schools something to aim at, and simply to allow schools to compete with each other: the original Oxford and Cambridge 'locals' developed out of a contest. In Britain too the system became elaborate, disjointed, and disconnected so that it had to be severely pruned – when the school certificate was introduced in 1917. The Americans did not abandon examinations fully (though the SAT as a requisite for the best universities was not introduced until the 1920s), but more important they introduced testing and guidance: two very important mechanisms of selection but more appropriate to the discussions of the next chapter.

When we turn to the Russian Empire in the second half of the nineteenth century we find that despite its backwardness, progress has been made and in ways which are significant. As we saw earlier, Russia was not undeveloped in 1850 – she was backward. Furthermore certain encouraging economic developments had already taken place (e.g. in textile production) and these continued, albeit slowly at first but then with increasing acceleration, as the twentieth century approached. Production tripled in the 1880s, and by 1914 Russia had one of the fastest growing economies in the world with a growth rate of 8 per cent per annum.[41] The abolition of serfdom in 1861 marked the turning point because modern developments on a major scale were certainly not possible whilst slavery prevailed. However, despite the fact that for most peasants the abolition made very little difference because of the operation of a collective way of working, known as the *mir*, some of them were able to move to the towns and to take on new occupations. Indeed the growing proletariat which increased to as many as three million, 2.3 per cent of the population by 1900, was composed mostly of them and became a potent force in the events of the next two decades.

Another factor which permitted industrial development was the establishment of the railway system. This began partly as a response to the failure of Russia in the Crimean War which brought home even to the complacent and inefficient Czarist government the extent of Russian backwardness. The 1,600 kilometres of track of 1860 had increased to 81,000 kilometres by 1917. Considering the size of the Empire this was still no great amount but most of it was in European Russia and established links between the all-important centres, such as St Petersburg and Moscow, and the Ural Mountains, so important for coal and steel. In these two latter fields there were tremendous improvements in production, mostly towards the end of the century. Less than half a million tons of coal were mined in 1861 and over 36 million tons by 1913,[42] but it was steel production which was truly remarkable because it rose from 7,000 tons to 5 million tons in the same period. The populations of St Petersburg and Moscow expanded rapidly, each having well over a million inhabitants by the turn of the century. Factories developed in both cities; consumer goods were produced. In fact the forms of mechanization which were brought in were not those of eighteenth-century Britain. This was a nineteenth-century industrial revolution and many of the concerns, backed as they were by Western capital (very often French), were very large. Social change was taking place. Meissner writes:

> in 1913, the upper and middle classes, including the trading sector and the *kulaks*, constituted 15.9 per cent of the entire population. Workers and white collar employees totalled 16.7 per cent of the population, while 65.1 per cent was made up of individual peasants and home-workers.[43]

So the sections which matter to the sort of social and occupational changes which we saw in Britain, France and the USA are quite substantial here. Both Hans[44] and Anweiller[45] maintain that the all-important intermediate strata were falling into place. It must also be remembered that the abolition of serfdom had also affected adversely some of the lower ranks of the nobility whose children then required an education which had some value in the market place. Administrative jobs increased, though nothing like as rapidly as in the West. The central government increased its staff (though many of them seemed to be policemen or spies!) and local government reform led to opportunities for appointment: 'reforms in the judicature and the institution of the *zemstvos* (county councils) and the organs of municipal government actually opened up careers in a number of new directions'.[46]

The number of teachers, at all levels, also increased. The creation of the *zemstvos* was an indication of the changing power structure within Russia, but, again, circumspection is required when dealing with Russia. The situation there was so contradictory because though modernization was actually under way, thus forcing change, the Czarist regime was so incredibly reactionary. Nevertheless, there was representation of all classes on the *zemstvos*, from 1864, when they were first set up. Six years later equivalent organizations were established in the towns, though the Romanovs then seemed to spend the rest of their time in office trying to undo the good they had done. The first and second *Dumas*, the nearest the Russians ever got to legislative assemblies, though both short-lived, were elected on a fairly broad franchise. The third and fourth *Dumas*, though more durable, were not really very representative and all but powerless, though they did manage to increase the amount of money spent on education. Obviously the political situation in Russia before 1917 was such as to make comparison with the other countries of this study very difficult. However, opposition to the regime continued to grow, though it took on increasingly more desperate forms, and the government managed to prevent it from consolidating, the 1905 Revolution being exceptional. However, the power of the Czar and the nobility was on the wane and the very repression is a sign of this. It underlined government weakness and incompetence. The existence of soviets from 1905 onwards and the creation of trade unions showed that other centres of power were beginning to form.

Generally speaking, education in Russia was inadequate but the main features of a modern system did exist and there were signs that the changes which took place between 1861 and 1917 could have produced a healthier situation. Unfortunately, the obsession of the regime with security and the preservation of autocracy acted too often as a blight on education as on everything else.

Elementary education made progress, inspite of the Holy Synod and the reactionary attitude of most of the ministers of education who held office between 1861 and 1917. The literacy rate rose considerably and had reached 21.1 per cent by 1897, but this figure conceals much achievement. The figures for men were higher than for women; those for the young (below the age of forty) were far better than those for the old; and the western provinces, with the cities outstanding, were much higher than the eastern provinces and the countryside. The fact that the church controlled half the schools was not an advantage but because the *zemstvos* were given a measure of authority over education, the situation improved and over 5 million children were in school by 1914.[47] Moreover, though the official instructions on elementary schools made them organs of social control in a much more explicit way than did their Western counterparts, the curriculum of the schools actually became more liberal as the century wore on.

In secondary education there were three types of gymnasium. The first was the classical school where the ancient languages were taught, and where Greek still held its place because of Russia's cultural heritage. Other subjects were, however, taught. Then there were gymnasia where Latin but not Greek was taught and finally, following the example of Germany, there were 'real' gymnasia. This last type was the most important as far as the future was concerned because it offered a more 'useful' curriculum than the others and concentrated on mathematics, physics, natural history, drawing, and design.[48] However only a little over 1 per cent of males and less than 1 per cent of females had secondary education in 1897,[49] though this was a considerable improvement on earlier times. The percentages for higher education are much smaller but the numbers of students and the variety of courses available were both increasing. Of new institutions in higher education founded during the period, several were technological, e.g. Kharkov Technological Institute in 1885, the Electrotechnical Institute (in St Petersburg) in 1886, the School of Engineering (Moscow) in 1896, and the Polytechnic Institute Sosnovka (St Petersburg) in 1902.

However, Russian students were noted for their poverty and there were almost ceaseless disturbances towards the end of the period, though most of them seem to have been provoked by the government. Trade schools existed in Russia before the Revolution but not in any great numbers, though technical education in Russia must have been better than most people thought because at the beginning of the First World War, she had more aeroplanes than any other combatant.

During the war, proposals for the reform of education were put forward – by Ignatiev, the then minister of education. Not surprisingly, he suggested a properly co-ordinated system with the kind of articulations already being formed in Western countries. Primary education would be compulsory from the age of seven until the age of eleven. Then there would be a form of selection so that only a proportion of children would go on till fourteen. Then another selection would be made of those to go till seventeen. Despite Bolshevik claims that they introduced the first measure of co-ordinated education in Russia, the Ignatiev model was to remain influential. Selection was to be an important function of Soviet education from the beginning.

Part 2

Education becomes the most important agent of selection in industrial societies

4

Industry and education in the first half of the twentieth century: selection by differentiation

Even had the First World War never taken place, the economic and social developments which occurred in all these countries in the early twentieth century would have been remarkable, but the effects of the war on them, and especially the three in Europe, were incalculable. Nor were the terrifying losses of manpower, the widespread devastation of homes and industrial plant, and the enormous, and especially in the case of Britain, crippling expenditure of capital and resources in themselves the causes of the most important change.

In some almost unaccountable way the total experience of the war meant that the world could never be the same again. There seemed to be more than four brief years between 1914 and 1918, because how large numbers of people thought of themselves, viewed each other and considered their relationships with each other, changed profoundly in those years and nowhere more so than in Russia, where the war finally brought to a head all those forces making for revolution. However, precisely what were the causes of such changes in attitude are difficult, if not impossible, to disentangle and it is better, perhaps, to adopt the careful and measured terms of the historian:

> The war of 1914–18 brought into relief the hidden and unresolved tensions which had been gathering strength since the closing years of the nineteenth century; it weakened the framework of society and made it easier for new forces to make themselves felt.[1]

Nevertheless, it is safe to say that what was expected of

education became more confused because of those tensions and forces and the way the war acted on them. Barraclough also says later:

> when the decisive changes began towards the close of the nineteenth century, they had done so in a world which, for all its expansiveness and in spite of symptoms of *fin de siècle* malaise, was securely anchored to two fixed points: the sovereign national state and a firmly established social order stabilized by a prosperous property-owning middle class. Both characteristics proved remarkably tenacious.[2]

Consequently, the ways in which industrial societies were stratified were still important, and the distribution of power, in so far as it was related to class had not changed so much as might have been expected. Status, however, had changed a great deal because the war had enabled classes to become better acquainted with each other at a personal level and because the so called lower orders were less deferential towards their supposed superiors than they had been before the war. Therefore, dislocation between class and status was more pronounced than it had been at the end of the nineteenth century, because the war had also speeded up those structural changes in industry which were to affect the production of consumer goods as well as accentuating changes in attitudes towards personal relationships.

In such circumstances education became more easily recognizable as a means of social mobility: the desire for upward mobility was enhanced, and with it the demand for education beyond the elementary level. Indeed, the dilemma faced by education systems of modern industrialized societies, already seen beginning to emerge in the second half of the nineteenth century, became more apparent during the first half of the twentieth century. One horn of the dilemma was that further industrial developments increased the pressure on education not only to expand but also to make possible the acquisition of a greater variety of skills and at the same time cater for the higher aspirations of wider sections of society. The other was that education had to elaborate its selective function because of the increasing numbers going on to some form of post-primary education. Had something like the conditions suggested by Davis and Moore[3] prevailed (where personal endeavour and persistence are supposed to ensure the selection of the fittest) then the dilemma might never have arisen. However, because social class as a determinant of educational success continued to exert great influence on who was selected for which job, then the contradiction became more and not less problematical.

Though the period under discussion was marked by economic depression, the trends observed earlier continued but in a more pronounced form. The old staple industries, so important in the early stages of industrialization ceased to dominate the industrial landscape (except in Russia where heavy industry at the expense of consumer-oriented industry was deliberately overemphasized to enable the new Soviet Union to catch up with its Western rivals). Furthermore the newer industries were less labour-intensive and demanded both greater technological and greater organizational skill from their employees. Probably the most striking industry to emerge clearly at this time was the automobile industry, though again its roots were firmly in the nineteenth century. However, its twentieth-century expansion was important, not only because of its reliance on engineering skills but also, at the first sight paradoxically, because of its assembly-line methods of mass production. These could be seen as requiring less skill from workers. However their effects were similar to those of a forerunner, the ASM:

> The rise in a highly mechanized industrial sector, marked by tremendous powers, did not mean that a rapidly growing portion of the American working force was subjected to the harsh discipline of the assembly line. On the contrary, it made it possible for more and more labour to be switched from onerous tasks, whose output was enormously leveraged by industrialization, into other less physically demanding tasks.[4]

Moreover, the assembly-line methods were also important because they were copied elsewhere and because they made the motor car more widely available, thereby contributing to those social developments which so affected people's notions of their own status. This social impact of the motor car was much more obvious in the United States. But substantial developments took place in the motor industries of France and Britain. The French car industry had begun earlier than most. In 1905, competitors in the last of the Gordon Bennett races complained that they were allowed to enter only three cars when French production of automobiles outnumbered that of all other countries put together[5] and by 1913 their production at 45,000 cars per annum was almost double that of Britain (though only one-tenth of American production). The war, with its heavy demand for motorized vehicles of all kinds, obviously boosted production and several companies, such as Citroen, probably would never have existed but for the war, yet this company was producing 400 cars a day by 1928.[6] Total British production at about the same time stood at over 1,000 cars and 500 commercial vehicles a day.[7]

The motor industry also provides a good example of what might be termed a modern industry. It is obvious that technical know-how and scientific knowledge were both important to the industry, particularly in its initial stage of growth. The internal combustion engine itself is much more sophisticated than the steam engine, puts greater demands on the precision skills of its engineers, and combines features from a number of scientific and technological fields. Put at its simplest, there are more parts to a car. The education required of men working on the assembly line was not high, but as Heilbroner has pointed out, those actually assembling cars were in fact only a minority of those engaged in the industry: a great deal of often highly skilled work had already been done to make the parts being assembled. The industry also carried a larger administrative sector than many of its forerunners; advertising and sales were more important to it. Furthermore, once the cars, lorries and buses had left the factory, they generated more work – often not considered by the casual observer. Fuelling and servicing employed more people by 1939 than did the strictly productive section of the industry. Moreover, a large proportion of these people were skilled and saw themselves as having higher status than factory workers.

The question of status at this time is an interesting one particularly in circumstances of the kind described above. The assembly line might have paid good wages but its prestige was not high because the division of labour within it had become even more fragmented, influenced as it was by the principles of 'scientific management' enunciated by Frederick Taylor at the end of the nineteenth century. His work had a profound effect, especially in the USA in the early part of the twentieth century, not only on the factory floor but also in the administration sector (and not only in manufacturing) to which many of the increasing number of American high school graduates were attracted. They were in no doubt of where prestige was to be found, despite any routinization of work which might be taking place there. This all seems to show that status is greatly influenced by what people want to perceive about their own situations. Routine work was to be found in white-collar as well as blue-collar positions in new developments like the motor industry, and yet it was interpreted differently in the former case.

Important though the motor industry was, there were other developments, just as significant, which had similar effects on both occupational structure and patterns of consumption. Electricity as a source of light and power became increasingly important in all these countries during the first half of the twentieth century and more and more people became involved in its generation. Even Russia, despite the chaos of war, revolution, and reorganization, was producing two and a quarter million kilowatts by 1929. One reason for the increase in demand for electricity was the more widespread use of the electric motor in industries of all kinds and this not only permitted changes in the design of workplaces but also led to the extension and elaboration of those occupations which come under the heading of electrical engineering, with obvious consequences for education. Moreover, the use of electricity in industry (as well as in the home) was cleaner and also allowed greater flexibility, which was an important factor in the stimulation of the new forms of production so vital in countries where what had once been considered as staple industries were of declining importance. Dunning and Thomas point out that between 1930 and 1939 the numbers working in British basic industries fell from 34.6 per cent to 27 per cent of the working population. They go on to say that, 'almost exactly counterbalancing this trend was an expansion of 450,000 in the labour force of the newer industries of motor vehicles, electrical engineering, scientific and industrial instruments, constructional engineering, heating and ventilation appliances'.[8] This was, in effect, doubling the numbers involved. They also list other areas of growing importance in both Britain and the United States and mention chemical products, artificial fibres, and developments in the uses of stainless steel and aluminium.

Most of the newer industries required more skilled workers, often with technical qualifications as guarantees of their expertise. Indeed, expertise of all kinds was becoming more important and more widespread – and not only in science and technology but also generally throughout the populations, certainly of the three Western countries. All aspects of life were becoming more complex. There was not only an increase in the number of chemical, mechanical, and electrical engineers, but also in the numbers of civil and structural engineers, civil servants (at both local and national levels), solicitors, accountants (and others dealing with finance), insurance workers at all grades from underwriters to agents, doctors, radiologists, teachers, and those who offered higher-level services such as restaurant proprietors and managers.[9] These trends can all be traced back to the nineteenth century but Marsh cites Carr Saunders[10] who showed how difficult it was to define the meaning of 'professional' in the twentieth century as compared with the earlier period. Nevertheless, Marsh says that between 1931 and 1951 in Britain:

> The growth in the numbers engaged in professional and technical occupations by about 76 per cent symbolizes the increasing specialization required in this technological age, and the more widespread demand for professional status. It is by no means easy to define satisfactorily 'professional' and it would certainly be difficult to obtain universal agreement on which occupations should be classed as professions, but if we accept the census method of classification which is based in the main on the possession of technical qualifications, then it is apparent that the overall increases obscure quite marked variations in the professional group.[11]

This was because certain groups, such as clergymen, declined in importance. Many others increased.

This all points to definite underlying trends in the occupational structure of the four countries. Indeed it was in this period that, as a result of such developments, certain economists began to discern what they claimed was a pattern of industrialization which all advanced countries would follow. Kumar, though writing of a later period, shows how important were the inter-war years:

> Accepting the conventional sectoral division of the economy into primary (mainly agricultural), secondary (mainly manufacturing), and tertiary (services), there is no doubt that, in all industrial societies, there has been a long-term tendency whereby the majority of the working population has come to be employed in the tertiary, service, sector. Developments, in other words, have borne out a celebrated analysis of Colin Clark in *The Conditions of Economic Progress* (1940). Clark argued that there was a trajectory along which every industrialized nation would pass, following which, because of the sectoral differences in productivity, and the increasing demand for health services, recreation, and the like, as national incomes rose, the greater proportion of the labour force would inevitably move to the service sector. As a category, by reason of its heterogeneity, the service sector is notoriously difficult to define precisely. But there seems general agreement that it is best thought of as a residual category, comprehending for instance trade, finance, transport, health, recreation, research, education and government.[12]

Another important feature of the industrial developments which occurred in this period was that so many of them were geared to the production of consumer goods such as household wares and appliances, which had a profound effect on life styles. This was a trend noted earlier, but at this stage it was charged with much more cultural significance, for it often involved products such as paperback books, wireless and gramophones - all artefacts of the growing mass culture which in its turn had the effect of blurring the distinctions between people. The sort of changes noted earlier in organization of the food and drink industries progressed even further as did the production of clothing and furniture. Methods of mass production were adopted on a wider scale and distributive trades became more clearly defined and were increasingly important and even during the worst years of depression the numbers engaged in transport and distribution continued to increase. For example, in Britain between 1929 and 1937, they rose by 18 per cent.[13] Such trends were also to be found in France and the United States. In the USSR the numbers engaged in transport certainly increased but, because of the bias towards heavy industry in Stalin's Five-Year Plans the distribution of consumer goods was clearly not so important in the Soviet Union.

Other developments also affected life styles and David Marsh says that 'building and contracting occupations have been expanding continuously over the past eighty years and they probably reflect the changing standards of living of an economically developed community. The demand for buildings of all kinds has been continuously growing'.[14] Marsh was writing about Britain but what he has to say would also be true of France and the United States. Again, as for transport, the long-term trend was that the numbers involved increased, despite any temporary problems caused by the periods of depression which marked the years between the wars. The economies of all countries were continuing to evolve and the variety of buildings required, as well as their number, increased. The social effects were bound to be important: workplaces were being transformed. But what was more important, especially in Britain and in the USA, was that more people felt that it was possible to own their own homes and this meant that the 'property-owning middle class' referred to earlier by Barraclough was expanding throughout this period (though the really important expansion came after the Second World War and has since then affected France as much, if not more than the other two Western countries). There were also other important indications of changing social attitudes. The number of pawnbrokers and money lenders in Britain dropped from 11,000 in 1901 to 4,321 in 1931.[15] Hire purchase began to make an important contribution to how people consumed, and this was bound to affect how they thought of themselves. So, not only were class relationships beginning to change more rapidly as occupations proliferated, but so did the status systems, as the pattern of consumption affected life styles. These trends will be picked up again in the next chapter because they became even more pronounced after the war.

Something should now be said about what was happening in Russia at this time because it was rather more striking – but then so were the changes to the Russian economy. Khachaturov says that:

> the pre-war Five-Year Plans were in fact plans for a technological revolution, for the transition from the contemporary dominance of manual labour to mechanization. Under these plans the industrialization of the national economy, the establishment of national machine building, metallurgical and chemical industries was accomplished. . . in the process of industrialization a technological revolution covering all branches of the national economy was achieved.[16]

Earlier experiences had shown that rapid industrialization would not be easy and the adoption of War Communism, though successful in that it enabled the Bolsheviks to harness sufficient resources to win the civil war, had alarmingly detrimental effects on both industry and agriculture. Indeed a reversal of the trends seen earlier can be perceived and Gregory and Stuart note:

> the result of this egalitarianism was an insufficient pool of qualified labor in industry. Instead of being drawn into the factories, labor was flowing out of them during War Communism. The number of townspeople declined from 2.6 million in 1917 to 1.2 million in 1920. Morale was poor, worker shortage rampant, absenteeism high, and the tenuous loyalty of specialists was slipping. These developments were especially ominous in view of the dearth of skilled industrial labourers during this early period.[17]

Even before War Communism was dropped and the New Economic Policy was introduced the Ninth Congress of the Communist Party (1920) declared that incentives would have to be introduced, and the NEP was really a return to capitalism with the government controlling the 'commanding heights' of the economy. As a result of it, recovery was rapid and a return to pre-war levels of production was accomplished by 1928. However, the really big changes began in 1928 with the Five-Year Plans, though these were introduced only after a prolonged debate on how rapid industrialization ought to be undertaken.

Stalin opted for the stimulation of heavy industry at the expense of light industry, agriculture and services because, he argued, that sector provided the base on which to build the others (even though, historically the reverse appeared to be true). Furthermore, heavy industry was essential to the development of military power, without which it seemed unlikely that the Soviet Union would survive. Whether or not the order of priorities was wise, the Soviet economy did develop rapidly, even if the cost in life was high, especially so because the collectivization of agriculture took place at the same time. Heavy manufacturing's share of the net product doubled between 1928 and 1940 while that of light industry was halved. These facts are derived from figures quoted by Gregory and Stuart who go on to say that agriculture's shares of the net national product declined from 49 per cent to 29 per cent, and of the labour force from 71 to 50 per cent between 1928 and 1940, whereas industry's product increased from 28 per cent to 45 per cent and its share of the labour force from 18 to 29 per cent during the same period.[18]

Looked at from another point of view, the production of steel rose from 4.3 million tons in 1928 to 18.3 million tons in 1940, coal from 35.5 million tons to 166 million tons and oil from 11.7 million tons to 31 million tons in the same period.[19] By 1940, the Soviet Union was also producing 31,000 tractors and 145,000 motor vehicles per year and indeed, only the USA produced more trucks in that year.[20]

It is quite obvious that such rapid developments were bound to be accompanied by gigantic social changes. Meissner says that between the census of 1926 and that of 1939, urban population increased by 112.5 per cent or 29.6 million and the number of large cities (100,000 inhabitants) from 31 to 82, some of them, like Magnitagorsk, arising seemingly out of nowhere.[21] Many of those moving into the swelling towns were peasants displaced by collectivization. Even so, the levelling of society which had occurred during the period of War Communism, and which had been reversed while the NEP was permitted, recurred during the initial stages of the Five-Year Plans and was accentuated by fluctuations in wage levels and the supply of consumer goods, both of which caused pauperization. This tendency was strengthened by the government's habit of conflating several social groups under the heading 'proletariat'. However, differentiation was unavoidable. Meissner is worth quoting when he says:

> The leveling of Soviet society furthered as it was by the blending of social groups and the pauperization of the toiling masses, was offset very soon by a countervailing tendency toward greater differentiation among white-collar employees and, to a lesser extent, among the workers themselves. This was partially a result of the very nature of an industrial society and partially also the consequence of the political 'revolution from above'.[22]

The number of *apparatchiki* or state employees, who generally enjoyed benefits unknown by manual workers or peasants, had increased to 2.4 million even during War Communism and doubled again during the period of the NEP. Meissner says that:

> They turned out to be technicians and administrators drawn mainly from the old intelligentsia and former upper and middle strata and proletarian members of the party apparatus. Growing numbers of university and advanced technical institute graduates, most of whom were from proletarian families, combined with the petty bourgeoisie to push the number of white collar employees up to 9.6 million people in the course of the first two Five-Year Plans.[23]

In 1931 Stalin not only called for an end to egalitarianism in the labour force but also introduced variation in salaries based on achievement. Personal responsibility was to be given a new stress. The result of all this was that, just as in the West, industrialization encouraged upward mobility by making new occupations, which carried both status and reward, available to larger numbers of people. If anything, this process was much more clear-cut in the Soviet Union because whole sections of the old class structure had been swept away in the turmoil of the years after 1917, and because state planning went much further than it ever went elsewhere.

Moreover, the link between social mobility and education was also more obvious. Stalin tried to avoid the embarrassment this caused, by claiming that the new intelligentsia was not a new class but merely an 'intermediate stratum', a term of impeccable Marxist respectability (see Chapter 1, p. 17). However, even the purges strengthened the position of this 'stratum' and its importance is indicated by the fact that whereas in 1939 it constituted 20 per cent of the Communist Party, by the end of the war it had risen to 50 per cent, whilst the representation of workers fell from 50 per cent to 25 per cent. Even as early as the Eighteenth Party Congress, Stalin had dropped the term 'proletariat' in favour of 'working class'.[24] Despite the obvious differences between the Soviet Union and the other three countries of this study, underlying trends, deriving their force from accelerating industrialization, and similar to those observed in the West, can be discerned. The process of increasing differentiation in occupation with concomitant changes in attitudes to how status is attached to jobs meant that levels of educational aspiration went up and also affected a wider cross-section of Soviet society. Moreover, Marxist ideology, as interpreted first by Lenin, and then more significantly by Stalin, actually encouraged this process. Again it must be stressed that, despite the continuing Russian over-reliance on manpower, even in those industries where capital investment was high, the changes taking place in the Soviet Union were twentieth- and not nineteenth-century ones: workers were becoming car mechanics rather than cotton mill operatives. Braverman maintains that the parallels are even closer and he says that:

> in practice, Soviet industrialization imitated the capitalist model . . . and the Soviet Union settled down to an organization of labour differing only in detail from that of the capitalist countries so that the Soviet working population bears all the stigmata of Western working classes . . . the technology of capitalism, which Marx had treated with cautious reserve, and the organization and administration of labour, which he had treated with passionate hostility became relatively acceptable.[25]

First Lenin and then Stalin advocated the 'scientific management' of Frederick Taylor!

Throughout this period, the education systems of all four countries were put under continual pressure to change, and yet they found adaptation difficult. The recurring economic depression reduced the willingness of the Western countries to invest adequately either in schools or in new ways of organizing them, even though certain sections of educational opinion in all of them claimed that, in part at least, the inability to cope with recession reflected the inadequacies of educational provision. In the Soviet Union, the problem was rather the inadequacy of the infrastructure which had been inherited from the past, though obviously there was also a lack of general resources even more serious than that experienced in the West. In Britain and France, traditional attitudes to education, based on social divisions which were no longer appropriate, also made change problematical, because it made it difficult to decide what education was for, particularly at the secondary level. The United States and the Soviet Union suffered to some extent from the same confusion, but it is in the two west European countries that the most obvious ramifications of the dilemma of the inter-war years can be seen.

As we saw in Chapter 3, elementary education had become universal. Secondary (including technical) education had begun both to expand and to become more elaborate, and the two forms had become more closely related to each other. In England and Wales, the disappearance of payment by results, the establishment of the new code of 1904 and the introduction of the enlightened *Handbook of Suggestions* meant that elementary education began gradually to take on a shape which could develop later into what we would call primary rather than elementary education. However, this was only in so far as it applied to younger children, and even then it was to be distorted by the scholarship system. Those older elementary school children not siphoned off (even more formally after the 1907 Act) into secondary education were still locked in a separate system described as 'education for followership' by Eaglesham[26] who goes on to say that this was what Morant, doubtful of the abilities and the inclinations of the lower orders, had intended the Code of 1904 to create. Morant, secretary to the Board of Education from 1903 (officially) until 1911 was much more interested in secondary education and influenced developments there in a way which was not to be wholly beneficial in the future. Inspired partly by Sidney Webb's pamphlet, *The Education Muddle and the Way Out*, he had masterminded the 1902 Education Act which had introduced a measure of coherence into the administration of education in England and Wales. He was also a very dynamic administrator. However, Morant's view of secondary education owed much to his own experience at Winchester, i.e. it was based on what happened in the best public schools. Moreover, he feared the increasing influence of technical education and had played an important part before 1902 in preventing further growth and development of the higher-grade schools and school board evening classes.

It was Morant who established the grammar school, as we know it, with his code of regulations for secondary schools because he excluded technical and commercial education from the curriculum and thus ensured that the grammar schools would remain elitist institutions geared more to the preparation of pupils for university than for anything else. Because of these regulations many grammar schools which had a vocational bias underwent changes before the First World War which made them indistinguishable from grammar schools proper. (Even a cursory study of the prospectuses of Bablake School for this period shows this happening.) Other regulations also restricted technical education of any real value to children aged sixteen,[27] at which stage Morant believed it could do less damage. He later changed his mind about technical education and even commercial education and went so far as to gather a team to be responsible for transforming elementary education into a kind of polytechnical education which would prepare pupils for 'industrial citizenship'.[28] Unfortunately, the work was never completed. The most damaging effect of Morant's work was that the division between elementary and secondary education was made worse just when the two should have been brought closer together. The Educational Provisions Act of 1907 appeared to build a bridge between them but this could be crossed only by the brightest children. Moreover, elementary education no longer had its own higher forms to which it could lead and Morant even tried to wrest technical education from it. Most of the members of the National Union of Teachers came to believe that the divisions were strengthened in this way by Morant because of his notion of the divisions of society, which he still saw in nineteenth-century terms.

What Morant created was inappropriate because the changes which had occurred and were continuing to occur in the structure of industry and commerce were causing serious changes in society. Indeed the new local education authorities, though they were dominated by people just as convinced as Morant of the superiority of their class, had to face up to those changes: they had to cater for the industrial, commercial and administrative needs of their areas and Morant's system was not capable of providing for these. Thus it was that so many of them developed 'continuation' education, or central schools, or junior technical schools, even when these were of doubtful legality, because that is what cities like London and Manchester (where these innovations first took place) needed so badly. It could be argued that what Britain as a whole needed in the years before the First World War, when the stresses and strains of the second phase of industrialization were becoming obvious, was a common system of schooling for all pupils where the only real division would be between primary and secondary. However, the structure established by Morant, and the grammar school in particular, proved to be so entrenched that even the cataclysm of the Great War itself could not weaken it. Indeed it was during the war that the school certificate, which further strengthened the grammar school, was introduced.

On the other hand, as we saw earlier, the war speeded up economic and social change and made clearer the connection between education and economic development. Indeed at the end of the war, Lloyd George said that 'an educated man is a better worker, a more formidable warrior and a better citizen. This was only half comprehended here before the war'.[29] Moreover, the war had the temporary effect of drawing the various classes together and the feeling was abroad that a vigorous programme of social reform which included education should be undertaken. Nevertheless, the Education Act of 1918, half-hearted in itself and a dead letter almost before it was on the Statute Book, merely serves to illustrate the contradiction between the needs of society (and the economy) in general and the interests of those classes with any real power. Instead of secondary education for all, the Fisher Act offered only the promise of continuation education for the working class. In the slump which followed the war, the promise was not kept. Continuation education was introduced in only a few places though, interestingly, one of the schools that did survive had strong links with a local modern industry, i.e. GEC at Rugby. The dilemma facing British education remained and was made all the more obvious by the publication of R.H. Tawney's pamphlet *Secondary Education for All*. But how could the grammar school be preserved as an elitist institution if all pupils were given secondary education? The answer emerged slowly through the three great reports of 1926, 1938 and 1943. Hadow, Spens and Norwood created the tripartite system, though they used forms of education already in existence.

The Hadow committee not only made adolescence 'official', it also realized that there already existed forms of secondary education other than grammar schools, i.e. those developed by the local education authorities by pressure of demand. It therefore recommended that elementary education should cease to exist and that all children should receive primary education up to the age of eleven, when, because of the onset of adolescence, they should all proceed to secondary education, but secondary education in differentiated forms, in order to preserve the grammar school. The report declared with unconscious irony that children:

> who do not go forward to 'secondary education' in the present and narrow sense of the word, should go forward nonetheless to what is, in our view, a form of secondary education, in the truer and broader sense of the word.[30]

There is no mention of why grammar school children should be deprived of such benefits! Reorganization on Hadow lines did begin in some areas but, as usual, financial stringency prevented the recommendations from being implemented on any large scale. The Spens Committee rediscovered technical education, and even castigated Morant for his neglect of it. It also criticized the narrowness of the grammar schools, but it could not bring itself to threaten their existence. It therefore recommended that technical schools should be inserted alongside grammar schools and modern schools into the Hadow scheme of things.

However it was the Norwood Report, written largely by the committee chairman, Sir Cyril Norwood, sometime headmaster of Bristol Grammar School, Marlborough College and Harrow School, which set the seal on the pattern of education which was introduced into England and Wales in the period after the

Second World War. Norwood 'discovered' that there were three types of children who would fit the three types of school evolved by Hadow and Spens out of the variety of forms thrown up in England and Wales by economic and social need. Despite heavy criticism, even from Sir Cyril Burt, the report was influential and along with the White Paper, *Educational Reconstruction*, also issued in 1943, shaped the thinking of the local education authorities when they carried out the reorganization of education incumbent upon them after the passing of the 1944 Education Act. The Act itself does not mention tripartism, though it does imply that it should be used and Butler himself obviously intended that it should. The partial reorganization which had taken place earlier also made it easier for the authorities to establish different types of secondary schools on Norwood lines. Moreover, they all had long experience of testing children for selection to the grammar schools. Such tests required little elaboration to fit the new system.

What was happening was that the education system was being transformed into a more efficient form of selection. Parental choice (of which school to send a child) still played a part in the differentiation which occurred at the level of occupation because the fee payers still dominated the grammar schools, and the public schools were very influential institutions. However, this sort of choice, which had been the chief mode of selection in the nineteenth century for jobs which required education, was no longer sufficient to the kind of differentiation required by the advancing economy. There was an awareness of this as shown by the Spens Report.

Moreover, the education system in its unelaborated form did not cater for the growing aspirations of ever-larger sections of society and this was indicated by the increasing demand for places in all types of school. Furthermore, lower-class parents were prepared to pay for places at times of high wages as, for example, during the First World War. Such was the pressure for places that the process of change in the structure of secondary education would have occurred much faster in the inter-war years, if it had not been for the financial stringency which followed each economic crisis – and for snobbery.

Nevertheless, the changes described here illustrate the ways in which the British traditionally elitist form of education was elaborated in order to accommodate both the changing needs of continuing industrialization but also the increased social mobility which went with it. Selection through education became therefore more important and also more complex, especially as it had to present at least the appearance of greater social justice. Similar developments took place in France, though they were obscured by the political and religious squabbles of the time.

Though there were clear signs that, by the end of the nineteenth century, education in France was changing in response to developments in social and economic life, the traditional basic divisions of French education still existed. While elementary education had thrown up its own higher forms and secondary education had become more elaborate, the two systems – elementary and secondary – were still separate from each other, just as they were in England. In 1899, Emile Boutary, commenting on the baccalaureate, maintained that 'it divides the nation into two classes: the one which has parchments, the one which does not'.[31] Secondary education was for the élite, elementary for the rest. Yet industrialization was in progress in France and with it the proliferation of occupations, despite the fact that agriculture continued to be so important. Moreover, just as in England, the old class divisions were not so clear-cut as they once had been, especially after the First World War: aspirations were changing. In such circumstances, nineteenth-century forms of education became inadequate. (In 1918, secondary education followed the pattern laid down in the 1902 reforms.) However, attempts to reform education in the first half of the twentieth century stirred up both political and religious difficulties which often obscured the real problems which underlay all the others, i.e. the need to extend secondary education to wider sections of the population and the need to bring the two systems together in some unified form or at least to articulate them in some way, because only then could the requirements of French society, as it was then developing, be fulfilled. Though would-be reformers of education and their opponents often seemed to ignore social and economic questions, these were the true causes of the need to change. The changes which did occur in French education can therefore be interpreted as responses to those underlying needs, but as responses which were also conditioned, and consequently to some extent shaped, by traditional notions of what education was for. In other words, just as in the case of Britain in the same period, they were compromises. They were almost attempts to look both ways at once: to bring elementary and secondary education together and yet to preserve their differences; to elaborate secondary education and to make it more widely available – and yet to keep it selective.

Indeed, the paradox at the heart of the dilemma can be seen in the writings of *les compagnons de l'université nouvelle*, who though not the first to raise such issues, can be regarded as the progenitors of the reform movement, coming as they did at the end of the Great War, i.e. at a time when reform was in the air. Talbot[32] draws attention to this contradiction and quotes from their publication *Les Compagnons de l'Université Nouvelle*: 'everyone must be taught', but 'the best must be drawn from the crowd and put in their real place, which is first'. In other words, there must be mass education (and more than the three Rs) *and* selection of the élite, if the education system is to serve as the well-spring of the productive forces of the country. Tawney interpreted the problem (at first) in the same way in Britain, as we saw earlier. In fact, the solutions *les compagnons* proposed were rather similar to those evolved in Britain through the Hadow, Spens and Norwood reports. They called for an end to the isolation of the primary school (in France, this means elementary) from the lycée and proposed a primary school for all – *l'école unique* – which would give everyone an equal chance to take the next step. This meant that the best would be selected for either the lycée or the technical school. Those not selected in this way would go on to 'post-school training'.[33]

Les compagnons had no monopoly of ideas for educational reform but they influenced all who came later. The radical, Edward Herriot, probably understood better than they that education organized on a basis of class was 'economically wasteful'[34] but he adopted their idea of *l'école unique*, and extended and even tried to introduce it. The Syndicalist, Ludovic Zoretti, whilst putting forward similar views, also drew attention to some of the ambiguities in the idea of *l'école unique*. However he is interesting for another reason because though he questioned the wisdom of granting subsidies to the confessional (mostly Catholic) schools, he also implied that the religious question was irrelevant when he said that the confessional schools could act as a healthy stimulus to the state schools.[35] He was right, the question was irrelevant but few agreed with him: religion remained a bar to progress and Catholics saw *l'école unique* merely as a pretext by which their opponents would introduce a state monopoly in education. The fuss created by the squabbles made the religious question appear central to the educational difficulties of the time. That it was not, is borne out by the fact that even within the Catholic camp at least one faction, the Lille group, favoured, in the name of social justice, developments in education similar to those contained in the Organic Statute (worked out by a committee of those in favour of *l'école unique*) and even to those put forward by the *Confédération Generale du Travail*, upon which Jean Zay, at a later date, would base his reforms and experiments.

Another area of controversy which obscured more fundamental problems was that of the classical languages which even *les compagnons* could not see as other than essential to secondary education. With hindsight it is possible to recognize the inadequacy of the arguments put forward at the time to justify the primacy of Latin. However, when even the teachers of modern languages and science had themselves had a classical education, change was difficult. Indeed, the position of Latin was strengthened in 1923 when a decree introduced by Bérard made it compulsory for all lycée pupils, but in the following years, François Albert introduced a return to a modified form of the 1902 pattern (see above p. 43). This change was significant in another way. Talbot says:

> For the first time, certain of the basic disciplines – French, history, geography, and sciences – were to constitute a common programme for pupils of all sections. The reform was a greater innovation than appeared at first sight. A *culture générale* based on the study of French and science became for the first time the fundamental characteristic of secondary education; the study of classical languages, keystone of the old classical curriculum, now became simply one option among others.[36]

This meant that, though classics continued to dominate the options even until after the Second World War, a curriculum more appropriate to modern needs was compulsory for all lycée pupils at least in the early stages of the course.

More significant, though they were moderate, were the changes made in the relationships between the schools. The notion of elementary education as a separate system for the lower orders had already lost much of its meaning by 1918. More and more, primary education was coming to be recognized as that which leads on to something else. Hence the belief on the part of most of its supporters that *l'école unique* meant a common primary school for all children. Many parents viewed such promiscuity with horror especially if they had children in the elementary sections of the lycées through which entry to the lycée proper seemed best assured. In 1913 only 22 per cent of those entering the lycée came from the state primary schools. It was not until 1936 that the numbers of those entering the lycées from state primary schools matched those from the preparatory classes of the lycées. Nevertheless, the first steps in bringing these two forms of primary education together were made in 1924 by putting the preparatory classes under primary inspectors and by making such classes open to primary children. This process was taken further first by Lamoureux in 1926 when he made one curriculum common to both schools, and then by Jean Zay in 1937 when the elementary preparatory classes became primary schools proper. That he did not abolish these classes completely was a disappointment to many of those in favour of radical change.

But to some extent, the hopes of *les compagnons* had been realized: there was a commonality about primary education by the time of the Second World War, even if *l'école unique* did not really exist. However, what had been achieved had not been brought about without a struggle. To pull together the various kinds of post-primary education in the same way would be even more fraught with danger because besides having anti-clerical overtones, such a process would appear not only to be an attack on French academic traditions, it would also threaten the monopoly held by the bourgeoisie on access to power. Hence the long debates on education in the Chamber of Deputies and the accusations of 'primarization' of education hurled at the reformers (and blamed, incidentally, on American influences). And yet changes did occur. François Albert, in 1925, made it easier for pupils in *écoles primaires supérieures* to transfer to lycées. Even such a minor change was controversial, but further developments followed. Urged by Poincaré to reduce the cost of education, Herriot (minister of public instruction in the coalition government) used economy as an excuse to combine certain courses, significantly French, modern languages, mathematics, science and physical education, in collèges and *écoles primaires supérieures* or technical schools (which had increased in numbers since 1919)[37] where the two institutions were in the same building. This also happened to be the case with certain lycées, but it was more likely to be collèges which were municipal secondary schools. Besides causing an outcry this decision also raised the vital question of tuition fees because it placed pupils who had paid fees next to those who had not, to be taught the same courses by the same teachers. Herriot believed he had taken the first step along the path to free secondary education (one of the main aims of the Organic Statute) and in one sense he had, because he was able to exploit this anomaly in order to make education free for the first three years (and then six) in such combined institutions. There were fifty-three collèges or lycées with *écoles primaires supérieures* or technical schools attached in 1926. However, that was as far as he got. Further progress was delayed until 1930 when the Radicals and the Left, able to exploit the political situation at the time, forced on the Tardieu government a decision to make education free in the first class of all secondary schools. Though this appeared to be merely experimental, it was extended to other classes and by 1933 to all seven which formed lycée education.

The appointment of Jean Zay as Minister of Education in Leon Blum's Popular Front Government of 1936 was important because though Zay's reforms were not as far-reaching as he had hoped, and though they were short-lived (because of Vichy), they were significant. The post-war Langevin-Wallon recommendations, on which all reforms since have been based, were much influenced by them. Zay's aim was to have all children in primary schools take the *certificat d'études primaires* at the age of twelve (not at eleven, nor at fourteen, as various rival groups had hoped). The certificate could then be used as a means of selection for the various forms of post-primary education – *lycée, école primaire supérieure, école pratique du commerce et de l'industrie*, or *cours complementaire*. However, all children would undergo a common first year in which orientation would be the key. From this orientation year would branch classical, modern, and technical courses, and allowances would be made for children to transfer into them later from the *cours complementaires* which would be a form of extended primary education. Secondary education would be organized in two cycles. The first would last four years and the second three, but technical education would have a first cycle only – there would be, as yet, no technical baccalaureat.

Zay knew that all this would have a difficult and long passage through parliament, especially since the euphoria, which had greeted the Popular Front initially, had melted away. He therefore proposed, and got accepted, a trial scheme in forty-five centres. However this ran into all sorts of difficulties. For example, instituteurs and professeurs did not always find it easy to work together, and some centres had not got all the necessary branches of secondary education, even though some small municipalities were already running what were virtually multilateral schools even before the reforms.[38] Furthermore, parental preferences caused difficulties: parents whose children did their year's orientation in a lycée did not take kindly to advice that their children should continue in a technical school. Even before the outbreak of war, Zay's experiment had run into national opposition. No further progress was made before the war.

It is unlikely anyway that the reforms could have been introduced nationwide because they would have been expensive and the inter-war period was a time of financial chaos in France, just as it was in Britain and everywhere else. However, it was not the depression which was used in France as an excuse for inertia in education: political and religious controversies held back its development. The fact that it changed at all is an indication of the economic and social pressures on it.

So education made no more headway in France than it did in Britain. Nevertheless, the changes which did take place were similar in each country. Primary education (up to the age of about eleven) was considered less and less as a process intended to gentle the masses and more as a basic form of education preceding secondary education. Furthermore, the two stages were linked more firmly through the development of scholarships in both countries. Access to secondary education was widened but by means of differentiated forms, and though this fell far short of introducing anything like equality of opportunity, at least it had the merit of catering more efficiently for occupational needs. To that extent opportunities did improve, but mostly for the lower middle class. Talbot maintains that this was the case in France and goes on to say that 'education was an almost certain means of upward social mobility and a family preoccupied with questions of social status would be quick to seize the advantages free secondary education afforded'.[39] The pattern of job opportunity being what it was, this was to be expected. France, in her industrialization, was at a kind of half way stage where the absolute necessity of secondary education for all had not become fully apparent. Indeed, Talbot uses Hoffman's expression, 'the stalemate society', to describe France at the time: 'the Republican synthesis. . . in which French society was the halfway house between the old rural society and industrialization.'[40] The new technical, commercial, and administrative occupations were of a kind which suited the petite bourgeoisie, and it was they who benefited most from the educational developments which had taken place. And those developments were, as much as anything else, a more refined set of mechanisms for selection. Again, as in England and Wales, parental choice was still important but we can see the schools playing a more important role, particularly where they became part of Zay's experiments, and those experiments were the culmination of the struggles between the wars.

Though education in the United States in the early years of the twentieth century was better placed to face the demands of industrialized society than in either Britain or France, it was not without its problems. Indeed, it could be said that the dilemmas which began to appear in America at this time were those which would later be recognized as inherent in the education systems of all advanced societies. In retrospect, it can be seen that during this period, Americans were in the process of developing a set of institutions which could provide for mass education beyond the primary stage and yet at the same time act as a means of selection.

American education, fortunately not so hampered as its

European counterparts by hide-bound notions of social class, had already thrown up the comprehensive high school, through which the aspirations of growing numbers of manual workers' children could be satisfied. Moreover, this institution was in the process of becoming a common school because its only rivals were not so important. Those private schools which catered for an exclusively rich clientele (counterparts of the English public schools) were very few in number and the parochial schools, though much more numerous, were themselves to become mere variants of the comprehensive school and attendance at them was to be socially of no particular advantage. Furthermore, vocational education – and particularly some of its technical forms – had already moved into the high schools.

Good and Teller, commenting on changes in education in the first two decades of this century, say that:

> by 1910 the high school had come to the smaller towns and the automobile was facilitating the building of quality rural high schools; the junior high school was developing; the programme of studies was still growing; and a broader more democratic, and more practical education was gaining favour.[41]

They go on to describe the work of the Commission for the Reorganization of Secondary Education which reported in 1918 under the title of *The Cardinal Principles of Secondary Education*, and they contrast its point of view with that of the Report of the Committee of Ten of 1894. Whereas this earlier committee – though it had recognized that the high school had to cater for many children who would not be going on to college – stressed academic courses, 'the later Commission made preparation for life the primary purpose'[42] of the high school. This was very different from the situation in Britain and France where, despite the increase in the provision of secondary education, elitist assumptions continued to dominate the grammar schools and lycée, and entry to higher education shaped the curriculum even for those who would enter work straight from school. Other kinds of post-primary schools had to be established in Europe to cater for occupational needs (e.g. central and technical schools) whilst in the United States even the surviving trade schools broadened their curriculum and some of them went so far as to become comprehensive high schools.[43] The consequence of all this was that, as the twentieth century wore on, secondary education in the comprehensive high school became an increasingly common experience for American children. However, though the establishment and development of such an institution went a long way towards satisfying the growing demand for secondary education, and undoubtedly reduced much of the build up of pressure from growing aspirations, it did not remove the need for selection, and here lay the real dilemma.

One way in which the dilemma was eased was by the introduction of the junior high schools. Though these schools are still not universal in the United States, they have increased steadily in numbers since 1910 when they first appeared. They were meant to make the transfer from elementary to secondary education easier for children and they have, to a great extent, been successful in this. They have also had an effect on the elementary schools, permitting them to develop a more child-centred approach to the teaching of young children, in accordance with the principles of so called progressive education. The schools themselves have tended to remain part of the primary sector of education but because they have been able to offer 'some choice of studies, exploratory and orientation courses, individual instruction and more expert guidance',[44] they have also been able to anticipate and therefore facilitate the differentiation process which occurs more fully in the high school proper.

If we consider the development of the junior high school along with the introduction of the junior college we can see beginning to take shape a system of schooling which can both select and permit aspirations. Admittedly, between the wars, the outline was not too clear but in the light of how American education developed in the late 1940s and the 1950s, these innovations were important. Burton Clark says that there were no junior colleges in 1900, 19 in 1915, 178 by 1930, 261 by 1940 and 329 with nearly half a million students by 1950.[45] He also points out that their spread was uneven. Even so, the beginnings can be seen here of what Ralph Turner[46] referred to as 'contest' mobility in education where schools are organized like an obstacle race but one in which all the early hurdles are easy to take so that most pupils stay in the race until towards the very end. We can see this in the easy movement of children from the elementary school, to the junior high school, to the senior high school and then junior college and perhaps university proper. Again, it must be pointed out that at this time the system was still only in the process of taking shape but its components were there.

Meanwhile, internally, the high schools still had to deal with the problem of mass education and differentiation. Where the junior high schools existed some pressure could be taken off, not merely because the younger children were in these other schools, but also because the junior high schools were preparing children for the decisions they were to make later in the senior high schools.

Nevertheless, the differentiation which took place in the senior schools was obviously the more important. To some extent the decisions could be left to parents and to the pupils themselves, and indeed the individualist myth remains a powerful part of American educational ideology. However, educationists find it difficult not to direct students, even if that direction is under the guise of advice. Furthermore, if 'scientific' reasons can be put forward to justify particular kinds of advice then teachers will use those reasons and this is why testing became so important in schools in the United States during the inter-war years. This sort of testing had begun in fact in France with the Binet-Simon tests, devised early in this century. They were translated and adapted for American use in 1910. However, their most successful adaptation was made by Terman in 1916 in the form of the Stanford-Binet scale. Tests were also used in Britain but not to differentiate between children within schools: local authorities used them to select those children who would enter grammar schools from the elementary schools, but of course in Britain there was no common secondary school.

Writing of the year 1922, Gumbert and Spring say that:

> after the war, Detroit launched a massive testing program that led to the classification of 60 per cent of the students into the average (Y) group, 20 per cent into a backward (Z) group and 20 per cent into a superior (X) group . . . the classification of children into different ability groups led to a differentiated program of studies.[47]

They also say later that 'while the testing movement never created a national eugenics program it did result in the schools defining as one of their important functions the selection and classification of students'.[48] Bowles and Gintis are less polite about eugenics but add to the last point by saying that:

> by 1939, no less than 4,279 mental tests were in circulation; a survey of 150 city school systems, in 1923, revealed that three-quarters were using 'intelligence' tests to assign students to curriculum tracks.[49]

It was in the same period that the scholastic aptitude test was devised by Carl Brigham (he was the secretary of the newly formed College Entrance Examination Board) and this test later became more important as one of the means of selection for higher education. Its existence has had an effect similar to that of the school certificate in Britain because aiming for it skews students' choices in certain curricular directions. Testing, however, was only one part of the selection process being adopted in America.

The notions of testing and vocational guidance can be closely associated. Bowles and Gintis quote Lewis Terman himself on this:

> an IQ below 70 rarely permits anything better than unskilled labour; the range from 70 to 80 is pre-eminently that of semi-skilled labour, from 80 to 100 that of skilled or ordinary clerical labour, from 100 to 110 or 115 of semi professional pursuits; and that above all these are the grades of intelligence which permit one to enter the professions or the larger fields of business. . . . This information will be a great value in planning the education of a particular child and also in planning the differentiated curriculum here recommended.[50]

Despite the gross oversimplification here, it can be claimed that the very desire for guidance is, in a way, an expression of the difficulty of co-ordinating the system of education with the changing patterns of occupation and that this problem is made all the more obvious where children attend common schools. The way in which guidance was discussed in America from the early years of this century is also an expression of the apparent contradiction between growing aspirations and the need for selection.

There are times when it appears as though guidance is being introduced solely for the benefit of the employers (or at least for continued easy development of the economy). There are other occasions when the needs of the individual child and his or her search for a full and profitable life are what appear to be important. It could be that the latter merely masked the former. If this is the case then a subtle form of selection was being legitimated. Educational and occupational decisions appeared to be those of the student or the parents but in fact served the interests of employers, especially where test results forced the issue. Whatever the case, one thing is certain and that is that the education system in the United States permitted children to move more easily into the world of work, and without doing severe damage to their aspirations and those of their parents. It *appeared* to be fairer than the systems of France and Britain. How the selection was legitimated is important. We will find American methods became widespread in all four countries after the Second World War. There was another development in America which ran counter to testing and guidance. This was the growth of equivalents which S.A. Rippa traces back to a recommendation of the Committee of Ten:

> In an effort to cope with one of the problems of mass education, the Committee adopted the principle of 'equivalents': a subject on an approved list was deemed just as acceptable as another, if it were studied for an equal length of time. Later the term 'unit' or 'credit' was used to designate a certain number of class hours of work. This procedure was soon followed in high schools and colleges, which began measuring educational programs in terms of units or credits.[51]

He goes on to say that this system has had a 'deleterious' effect on American education because it has led to the mechanical acquisition of credits without regard to the true value of what was learned. This may be true, but at least it counter-balanced the alternative danger encouraged by testing, tracking and guidance where theoretical and college-oriented subjects acquire a dubious prestige.

That there should be such contrary developments in American education in the first half of the twentieth century ought not to be surprising. Social and economic pressures had combined to establish the first system of comprehensive high schools in the world: that system had to live up to its promise, in the sense that it had to seem to offer opportunity to most children, because, otherwise, not enough of them would be encouraged to go through it and then go on to fill the roles developing in the new economic and technical circumstances. Yet looked at from the perspective of those who might subscribe to a conspiracy theory of history, the high school can seem like a confidence trick because though it is less easy to see it in Bourdieu and Passeron's[52] terms of stark social reproduction (when compared with the English or French systems of the period) it can still be done, as Bowles and Gintis have shown. What we can say with certainty is this: one way to ease the dilemma (or conceal the trick) is to make the system more elaborate – but in its horizontal not its vertical divisions. Another is to justify any differentiation which might occur in it by reference to 'scientific' testing. A third way is to 'massage' the pupils through the system by guiding them in what appears to them as the way they ought to go.

It would be foolish to claim that before the Second World War, American schooling had developed quite as described here, but these tendencies were present and could be developed further. At the time, other matters concerned educationists. Child labour was still a serious problem; the depression had all sorts of distorting effects on educational opinion; and for certain groups (e.g. Blacks) there was little evidence of improvement in educational opportunity. Nevertheless, American education was moving in a direction which would later influence other countries confronted with the same dilemma. In the meantime, in the young Soviet Union, American progressive ideas were having an immediate impact.

Flirtation with Western progressive notions of child-centred education was to prove short-lived. What was more important to later developments in Russian education was the pattern of schooling put forward by Ignatiev, before the Revolution, in 1916 (see above, p. 57). His three-tiered plan was to become the basis of the Soviet system because it would become more and more appropriate to the changing conditions brought about by the drive towards industrialization. Nevertheless, in the heady days of 1917, there was an attempt to put democratic ideals into practice, and there were even cases reported of children dismissing their teachers. Certainly, experiments in project work – or the complex method as the Russians called it at the time – were tried and these were based on the ideas of John Dewey and also those of Helen Parkhurst, whose Dalton plan was particularly attractive because it sought to eliminate all restrictions. Her laboratory plan which used heuristic approaches to science learning was also influential. Needless to say, the ideas of Russian educational reformers like Tolstoy were also current. However, though the Webbs were later to characterize Russian education as 'joyous Bedlam', the experimental practices were never really widespread and were confined to the urban areas. One cynical American comment[53] was that they were permitted merely to break the power of the traditional Russian teachers and that they were dropped once a trustworthy body of teachers loyal to the new regime had come into existence. What is certain is that the introduction of such methods added to the confusion at the time.

Progressive education was not the only source of confusion in education in the years immediately after the Revolution. The writings of Marx and Engels were another. It is obvious that these would be important because they could be, and were, used as a legitimating force in Soviet decision making. Unfortunately their ideas on education had never been fully worked out and in fact could be contradictory. For example, they advocated the democratization of education along with the development of equality of opportunity but also assumed that proletarianization would occur even though this implied reducing access to education for certain other classes. Furthermore, their educational formulations took it for granted that industrialization was the situation for which the schools prepared children even though this meant the proliferation of occupational roles and differentiation. No doubt a solution to such a paradox could be evolved, but not in a hurry. Consequently, in the Soviet Union, as in the other countries under discussion, contradictory forces were at work: ideological assumptions and industrial needs were difficult to reconcile.

So the dilemma underlying the education systems of all

countries moving towards more sophisticated forms of industrial organization can be observed in the young Soviet state and can be seen in the early attempts to reconstruct the school system. The unified labour school itself expressed the highest hopes of the Russians because its ideals were universalism, proletarianism, and technical needs of the new society. However, given the pre-Revolutionary pattern of schooling where the primary and secondary sectors were not linked in any systematic way, the poverty of resources immediately available and the continuing political dislocation, the unified labour school was not likely to succeed if only because it had to function in plant inherited from the past. So it was that, operating beneath the unified ideal, the pattern suggested by Ignatiev, and in part endorsed by the People's Commissariat of Education, Narkompros, in 1918[54] was the one that really took shape. Furthermore, the Marxist ideal of polytechnical education, though proclaimed as the hallmark of Soviet education by Krupskaya herself, was never very successful. This was partly because it had never been clearly defined and partly because it was interpreted differently at different levels and times. Theoretically it was intended to combine moral, academic and technical education in a way which would offer both equality of opportunity and a reduction in the division of labour,[55] but as we have seen, here lay the paradox, and one not easy to solve during a civil war.

There was, on the other hand, one important success to which the early Soviet schools could lay claim and that was the removal of illiteracy. This was due to the rapid development of the primary sector (often in a separate primary school, in many areas the only school) of the unified labour school. The notion put forward by Halsey and slightly differently by Laski[56] that extensive secondary education can evolve only after primary education approaches universality is borne out by the fact that the Russian primary school had already eradicated illiteracy (i.e. these schools were virtually ubiquitous) by the late 1930s. Various literacy campaigns and adult evening classes had made contributions to this but the most important factor in the success was the primary school. Without near universal literacy, modernization could not have taken place, and to have brought it about as early as the 1930s was the most significant achievement of the early Soveit schools. On this sound foundation a modern educational edifice could be built. Moreover, the contradiction between proletarianism and universalism did not matter at the primary stage because, within it, they both led to the same end: universal literacy. It was at the post-primary stage that dilemma came into play, just as it did in the USA, Britain, and France.

Access to secondary and higher education and whether or not it should be limited was not seen immediately as a dilemma, and the open policies declared in the early years seemed to be successful. The workers' faculties established in 1918 to help the working classes to enter higher education had much to do with this: 38.5 per cent of the higher education intake came from them by 1925.[57] However even though the new social system which was being forged was deliberately skewed in favour of the lower classes and to the disadvantage of white-collar workers, the latter still managed to obtain a disproportionate number of post primary places for their children. Anweiler[58] says that this was because the gymnasium (upper grades of the unified labour or general school) was still unfamiliar to the working class and calling it a unified labour school made little difference. Consequently, selection up to the time of the first Five-Year Plan was to a large extent still parental rather than being a function of the schools, a situation only to be expected at the time of the NEP.

It must also be remembered that entrance to higher education through the workers' faculties was not necessarily closed to white-collar workers, many of whom knew how to acquire the necessary credentials for entry to them. What was happening in the schools was that children were being prepared for occupations according to the number of years they attended. Those with (only) primary education tended to become low-status workers; those with lower secondary education moved into intermediate positions; and those with nine full years went into more prestigious positions, or went into higher education. However, with the first Five-Year Plan of 1928 more serious efforts were made to proletarianize the schools. The result was that by 1931 nearly 70 per cent of those in higher technical institutes were of working-class origin.[59] Furthermore, party, trade union and *komsomol* members were encouraged to enter the technical institutes and the universities proper so that the party could dominate education. Anweiler claims that at this stage a new intelligentsia had emerged,[60] and that a large proportion of it was working-class or at least had working-class credentials.

Nevertheless, it was the process of industrialization rather than proletarianization which was having the most profound effect on the shape of education in the Soviet Union, because besides the difference in levels of education actually acquired by different groups of children in the general schools, various forms of technical education had been developing throughout the period to provide for the technical requirements of the new state. The upper vocational schools (*technikums* or secondary specialized schools as they came to be called later) expanded very rapidly and between 1915 and 1927 increased their intake five-fold to 189,000. This was 505 more students than found in upper grades of the secondary schools proper,[61] which for a time they even superseded. This was not only because of the popularity of the schools but also because of a campaign against these grades of the general school carried out by *komsomol* which always pushed the notion of proletarianization more strongly than did *narkompros*, which was more liberal in its attitude to the question of who should be educated. The *technikums* were important not only in providing for the technological and administrative needs of the Soviet Union but also because they gave the opportunity of social mobility. But this was true of all forms of technical education at that time. It was so for the trade schools (pre-revolutionary institutions), which were expanding throughout the period.

These were joined by the factory apprenticeship schools set up and developed in the 1920s. By 1927, the combined intake of these two sets of schools was 243,000 students. In the countryside peasant youth schools were established to give both general education and some farm training. Furthermore there was a great deal of on-the-job training in factories under the auspices of the Central Institute of Labour. It was not simply that *komsomol* encouraged technical schools as a means of proletarianizing education in opposition to the more general education preferred by *narkompros* but also because local authorities, just as in Britain at that time, found such schools necessary in the face of industrialization. The proliferation of forms of education and the facilitation of more diverse selection for occupational roles made possible by such a process were the important factors, especially as aspirations were also aroused by this development. This is not to dismiss the political squabbles of *komsomol* and *narkompros*. They were indicative of the dilemma which arises when ideology conflicts with the need to select. However, confusion prevailed until Stalin, in his ruthless drive towards industrialization, made the system more coherent and at the same time more similar to its Western counterparts.

Though the dangers of revisionism and the ghosts of the bourgeoisie could always be conjured up for propaganda purposes, proletarianization was probably no longer a pressing necessity by 1931 when as we saw earlier (p. 71), Stalin called for an end to egalitarianism in the labour force. His 'intermediate stratum', so crucial to the continuation of economic development, was in place and was both loyal and committed to the communist system. Moreover it had high aspirations for its children. This meant that Stalin could concentrate on providing for the ongoing modernization of Soviet society. The necessary educational components for this were already in existence. Universal primary education could lead to a number of secondary and higher forms, all of which provided routes to an increasing variety of occupational roles. What was needed was a more reliable means of selection.

The trend away from upper secondary education of a general kind, which had occurred during the first Five-Year-Plan, was reversed. This was partly because selection for higher education had become problematical, there being no direct route from school to VUZ[62] and also because there was concern about falling standards.

Stalin formalized ten years as the period of full schooling in 1934. However, not all children received ten years education: many, especially in the rural areas, still attended only the primary stage. Many others left, as they had earlier, after seven years. Those who went on to complete the final three years were probably destined for higher education and this became the chief educational route into the élite, especially after the abolition of workers' faculties in 1940. Moreover, all signs of progressivism were dropped and the pre-1917 methods with their formality and bookishness were reinstated. Polytechnical approaches were also discouraged because they were considered to have lowered standards particularly in mathematics and science. Those children not going on to complete secondary education could either enter work or go to the various forms of technical education described above. Decisions about who should enter which sort of school were made easier by the introduction of assessment procedures, universally applied, in 1935. Furthermore, social origin was no longer considered as a criterion for entrance into higher education[63] and fees were introduced for grades VIII-X, *technikums* and VUZy in 1940. (This was not as retrogressive as it appears: many of the intermediate grades could afford the fees as could many factory workers whose wages were better than those of many white-collar workers.) Finally the Attestat Zrelosti, or certificate of maturity, was introduced into the tenth grade in 1944. It operated as an entrance examination for higher education.

That the Soviet system was becoming more like those of France and Britain should be quite obvious: Anweiler observes that:

> educational policy under Stalin, in contrast to the earlier egalitarian – democratic and proletarian – revolutionary phase of Soviet education tended to stabilize the emerging differentiated social order that was evolving in part out of the educational system.[64]

On the other hand, immediately before the Second World War there was an enormous increase in the availability of all post-primary forms of education,[65] thus increasing opportunity. Moreover, the introduction of the Labour Reserve Schools in 1940, though sometimes regarded simply as a ruthless means of drafting youth to where they were needed, did provide training for children who would otherwise have received none, and those between fourteen and seventeen who were receiving full-time fee-paying education were exempted. Also, although the shortest forms of this training were suspect, others were of value and could last two or three years. Fitzpatrick says that:

> the Labour Reserve system has sometimes been regarded as restricting the mobility of working-class children, but this conclusion is highly dubious. Most of the Labour Reserve students were peasants; and for peasant children – as for

> those of labourers and unskilled workers – the acquiring of a trade skill in itself constituted upward mobility.[66]

Besides this, when it is remembered that evening classes became widespread at this time as did all forms of in-service training[67] then claims that half the population was receiving education of one kind or another are not so ridiculous.

Nevertheless, no matter how events before and during the Second World War are viewed, it is clear that educational expansion and elaboration were geared to the exigencies of industrialization. Indeed, despite the idealism of the early years of the Revolution and the social engineering of the late 1920s, the effects of industrialization were more directly felt in Russian schools than in American schools and certainly more than in British and French schools where the inertia of traditional social structures held back necessary development. Even so, the same pressures were felt everywhere: continued industrial development and the social adjustments which went with it obliged all four countries to make changes in their systems of education so that those systems were becoming more similar. No matter how strongly traditional notions of class and status were held, or conversely, no matter how fiercely arguments for proletarianization were put forward, the complexities of organization required to run the multifarious institutions of advanced industrial societies meant the United States, the Soviet Union, France, and Britain had to expand their education systems and make them more elaborate. Moreover, they all had to arouse the aspirations of larger sections of their populations in order to ensure that the new occupational roles were filled. The consequence of this was that, because of their proclaimed political ideologies whatever selection took place would have to be justified more and more on educational grounds. This problem was becoming more important throughout the period between the wars. It was to become the most important question facing them after 1945.

5

Britain, France, the USA, and the USSR as advanced industrial societies

Despite the horror and destruction of the Second World War in the Soviet Union, France, and Britain, and the dislocation, even in the United States, it took none of them long to recover from it. Yet the war can hardly be regarded as a mere interruption of their economic development. In all of these countries, perceptions of the human condition had changed. One factor in that change was the importance of science which was underlined far more clearly by the Second than by the First World War. Paradoxically, considering the stalemate of trench warfare, the Great War had been one of mechanization which brought home the lessons of communication: this was exemplified clearly by Gallieni's defence of Paris when early communication of the threatening position of the German army was telephoned to him by an aeroplane pilot. Gallieni responded by commandeering Paris taxi-cabs to carry his troops out of Paris to attack the German flank.

But all these forms of communication – the aeroplane, the telephone wire, and the taxi – were clearly to be seen. Radar, sonar, and early forms of computerized fire power on the other hand were invisible. In the Battle of Britain, and in the Battle of the Coral Sea, what seemed to be science fiction had become reality. And radio, radar, and sonar were not the only developments the uses of which were accelerated. The rocket, the jet plane, and in the field of medicine, penicillin, were all introduced in a way which made it appear that science had all the answers. However, the dangers of this were also apparent. The terrifying significance of the atomic bomb was best expressed by Low's cartoon of the Scientist presenting the infant human race with a new and lethal toy. Yet it was not the bomb itself so much as the way in which it was made which is important here. That eminent scientists could be thus assembled and – supported by a huge team of second-line scientists, technologists, and technicians – could work in this large-scale way, was also very importtant. Governments could no longer ignore science; to survive they had to nurture it. Moreover, ordinary people also became aware of its influence.

Daniel Bell in *The Coming of the Post-Industrial Society* goes so far as to say that economic developments after 1945 were qualitatively different from what went before because of the influence of science. 'Science-based industries, unlike industries which arose in the nineteenth century are primarily dependent on theoretical work prior to production', and 'the ethos of science is the emerging ethos of the post-industrial society'.[1] Others, such as Krishan Kumar[2] suggest that Bell pushes the importance of the differences too far: recent developments in industrial societies are merely extensions of processes begun much earlier.

No matter which of these two perspectives we take, the Second World War seems to be a critical point[3] for each of the countries concerned: their economies did develop rapidly, especially in the 1950s and 1960s; the standard of living of all of their people improved (some more than others); new industries developed; greater concentration of industry occurred and so on. Perhaps we should look at these sorts of change first, because by themselves such developments had important implications for education, no matter what the position of science might be.

Even at the crudest level, development can be observed. Postan [4] says that British output increased by 3.5 per cent per annum between 1948 and 1963 and that of France by 4.6 per cent. For a similar period in the USA (1945-57) Bergson says that annual increase in the net national product averaged 3.7 per cent.[5] He maintains that during the period 1950-58 Soviet net national product rose by 6.8 per cent (of the 1937 level). [6] However, Russian calculations put the increases at double the figure. [7] Whichever statistics are taken, growth was impressive, especially as Herman Kahn has claimed that because a country with even the lowest of these rates would double its gross national product once every twenty-four years then all of these countries would be 'post-industrial' by the year 2000. [8] This gives some measure of the essential strength of each of them in the twenty-five years which followed the Second World War.

Yet they were obviously different from each other. The Soviet Union was still in many ways a backward country struggling hard to catch up with her rivals and to that end maintaining her high investment in heavy industry at the expense of consumer goods. Moreover, her ideological position affected the way she planned for the future. However, because the war left her in direct confrontation with the United States, in the form of the cold war, and because her declared aim was to surpass the West in economic power, then to some extent she followed the Western lead. Again it must be stressed that her backwardness was not that of an earlier period: in most respects she was a modern country with a modern economy.

Britain on the other hand had different problems many of which can be traced back to the fact that she was the first country to industrialize so that her economic development could be somewhat arthritic. At least one recent view of the British economy, as it developed during and since the Second World War, paints a dismal view of it, and certainly would take Britain out of Bell's category of a post-industrial society. Corelli Barnett portrays British industry as backward in comparison with any of the economies examined here, including that of the Soviet Union. Even a new industry like aircraft building achieved the results it did between 1939 and 1945 'not by a revolution in production but by deploying 111,500 extra machine tools and a million extra workers'. [9] He illustrates how backwardness in organization, in design of tools (Britain often simply relied on American supplies), in working practices, and so on affected the coal industry, ship building, the steel industry and even the production of modern equipment such as radar, in the same way.

Furthermore he claims that the continuation of attitudes more appropriate to the dark satanic mills version of industrial relations (i.e. both sides – workers and management) meant that the British economy was, and still is, a dinosaur. His array of evidence is difficult to argue with, and yet British output did increase after the war and her gross national product went on expanding, though not as fast as her rivals. Certain industries we know have gone into steep decline so that steel and ship building as well as motor production are in serious trouble, yet on other sets of figures (see below) Britain continued to make progress.

Moreover, there was greater social mobility: it might have been almost entirely structural but that is the burden of all that has been said so far. Even in a country like Britain, with management techniques based on outmoded and quite inappropriate class distinctions and a working population, as a result, capable only of 'lacklustre output, stoppages and go slows ... strikes and shoddy workmanship,'[10] changes did take place. The number and variety of occupations continued to expand – and there is plenty of evidence (see below, p. 125) from the 1950s to show that ordinary people wanted secondary education for their children. Not all were like those portrayed in Richard Hoggart's *The Uses of Literacy* in which he says they 'are not climbing' and 'only want the little more that allows a few frills'[11] – many were aspiring. This is not to deny that some of those described by Hoggart in the 1950s still exist even today, nor to deny that British economic growth has been sluggish, management techniques anachronistic, and working practices restrictive.

France, the country to modernize most rapidly over this period still had a large agricultural sector (often in small units) and problems with energy production because of her dependence on imports in this sphere. Other differences were to be found in the level of state control in each instance. The USA and the USSR appear to be very different from each other in this respect. However, if the positions of France and Britain are also considered then the Soviet Union's position does not seem so extreme. The French laid great store by central planning and direction and the French government can claim a share in the success of the economic miracle. Britain on the other hand never seemed entirely happy with the central planning which marked the late 1940s and early 1950s, certain industries being nationalized and then denationalized (steel and road transport). Looked at in this way, they can be seen as stretched along a continuum with the USA at one end and the USSR at the other.

Underlying trends can be found in the industrial development of all four countries. Firstly the production of all forms of energy, prerequisites of modern development, increased a great deal in all of them. The figures from the USA appear fantastic:

total energy consumption rose from 25,088 trillion BTUs (or equivalent) in 1940 to 62,423 in 1970. They combine the use of coal, crude petroleum, natural gas, and water and nuclear power. Over the period covered, coal became less important: it produced half the energy available in 1940, but this had fallen to a quarter by 1970, though the total mined had increased. The amount of oil increased by 250 per cent yet its contribution to the overall position remained about the same. Surprisingly, given the publicity for it through projects such as the Tennessee Valley Authority, the contribution of hydro-electrical power was quite low at 4.6 per cent in 1950 and still the same when combined with nuclear power in 1970. The really big improvement was in the production of natural gas, its contribution rising from 11.9 per cent to 38.9 per cent.[12] While none of the statistics for the other countries is as impressive as these for America, they are, nevertheless, substantial and the trends are the same. The coal industries in all of them continued to be important but were challenged by the use of oil which, because it is a more flexible and versatile source of energy, became more widespread.

Indeed the fortunes of the coal industries of France and Britain varied from decade to decade (i.e. until the oil crisis), as first they were put under enormous post-war pressure by demand and then challenged by oil. Nevertheless, modernization took place in both of them and in the 1960s productivity improved. In the Soviet Union, coal production went up year by year from 160 million tons in 1944 to 750 million tons in 1979.[13] The production of oil in Russia rose in a similar way, from 60 million tons in 1944 to 700 million tons in 1979. The petro-chemical industries in the three European countries followed the American lead and developed rapidly not only because of the use of oil in the generation of electricity and as fuel for road and rail transport but also because of the production of chemicals used in other industries and because of the variety of synthetic materials derived from oil. To this end, Britain and France developed large refineries at home, whereas before the war they relied on oil refined elsewhere.

Linked with the petro-chemical industry is the natural gas industry because gas too is not used merely as a fuel but also as a source of other chemicals and synthetic substances. As with oil, the Soviet Union is fortunate that it has large supplies of gas within its own territories. Britain and France obtain gas less easily and yet have greatly extended their use of it. Much of the increased use of energy went into the production of electricity. R.M. Robertson says that:

> at mid-century more than one fourth the coal and practically all of the water power were used to produce electrical energy; roughly 10 per cent of petroleum and natural gas were used for this purpose. For several decades the quantity of electricity consumed by American households and business firms has approximately doubled each decade.[14]

He says this will be the case until 1990. Similar trends are seen in the other countries. The USSR produced 60,000 million kw in 1944 and 111,000 million in 1979. [15] Though water power has proved disappointing for the Russians just as for the Americans, the former still show a penchant for grandiose hydro-electric schemes. Fears for the future and worries about fuel supplies have led all four countries to develop nuclear power stations. However, in none of them has this source fulfilled its early promise except in France and worries about its safety increase year by year.

Just as important as power to the economies of the USA, France, Britain, and the USSR is metal production – and steel is often taken as an indicator of the strength of an economy. Russian production of steel increased from 16 million tons after the war to 150 million tons in the 1970s. Britain's progress was rather more patchy: capacity was raised to 16 million tons in 1950, to 20 million in 1957 and 29 million in 1962. A plan introduced in 1966 aimed at a capacity of 35 million tons by 1975. However, despite improvement in productivity and the introduction of new techniques and processes, difficulties lay ahead and S. Pollard from whom these figures are taken says:

> the loss of technical leadership and the gap opening out between the lagging technology of the British industry as a whole, and its rapidly advancing chief foreign rivals, were among the most striking of any industry.[16]

Writing of France in the 1950s and 1960s François Caron notes:

> Iron and Steel underwent two 'surgical operations' each of which brought about a sudden spurt. The first, immediately after the war, involved modernization and restructuring, and made possible the brilliant boom of the 1950s. The second, in July 1966, took the novel form of a contract between the state and employers (who) . . . undertook . . . to concentrate on huge projects (e.g. Dunkirk and Fos) so as to achieve the best possible increase in productivity. . . . Production of crude steel, which had stagnated between 1964 and 1967, increased by 28 per cent up to 1973.[17]

The implication of this juxtaposition of quotations is that British decline need not have occurred. This period is also marked by an increasing use of other metals, aluminium in particular, but also magnesium and titanium as well as super alloys such as ferro alloys which:

> have grown in importance over the past fifty years until today they constitute over 10 per cent of steel tonnage and are absolutely essential to the equipping and tooling of the petroleum, chemical, electrical, aircraft, and armament industries.[18]

Also essential to this upsurge in activity was engineering. In France 'the engineering industries were the chief constituents of the sector which Desrosières has called the "equipment industries", a sector which between 1952 and 1972 showed the most rapid growth in volume'.[19] The same was true of Britain even though technological change there was slow. Pollard quotes the Ministry of Labour *Gazette* and shows that there was an increase of 555,000 people employed in 'engineering, electrical and shipbuilding'.[20] The figures for the United States, as would be expected, show the same trend:

> The employment of engineers increased by more than 80 per cent between 1950 and 1966 rising from an estimated 535,000 to about 1,000,000, the chief reason being the expansion in this period of the science-based industries such

> as electronics, space, missiles, scientific instruments, nuclear energy, and computer technology, and the longer time required to develop and produce products because of the increasing complexity of the production processes. About half of all engineers work in manufacturing, another quarter in construction, public utilities and engineering services.[21]

It was not the glamorous new industries that were important here, but the general run of industrial concerns: engineers were and are ubiquitous. Industry cannot run without them: they make the machines and service them. A measure of their importance can be gathered from the Russian situation. Khachaturov uses official Soviet statistics from *The National Economy of the USSR* for 1960 and 1973 to show that in that period the production of power machinery increased by 284 per cent, working machinery (manufacturing) by 297 per cent, measuring and adjusting instruments and gear and laboratory equipment by 393 per cent and other instruments and tools by 237 per cent.[22] One of the industries affected by this was motor transport. We looked at this industry in the last chapter and saw how it exemplified the notion of a modern industry. In the twenty-five years after the war and before the Japanese challenge came, the total production of cars, trucks, buses and tractors in Britain, France and the United States soared, benefiting also those industries which serviced the motor industry, from rubber and sheet metal to electrical accessories. Though the production of motorcars in the Soviet Union is still far below that of the West (412 cars per 1,000 people in the USA, 5 per 1000 in the USSR), [23] production of other forms of motor transport is just as impressive as the West's.

Motor transport then, continues to make its impact on society, again something observed in Chapter 4 for the period between the wars, though its more thorough-going effects then were seen in the United States only. In Europe before 1939 it was the motorbus rather than the motorcar which was important for the majority of people because it augmented the effect already felt through railways in giving people greater geographical mobility: it was a more versatile form of travel. As can be seen above, in the Soviet Union this is still the case because of the short supply of cars to the home market. But this is changing. Moreover the bus, trolley bus and even the taxi (still relatively cheap in Moscow and Leningrad) have affected Russian life styles. But it is to Britain and France that we must turn to see the biggest impact of the motor car. Few people in 1945 could have believed that the motor car would be almost universal by 1970. However, the car is merely the most expensive part (after a house) of the affluent life style (especially in the days of nearly full employment before the depression and ignoring the submerged tenth) which became so common as both countries pursued the United States' lead.

What, of course, made the difference between the 1960s and the past was the unbelievable increase in the number and variety of goods made available from refrigerators, televisions and other electronic gadgets down to nylon tights and the myriad forms of plastic goods. In America, the abundance was much greater especially for the very affluent sections of society. But even in Russia where consumption was much lower, the 'beneficial' effects of industrialization were felt by the mass of the population. For example, cotton products increased (in Britain, France and the USA this industry declined despite improved productivity) from 2,745 million square meters in 1950 to 5,499 million in 1965.[24] Over the same period woollen goods rose similarly, but more interesting was the increase in silk and artificial fibres from 106 million square meters to 801 million. This was mostly artificial fibre production which had been low in the USSR and limited almost solely to viscose, because the Russian chemical industry was weak. This was changed by Khruschev's reforms. He was interested as much in agriculture as in industry but he attacked the problem of agricultural production on several fronts, and one of them was the production of fertilizers. From 1960 onwards the stimulation of this led to a wider development of the chemical industry and thus to the production of more sophisticated materials. 'Khruschev in his turn began to emphasize agricultural development, then housing and later the contribution which an expanded chemical industry could make to consumer welfare.'[25] Total chemical products increased by over 700 per cent. But this also links up with the production of oil and gas which is where this chapter began. Dewdny says economic growth in Russia:

> has been accompanied by rapid technological advance as part of the general modernization of the Soviet industrial structure during the sixties and seventies. Above all, growth has been stimulated and made possible by the tremendous increase in the output of oil and natural gas. While chemical processes based on traditional raw materials are still by no means unimportant, a large and growing proportion [is] based on oil and gas, which have encouraged not only a general increase in the output of chemical products but also a diversification into an ever-widening range of commodities.[26]

There are many inadequacies in this overview of the development (for example, it neglects the space race) of the industrial sectors of the economies of these four, often very different states, but it is hoped that it will illustrate that their economies had become very complex by 1970. Even if we consider the least advanced we find complexity anyway. P.R. Gregory in discussing the need for reorganization in the Soviet Union says:

> A fourth interest in reform is the growing complexity of the Soviet economy, i.e. the expanding number of interconnections among producers, consumers, suppliers and so on, all of which significantly enhance the difficulty. Recent censuses reveal over 50,000 distinct industrial enterprises.[27]

It could be said that what is being described here is simply more of what occurred before 1940. Nevertheless the increases in production in all four were so enormous and the rate of change so fast that all sorts of organizational problems were raised and even larger sections of society were called upon to play more sophisticated roles than they had in the past. This is in the nature of an advanced industrial society, and no ideology can ignore the fact.

One of the consequences of greater complexity or interrelatedness, perhaps interdependence, was greater concentration of industrial power. This was not new, as anti-monopoly and anti-trust laws from earlier periods in the West indicate. However, the process continued in spite of the legal restrictions. Between the wars in the United States mergers had been usually of smaller firms against one or maybe two larger ones. Robertson gives the example of United States Steel's share of the market dropping because Bethlehem and Republic increased theirs after a merger. [28] In this way there was a shift from near monopoly markets to oligopolies. Mergers of this kind continued after the war with little evidence of monopoly power increasing. Robertson points out that large firms grew larger but, because of the sort of expansion we discussed earlier, so did smaller firms and they even increased their relative share of markets.[29]

A similar process can be seen in both France and Britain where the most striking mergers were in the motor industry. In Britain it began with the merger of Standard and Triumph in 1945 and went through several phases till Leyland and BMC merged in 1968. Since then the industry has been dominated by British Leyland, Ford, Vauxhall (and foreign competition). Meanwhile links were being made with body manufacturers, e.g. BMC and Fisher and Ludlow in 1953. The suppliers of components also merged so that each aspect was dominated by one or two companies, e.g. Lucas for electrical equipment and S. Smith and Champion for sparking plugs. In France similar developments occured: Renault (which made 40.4 per cent of French private cars in 1973) gained control of Saviem and Berliet. Peugeot and Citroen merged in 1974. The only other home-based rival was Chrysler France, but there are technical and research agreements between these companies.[30] Concentration was found not only in the capitalist West. Khachaturov writes:

> The growing concentration of production is one of characteristic features of the development of Soviet industry. This can be judged (a) from the growth of production and (b) from the shares of very large enterprises (in terms of volume of output, number of workers and size of assets). In 1964, 9 per cent of industrial enterprises had a gross product of over 10 million roubles, while in 1968, 11.7 per cent were in this category and in 1973, 16.2 per cent. In 1964, these large enterprises produced 63.4 per cent of all output, 70.8 per cent in 1968 and 77.3 per cent in 1973.[31]

He adds that economy of scale was the most important objective of concentration but he also comments that it was easier for large establishments to set up laboratories, design offices, auxiliary workshops and even waste-processing plants. On the other hand he discusses the benefits of having smaller enterprises for some products such as radios and watches where complex assembly processes are used or where the skill of the workers is very high. Concentration then can be counter-productive and one of the worrying factors about mergers in the West is that what has become more prevalent since the war is the conglomerate. A company producing diverse products is not new, but in the past the various parts of diversification were usually related in some way. The conglomerates of the 1960s and 1970s were not motivated in this way but by considerations of finance and nothing else, a situation unlikely to change where Wall Street, the Stock Exchange and the Bourse are so influential.

Though concentration has either reduced the labour force engaged directly in production or at least pushed up productivity with the same labour force, it has also extended the administrative sectors of the enterprises involved (only relatively recently has computerization of office practices threatened this sector of work and even now no one is really certain of the extent to which it is doing this). Again, this process began much earlier, but in the post-war years the number of people involved in administrative roles increased very rapidly. Furthermore, because so much of the industrial development discussed here could be termed science-based or science-related or highly technological then the technical staff of these concerns not only grew larger but also more varied than in the past. Also the marketing and distribution systems which we saw developing before the war also expanded rapidly after 1945 and they became much more sophisticated and labour-intensive.

The affluence of high employment and good wages further stimulated the economies of these countries. Housing remained a problem in Europe because it had been neglected in the adverse economic circumstances of the pre-war period and because of wartime destruction. The result was that large numbers of dwellings had to be built (from the immediate post-war prefabricated houses to the tower blocks of flats later). How successful this was is now a matter for debate but the building industry with all its associated skilled trades was boosted. So was the production of building materials (e.g., in the USSR cement production rose from below 2 million tons per annum in 1945 to 85 million tons in 1967).[32] Private houses in the West were built in large numbers. Affluence also allowed people to call upon services which they would not have used, or used only irregularly, in earlier periods. So expansion in this sphere ran alongside the other developments. Much more important however was the expansion of medical services and education: these two areas account for a considerable proportion of the increase in the tertiary sector. Added to this must be the bureaucracies of central and local government which expanded as society became more complicated in its relationships.

Whether these changes were different in kind from earlier ones, or whether they were merely the same but writ large does not really matter. What is significant is that changes in the social structure which, as a result of further industrialization, have been occurring since the nineteenth century were very much accelerated in the second half of the twentieth century. Perhaps the underlying divisions in society were not altered so radically as some commentators seem to imagine, as we will see in Chapter 7, but most people's perceptions of their own status and the status of others changed sufficiently for their aspirations to be enhanced. The availability of new and more diverse forms of employment made this certain. We saw this happen earlier: it happened much more after 1945. Bourdieu and Passeron[33] have shown that even in very advanced societies classes reproduce themselves, and other writers (e.g. Goldthorpe, Llewellyn, and Payne)[34] have demonstrated that most social mobility has been structural, i.e. dependent on the proliferation of occupational roles, many of which carry not only high salaries but also high status. Even though the deeper class divisions may appear impervious to change, the structural mobility which automatically follows from the introduction of more complex forms of production, distribution, and servicing, is sufficient to lead people to believe that they are part of a much more open society, where opportunities are more equally distributed than in older or less advanced societies. Actuality is not what matters as long as chances appear to be present. This is very important to the way education develops in these countries. However before we turn to the changes in the education system of Britain, France, the USA, and the USSR it might be profitable to consider in a little more detail the changes in the social structure which accompanied advanced industralization.

A.L. Stinchcombe[35] uses sets of figures compiled from statistics provided by the US Bureau of Census between 1900 and 1979 to show the general trends of change in the composition of the American labour force. Already by 1940 over 50 per cent of the working population were engaged in trade, transportation, services (including education), and government. By 1979 this had risen to 66.2 per cent whereas only 3.6 per cent worked in agriculture, forestry, and fisheries. 30.2 per cent were engaged in manufacturing, mining, and construction, this sector having remained fairly stable throughout the twentieth century. These figures seem to show that the biggest changes in American occupational structure took place before the Second World War and in gross terms this is undeniable, throwing into doubt the Bell thesis that a qualitative change had taken place in the occupational composition of American Society since the war. However it could be argued that the increase from 50 per cent to 66 per cent is in some way crucial to how most people perceive both themselves and the society in which they live. Moreover, Stinchcombe goes on to show that these broad sets of figures tell only part of the story because other changes had also occurred:

> agriculture was less than 3 per cent professional workers in 1970 while education and public administration were over 40 per cent professional. Thus, as agriculture declines and education and public administration grow, we will expect the percentage of all workers who are professional to grow. In addition to this change, there has been professionalization within each of the sectors.[36]

He then gives figures to illustrate the increase in the proportion of professional workers throughout the labour force: from 4 per cent in 1910 to 7½ per cent in 1940, and then to 11½ per cent in 1960 and 15½ per cent in 1979. Because this last figure means that one in seven of the present population is a professional, it could have a disproportionate effect on the aspirations of others, especially as the proportion of younger people with professional qualifications is higher than for the population in general: it makes the importance of education more obvious.

The same sort of trends can be seen in all the other countries. In France those engaged in the primary sector dropped from 28 per cent in 1954 to 16 per cent in 1968, and this in an advanced economy with what is regarded as an unusually large agrarian sector. Meanwhile those employed in the secondary sector rose from 30 per cent to 39 per cent and in the tertiary sector from 33 to 45 per cent.[37] In the same period, according to the National Institute of Economic and Social Research:

> it appears that in the United Kingdom there was a tendency for service employment to grow faster than goods employment in the interwar years . . . . Since the war and especially since the 1950s, the comparatively faster growth of service employment has been renewed.[38]

However, dividing a working population into these three rough sectors could be misleading because, as Kumar[39] warns, many jobs in the service sector can be unskilled, dirty, and dangerous and require only a very low level of education.

The increase in white-collar occupations since the war has been in areas which do require higher levels of education and training. Between 1951 and 1971 in Britain the percentage of white-collar workers in the total occupied population rose from 30.9 per cent to 42.7 per cent. At least two-thirds of this increase was taken up by managers and administrators, higher professionals, lower professionals, and technicians.[40] A similar breakdown can be made of Marceau's figures for France and this implies that the same sort of qualitative change which Stinchcombe described for America was taking place in Western Europe. It was also occurring in the Soviet Union, though perhaps not so extensively. Lane and O'Dell give figures to show that between 1960 and 1976 the primary sector's share of occupations fell from 39 per cent to 23 per cent whilst the secondary sector's rose from 32 per cent to 38 per cent and the tertiary from 29 per cent to 39 per cent.[41] Littlejohn, commenting on these figures, points out that this division in 1976 resembled the pattern found in Italy and Austria sixteen years earlier, but says that this might be due to 'technological lag' in

Russia.[42] So the process was unfolding more slowly, but it was there. Meissner describes the same changes, though by reference to the various strata in Soviet society. His description of who fits in which stratum shows the increasing importance of education and training in the higher strata and how these are either in the tertiary sector or in the non-manual section of the secondary sector.[43]

However, care has to be taken in dealing with the meaning of shifts from one economic sector to another. Kumar's warning about the number of jobs in the service sector which are low-level and low-paid has already been mentioned. We must also take into account the work of commentators such as Braverman, whose thesis is that advanced industralization (of the capitalist mode) and the large-scale organization which it so often employs lead to de-skilling and not only in the manufacturing processes but also in the engineering on which it depends and in the administrative component. He accepts that by the early part of the twentieth century the increase in commercial, administrative and technical labor seemed to cut across Marx's bi-polar class structure.[44] He recounts, however, from his own experiences as a craftman, how technical skills which had still been important in the early decades of this century were in decline as a result of Taylorism – which also had an effect on other areas such as office practice. But the really serious threat to skilled labour began in the 1950s and has increased since. Braverman describes how the silicon chip and the integrated circuit can control a machine (say) for complex metal cutting and then he goes on:

> numerical control is thus used to divide the process among *separate* operatives, each representing far less in terms of training, abilities and hourly labour costs than does the competent machinist. Here we see once more the Babbage principle, but now in a setting of technical revolution. The process has become more complex, but this is lost to the workers, who do not rise with the process but sink beneath it.[45]

He shows, too, how the computer has had the same effect in other spheres.

> Secretaries, clerks and bureaucrats were once grateful for having been spared the dehumanization of the factory. White-collar jobs were rare; they had higher status than blue-collar jobs. But today the clerk, and not the operative on the assembly line, is the typical American worker[46]

but the

> computer system . . . is the chief, though not the only, instrument of mechanization of the office. Its first applications were for large-scale routine and repetitive operations which to some extent were already performed mechanically: payrolls, billing, accounts payable and accounts receivable, mortgage accounting, inventory control, actuarial and dividend calculations, etc. But it was soon applied to new tasks, such as elaborate sales reports, production – cost accounting, market research information, sales commissions, and so forth, all the way up to general accounting, at which point the corporation's books of record are put into computerized form.[47]

The result is that

> such positions (as clerks) offer little in the way of prestige . . . the Survey of Working Conditions found much of the greatest work dissatisfaction in the country among young well-educated workers who were in low-paying, dull, routine and fractionated clerical jobs.[48]

The micro-processor causes the same problems everywhere, as Abercromby and Urry found in Britain.[49]

This is something of an embarrassment to the argument put forward in this book – that as industrialization developed further, it required greater levels of skill from more people. Now Braverman himself admits that to be true for the first part of this century. The case was, very probably, that both trends (skilling and de-skilling) were occurring at once: they always have and they always will. Some skilled tasks are downgraded, new ones come into existence – as we saw with the introduction of the ASM – and for each stage of industrialization. Several new kinds of skilled occupation have been created because of the computer. Futhermore, the effects of the changes described by

Braverman are not, so far, as widespread as he suggests. And how far the proletarianization of white-collar work has gone is still debatable. Moreover, the professionalization discussed by Stinchcombe earlier has also to be considered, as have a whole host of new service roles in leisure industries like travel and tourism, which are only partially affected by the computer. However, what Braverman describes may well overtake us: notice that the disappointed office workers he refers to were well-educated. Education had become a prerequisite even for the work they were doing. This raises the issue of credentialism because either those workers had been badly advised or their qualifications were undergoing some kind of debasement. This is a point we will have to take up later, because it is part of the cooling-out process which is integral to how selection now works. Whether de-skilled or not, these people were affluent – and for the same period Etzioni-Halévy describes the increase in the value of real wages in the United States, France, and Britain.[50] Of the Soviet Union, C.E. Black writes that

> families after the 1950s, as they grew accustomed to fatter pay checks, turned their attention to new patterns of consumption and leisure typical of highly modernized societies. Even more anxiously than before, they sought to place their children at the desired step on the educational ladder.[51]

Here again we can see how perceptions were changing, perhaps faster in the Soviet Union than anywhere else because the link between education and prestigious and better-paid jobs was more obvious than in the West. Such pressure was, nevertheless, seen in France and Britain where great dissatisfaction was expressed at the limitations put on children's opportunity, particularly by premature selection.

But it was not only individual families which put pressure on the education systems of these countries. As their economies developed, all four governments became much more concerned with the relationship between education and economic well-being. This can be seen in the reports on education in Britain in the 1950s and 1960s, all of which at some point deal with this question. In France it is seen in the increasing importance given to education in each successive Five-Year Plan and in the United

States in the panic which followed the Russian launching of the first sputnik. Soviet concern can be seen in the fact that education was discussed more openly in this period but particularly at the time of the Khrushchev reforms when the relative merits of polytechnical education (in its widest sense) and labour training were considered against the background of the USSR's economic performance. Moreover, this national concern with education in all of these countries was increased by the belief, discussed at the beginning of this chapter, that science and advanced technology were key factors not only for economic well-being but also defence. Consequently, governments were much more prepared to expand and develop their education systems at all levels. This in turn provoked a response from all classes of people within these four societies, at a time when they felt they could afford to prolong the education of their children.

From the second half of the nineteenth century, the educational aspirations of ever-wider sections of these societies developed steadily. This is understandable because each successive phase of industrial development has led to an increase in the number of occupational roles available for people to aspire to, either for themselves or for their children. Furthermore, throughout this period education has tended to feed on itself: each expansion of provision led to an increased demand, especially when growing affluence accompanied such development. People's perceptions of themselves also changed as a consequence, and they began to see education as a right. This process came to a head in the period after the Second World War when notions of status also underwent serious change.

In Chapter 1, the relationship between class, status and power was considered (in Weberian terms) and it was claimed that in the 1860s these three components of stratification fitted each other well. Now, even if we accept the arguments of Bourdieu, or Bowles and Gintis, or Goldthorpe *et al.* that the underlying class structures of these societies have not changed to the extent where there can be anything like absolute equality of opportunity, we can still see that the relationship between class, status, and power has changed. The above commentators would admit that there has been structural mobility, because of the changes in occupations. But what is more important is that people's perceptions of the relationship have changed. This argument is given further force by the nature of the distinction which Weber made between class and status. Classes he described as stratified according to their relation with the production and acquisition of goods; whereas status groups are stratified according to the principles of their consumption of goods.

If the first refers to the way people earn their living then it is obvious that this has changed. There are many more ways of earning a living and in many of them subservience found in earlier forms of employment seem to have disappeared. What, however, is much more important is the way people consume and what they consume. If we take the twenty-five years after the Second World War (i.e. before the spectre of unemployment, and the poverty consequent upon it, returned) then we can see the increasing affluence throughout most of society has meant that patterns of consumption have become even more similar across classes than they ever were in the late nineteenth century. This is what really changed people's perceptions of not only their own status but that of others in relation to them. Again, this can be referred back to the nature of advanced industrialization which led to both the proliferation of jobs (whether de-skilled or not) and also to the production of a greater variety of accessible consumer goods. For the jobs to be filled, education had to become both more elaborate and more widely provided; in order to obtain the goods, people also demanded greater access to that education and especially its higher reaches. Again, it must be stressed that perceptions are more important than reality. The all-important relationship is that between class and power, but the changes in status have led many people to ignore that fact, because they confuse class and status even to the extent in some cases of denying the importance of class altogether as we saw even amongst American sociologists (see p. 22).

Nevertheless, except perhaps during relatively brief periods of violent turmoil, class is still very important because it is usually the chief means of access to power. This access may have become wider as the structure of classes in advanced societies has become more elaborate, and this certainly appears to be the case if the conditions of the second half of the twentieth century are contrasted with the second half of the nineteenth, but, even so, access to power is greater in the higher levels of the stratification systems. Yet because status often reflects class position and therefore access to power, a change in it can lead those affected by such a change to perceive themselves as having greater access to power or at the very least as not seeing themselves as subservient. Moreover, if education is recognized as in some way connected with this development then access to it will also be desired. In such conditions, societies not only begin to appear more open, they are probably more open in reality.

One way in which this openness is demonstrated is in the extension of political power to wider sections of the populations of these countries. As we saw in Chapter 3, the franchise was extended in the Western countries from 1860 onwards and by the end of the First World War there was universal suffrage in all of them. In Russia the changes which took place in this direction were minor before the Revolution and dominated by one party after it, though the election in November 1917 to the Constituent Assembly 'was reasonably free and fairly expressed the opinion of the country'.[52] In Britain, the fact that the Labour Party held office twice, albeit as a minority government each time, between the wars was significant because it indicated how aspirations were building up in the lower strata of British society. And after the Second World War the landslide victory of the Labour Party was an even stronger expression of the hopes of large sections of the populace that post-war reorganization would give them greater influence over their own destinies.

Similar developments took place in France as exemplified by the election of 1924 and then more importantly by the setting up of the Popular Front government in 1936. On the other hand, the immediate post-war situation in France did not seem as hopeful for ordinary people as did that in England and Wales despite the election of a left-wing majority to the French Parliament in 1946. This was because France was still suffering from the effects of the defeat in 1940 and Marwick says that, 'the likelihood of a powerful ministry governing in the interests of the working class quickly vanished as fissures opened up between Communists and non-Communists, and Catholics and non-Catholics'.[53] Nevertheless, he goes on: 'The aborted reforms, and the frustrated emotions of the Popular Front were now, as the main features of the Resistance Charter became law, institutionalized, so that the working class would never again occupy the outsider position of pre-war days'.[54] What can be added to this is that they would become later more conscious of the contribution they could make. Ardagh says that:

> at first the new ethos of reform and modernization was confined to a few pioneers in key posts, like Monnet and his team, and to local élites that sprang up sporadically around the country, like the Young Farmers. The rest of the nation stayed with its eyes on the past, protecting its '*positions acquisés*'. Gradually, however, over the past thirty years (i.e. to 1977) the new spirit has spread more widely to infect public opinion as a whole. This is the greatest change between modern and pre-war France: ordinary people now believe in progress, and accept the need for change.[55]

Thus the similarities in developments in the Western European countries are fairly obvious. What of the two countries destined to become the super-powers?

In the United States of America, where there was a longer tradition anyway of populist political appeal, Roosevelt, through his use of radio for his 'fireside chats', at least made it appear, firstly, that he was taking the majority of the population into his confidence and secondly, that the New Deal was being introduced and developed in their interests. The war strengthened the unity of the nation.

> As in Britain and France, then, though in different degrees, the war both assisted the consolidation of classes and the disintegration of overt class distinctions. It also affected those facets of American life which tended anyway to cut across class. The war was a central phenomenon in bringing a new status and a new self-consciousness to the black American, and indeed helped to bring to birth the whole contemporary Civil Rights movement. A landmark in the shift of official opinion was the establishment by Truman of the Committee of Civil Rights.[56]

This is a statement by Marwick who also points out that though racial bigotry was still powerful in America, the upper classes were less dominant and he cites the defeat of Taft by Eisenhower in the 1952 presidential election as indicative of this.[57]

Even though the situation in the Soviet Union was very different from that in the United States, there are times when greater openness appears, if only fleetingly. In the confusion of the early years after the Revolution and particularly during the period of the NEP, this was the case, especially as parties other than the Bolsheviks still existed and within the Party itself there were sections opposed to certain of Lenin's policies. However, when Stalin took control he worked through the security services and through a limited number of trusted henchmen and with such ruthlessness that it can be claimed that he waged war not only on the nation but even on the Party itself.[58] It is ironic that during the period of the worst terror a constitution was proclaimed (in 1936) which had it ever been put into practice would have safeguarded the rights of the individual against Stalin. During the war, Stalin found it politic to relax the regime but he applied it again with severity after 1945. Later, after his death, the situation improved with:

> the . . . measures taken by Malenkov to accommodate the popular demand for more consumer goods, more legal security, and more freedom in intellectual–cultural affairs. The dissolution of most forced-labour camps was significant in this regard, as were the more deeply felt 'material interests' of working people in city and country, as well as the 'thaw' in the literary–artistic sector.[59]

However, Malenkov would have kept real power in the hands of a small coterie. Khrushchev, on the other hand, set about the restoration of the party as: 'an organ for the formation of élite opinion.'[60] As the party also grew in size during the Khrushchev period, larger sectors of Soviet society had some voice in affairs. Moreover, Khrushchev's attempts to improve both industrial and agricultural performance led him to introduce further liberalization.

> the Soviet leader was under fire to move forward to a more open society by disavowing Stalin's isolationist policy and by tolerating once again a measure of social pluralism.[61]

Though Khrushchev was to run into severe difficulties because of the contradictions in what he was trying to do, there is no doubt that the Russia of his day was much more open than Stalin's. Brezhnev, in the long run had a depressing effect on Soviet society but as we are now witnessing, Gorbachov believes that the economy can recover only if he pursues a policy of 'glasnost', i.e. greater openness.

It should now have become clear that the pressures for change in education became much stronger in this period. The economies of all four countries required it. The increased aspirations of growing sections of their societies demanded it and their proclaimed political ideologies meant that it could not be avoided, especially in the more open climate which developed after the war. Moreover, to some extent, these pressures, economic, social, and political, pushed in the same direction – but only up to a point, after which a number of contradictions set in. Therefore, what has happened to their education systems since 1945 can be explained in terms of these pressures and of the contradictions consequent upon them.

6

Education for advanced industrial countries

In Britain the end of the war coincided with the passing of a very significant education act which was the culmination of earlier developments. These, as we saw in Chapter 4, were leading, almost inevitably, towards secondary education for all, but in differentiated forms, and this was the most important provision of the Butler/Ede Act. It also brought an end to elementary education and set up the modern primary school. It must be remembered that this Act was dealing with pressures which had been felt during the inter-war years. It was an attempt to provide for the economic needs of the country as they were experienced then. Although it was realized that the economy could not develop healthily if secondary education was restricted to the few, it was still difficult to extend it in wholesale fashion. Indeed, the act was really only a codification of what had happened in the wake of the Hadow and Spens reports, and as we saw, neither of these could go as far as recommending anything like *equal* secondary education for all because the desire to preserve social distinctions was still strong, despite – perhaps because of – the heightening of social aspirations. While the 1944 Act was hailed at the time as an important advance, it was still not adequate to the economic and social needs of the country. Even though the Act, and the grammar schools, were vehemently defended by the first two Labour ministers, Wilkinson and Tomlinson, it was not long before the tripartite system of schooling which it created, but never mentioned, had to be modified. The reason for this, as we have seen in Chapter 5, was that the changes in the economy and the social reconstruction attendant upon them were much more striking than those between the wars.

Moreover, just as the First World War had changed people's perceptions of each other very rapidly, so the Second World War took this process further. Thus the social climate of the 1950s and 1960s was much more egalitarian than that of the 1920s and 1930s, though this was not immediately apparent. During the earliest phase of post-war reconstruction, therefore, the tripartite system of grammar schools, technical schools, and secondary moderns was established. That was how most local authority politicians and administrators understood reorganization (especially where attempts had been made to do this before the war). There is no doubt that they were influenced by the Norwood report and the White Paper, *Educational Reconstruction*. Both recommended separate schools – as did the HMIs who travelled the country advising LEAs. Furthermore the system of testing children to decide which type of school they should attend had already been perfected, i.e. it seemed to convince most of those involved that it was valid. It was merely a question of extending it to more children. And this appeared to happen. The children who entered the grammar schools were certainly from a wider section of society than in the past.

Nevertheless, there were early signs that the education system would be put under strain by the demands of the economy. This was made clear by the Barlow Report of 1946 which Maclure says:

> owed its origin to the awareness that industrial growth demanded more highly trained scientific and technological manpower. The experience of the war years had shown that this had to be organized rather than left to chance.[1]

This was followed by the establishment of the Advisory Council for Scientific Policy in 1947. The most important report of this body was that published in 1955 (the Zuckerman Report) which was one factor leading to the issue of the White Paper on technical education in 1956.[2] Another was Churchill's speech at Woodford in 1955, 'in which he drew attention to Russian advances in technology and technical education'.[3] This White Paper made it quite clear that the future of Britain depended on extending the provision of education. It is worth quoting at length:

> The aims are to strengthen the foundations of our economy to improve the standards of living of our people and to discharge effectively our manifold responsibilities overseas. Success in each case will turn largely on our ability to secure a steady increase in industrial output, in productive investment, and in exports of goods and services of the highest quality. . . . We face, then, an intense and rising demand for scientific manpower and by no means only for men and women with the highest qualifications. Every technologist relies on technicians and craftsmen to translate his plans into products. It would be a great mistake to increase the output of technologists without adequately supporting them at the lower levels from which in any event many of them are drawn. Much therefore depends on strengthening the base of the pyramid of technical education by improving education *in the schools* and raising the numbers of school leavers who are able and willing to take successfully the courses offered at technical colleges.[4]

The Crowther Report of 1959 also stressed the importance of education to the national interest. The committee's recommendations for expansion were underlined by the statement: 'We cannot in conscience advise that anything less is necessary if the national education system is to meet the requirements of this tumultuous and dynamic century.'[5] Furthermore, William Taylor's seminal study of the secondary modern school, which appeared in 1963, emphasized the need to expand and improve secondary education, because:

> during the 1950s there have occurred fundamental changes in the methods of production and industrial and commercial processes which render concepts of educational provision out of date. These changes make it imperative that education be viewed as capital investment rather than as a form of charitable or luxury expenditure.[6]

His references to other authors such as Shonfield, [7] Liepmann,[8] and Drucker[9] show that concern for this problem was widespread at the time.

But it was obvious that the tripartite system was inadequate: it could not provide for the nation's economic needs. Too few pupils attended the grammar schools, which in any case were not the institutions they have often been proclaimed to be in this respect since they gave the wrong education. What was worse was the depressing effect they had on the technical schools, which, as they dwindled in numbers, aped the grammar schools, and on the secondary moderns which rarely operated as they were intended, but instead as upper elementary schools. The Crowther Report:

> We do not think that the figure of about 12 per cent of the age groups still in full-time education at the age of 17 and of 6 per cent at 20 is nearly good enough. The education that is provided for the great mass of children is inadequate both in its quality and in its duration. In the middle, between brightest quarter and the great mass of ordinary children, the deficiencies relative to the need, are the greatest of all, for it is in this 'second quartile' that the richest vein of untapped human resources lies, which will have to be exploited if this country is to keep a place among the nations that are in the van of spiritual and material progress.[10]

The system failed to satisfy the economic needs of the country. Its deficiencies as far as social aspirations were concerned were even worse. This become clearer as parents became more aware of the increased possibilites of their children achieving more prestigious occupations as the economy developed. David Glass reported in 1954 that in Hertfordshire only 16 per cent of parents claimed to prefer the secondary modern school.[11] Rubinstein and Simon quote the scholarship statistics for Nottingham in 1954 to show how frustration was building up. Junior school heads picked 1,321 children to enter for the examination, parental pressure added another 1,395 names but there were only 477 places available,[12] and a disproportionate number of them were for boys. Just how many places were available in any locality was as much a historical accident as anything else and much higher proportions of the age cohort got grammar school places in Wales and the South East than in the Midlands and North.

Furthermore, other forms of inequality were unearthed by

the research of the 1950s. Halsey and Gardner claimed that working-class children were under-represented in the grammar schools.[13] They threw doubt on the eleven-plus as an instrument of selection, and that doubt deepened when the British Psychological Society reported that it found the categories of intelligence expressed in the Hadow and Spens Reports inadequate.[14] Moreover, Yates and Pidgeon reporting for the NFER showed that as many as 70,000 children were 'wrongly' allocated to schools each year because of errors in the assessment of them.[15] It is not surprising that in these circumstances pressure groups began to form amongst both parents and teachers.

In France, the situation was the same, because what was re-established in 1945 was the pre-war system of education, on which the reforms of Jean Zay had had very little impact. In effect, the French had a common primary school followed by a tripartite system. The lycée was placed, as before, in a position of eminence, whilst the majority of children entered upper elementary classes. Some however, could enter the *cours complementaries,* which were what the English secondary modern had been designed to be – central schools with a strong vocational bias.

This structure was inadequate. Even before the end of the war, the Algiers plan had said education ought to be expanded. This was made clearer by the Langevin-Wallon Report of 1947, the main theme of which was the shape which education should be given in an advanced society and so it recommended not only the opening up of secondary education to all classes but also the widening of opportunities for higher education. Moreover, it drew attention to the growing importance of science and technology and said that education should be more closely related to a modern pattern of occupations. Unfortunately, the recommendations could not be implemented because of opposition from the agrégés and certain other sectors of the academic profession. But the apparent stagnation in education was also due to the weakness of the coalition governments of the years before De Gaulle came to power. Even so the problems would not go away: the drawbacks for the economy of France became more obvious and this can be seen in the way each successive national plan stressed education more than the last. The first (1947–53) was much more concerned with the development of basic industry and the material requirements of recovery, but 'it should be noted that concern for faster growth of government investment appeared from the second plan onwards (1954–7), particularly in relation to the schools'.[16]

Moreover, the Commission on Education of the Planning Commissariat discovered an increasing deficiency in the supply of scientists and engineers in 1952, a problem referred to again later (in 1956) in the Landucci Report. So the third plan (1957–61), no doubt also influenced by new pressure groups such as the Permanent Committee on Scientific Research, set about deliberately encouraging the production of more scientists and engineers. However, this could not be done without changes in the pattern of secondary education where the real weakness lay, and this was admitted in the fourth plan (1962–5) 'which contributed to securing recognition of priority for education'.[17] By the late 1950s few could argue that economic development was independent of education: the role of technical qualifications in the labour force from the mid 1950s onwards assumed increasing importance.[18] But De Gaulle, when he came to power, saw education as being important not only to economic resurgence but also to cultural survival. In an address to the nation in 1964, he said:

> It is clear that it is necessary to produce always more, always better, to save and invest constantly and even more to push relentlessly our technical and scientific research, in order to avoid sinking into bitter mediocrity and being colonised by the activities, invention and capacities of other countries.[19]

Moreover, as in Britain, the social demand for education increased very rapidly in this period, as even a cursory glance at the figures for staying on at school after the age of fourteen shows. Cremieux-Brilhac says that this was because the improved standard of living in all family settings created the psychological and material conditions which favoured the prolonged schooling of children and that tehnical progress aroused a growing demand for better and better-qualified manpower which required of all workers a general culture and a professional drive which only the schools could give.[20]

The possibility of a lycée education was unimaginable for the vast majority of children after the First World War, whereas after the Second World War it was more likely to be expected – especially by a child who was gifted, even one from the lower social classes. Two studies carried out by the National Institute of Demographic Studies in 1952 and 1962 show just how much demand for education had expanded. Furthermore, they show that the children of agricultural and industrial workers were to be found in increasing numbers in the secondary schools proper, even if their chances of obtaining higher education were still far below those of the children of the white-collar and professional classes.[21] But herein lay the contradiction: the very structure of education encouraged aspiration (in a climate of economic expansion) because through entry to the lycée it seemed that upward mobility was possible – for the individual. But the structure, considered in global terms, frustrated aspirations and still did not provide adequately for the economy. Natanson and Prost express the contradition well. They say:

> Let us rejoice in the fact that for the first time the aspirations of men and the exigencies of the economy reinforce each other instead of combatting each other. . . . Our education in fact is still moulded in forms inherited from the nineteenth century: primary school for the mass and secondary for the bourgeois elite . . . the real difficulty is situated at the level of entry into the *sixième* and takes the form of a cold war between primary and secondary. The rivalry between the *lycées* and the *colleges d'enseignement général* is at the heart of the controversies over the reform of education.[22]

And this statement was made after a partial reform of education.

In the Soviet Union, where the devastation of the Second World War was even greater than in France, the chief aim after 1945 was to rebuild the lost schools. However, by the 1950s, the same concern as in Western Europe, for the economy and education's contribution to it, was being expressed. In his memorandum to the Central Committee of the Communist Party in September 1958, Khrushchev stated quite clearly that: 'the role of education is particularly great in our time, when without the widest use of the latest achievements of science and up-to-date technology the successful development of the country's national economy is impossible.'[23] But Khrushchev's memorandum was really only the culmination of a long process because doubts about the relevance of Soviet schools had been expressed as early as 1952 at the Nineteenth Congress of the Communist Party. This theme was picked up by Khrushchev at the Twentieth Congress of the Party in 1956 and was frequently discussed in the two years before his memorandum was published. There was then further discussion followed by a declaration by the Central Committee before the law reforming the school system was introduced.

Though these reforms were directly related to the economic needs of the Soviet Union, as these were perceived by Khrushchev and the other Russian leaders, the problems facing them were not quite identical to those facing France and Britain. In the West, there were manpower shortages, especially in the various skilled categories. In Russia the labour scarcity was again felt in all sections, but particularly at the level of the unskilled. This was due partly to the labour-intensive nature of Russian industry and partly to the larger percentage of the population lost in the war, with the latter leading to a fall in the birth rate, the effects of which were still being felt in the late 1950s. Moreover, whereas in France (to use again the words of Natanson and Prost quoted earlier) 'the aspirations of men and the exigencies of the economy reinforce each other', the Russians were experiencing dislocation in this area, because in a way, the school system set up by Stalin had been *too* successful in raising aspirations. This was expressed by Khrushchev in the memorandum when he wrote that:

> boys and girls who have finished secondary school consider that the only acceptable path in life for them is to continue their education at a higher or, at least, a specialized secondary school. A number of pupils passing out of ten-year schools show an unwillingness to go to work at factories, mills, collective farms and state farms, and some of them even consider this to be below their dignity.[24]

Perhaps he was exaggerating the size of the problem, especially as the attitudes he described ran counter to Soviet collective ideology. Though aspirations had been aroused to benefit the state, families exploited the opportunities in an individualistic way. This is not really surprising because, despite early claims by party functionaries such as Strumilin of 'the dying of the family under communism',[25] the integrity of family was protected almost from the beginning. Even so, by 1936, Stalin considered too easy divorce was having an adverse effect on the stability of Soviet society – the family was strengthened and, inter alia, parental responsibility for education was stressed. This trend was given further emphasis by legislation in 1944. Those parents interested in the education of their children realized the advantages of Stalin's school system and encouraged them to take the opportunities offered. It was this which had given rise to the situation of which Khrushchev wrote. How the pressure built up is summed up by de Witt when he says that:

> it was not until 1952 that enrolment in grades 8–10 exceeded the pre-war level, and the expansion intensified through the mid 1950s. It was the sudden and substantial surge of these people into grades 8–10 that brought into focus the prospect of excessive numbers moving towards higher education at a time when the number who would be expected to go to work after the seventh grade was beginning to fall off.[26]

So then the details of the problem were different in Russia but the dilemma was the same as that in France and Britain, i.e. the aspirations of more children (and parents) were being aroused than could be coped with by the schools as they stood, yet the exigencies of the economy made it difficult to avoid the problem.

Even before the Second World War the Americans had already begun to develop a form of educational organization elaborate enough to deal with this very dilemma (see p. 87). Many Americans were, indeed, complacent about their schools for not only had they evolved the comprehensive high school but they also managed to put the majority of the age group through it. Nevertheless, concern was expressed about the schools and their relationship with the economy. This was so even before Sputnik in 1952 threw some commentators (e.g. Admiral Rickover) into a panic. For example, during the war, the examinations for entrance to the Naval Reserve Officers' Training Corps showed a surprising failure rate in basic arithmetic and there were estimates, after the war, of high levels of functional illiteracy in some large cities. Even the *New York Times* expressed alarm at the ignorance shown by some college graduates.[27] It was against this background that the Americans discovered that the Russians had stolen a march in the space race.

In the ensuing debate about the comprehensive high school the danger was that the proclaimed egalitarianism of the high school might be abandoned for some elitist model of the kind advocated by reactionaries such as Rickover. However, one of the sternest critics of the high school, James B. Conant, actually endorsed these schools. Although, in his report to 'interested citizens', made under the auspices of the Carnegie Corporation, he highlighted the deficiencies of its curriculum and its teaching, he did say:

> I believe no radical alteration in the pattern of American education is necessary in order to improve our public high schools. If all the high schools were functioning as well as some I have visited, the education of all American youth would be satisfactory.[28]

Conant completed his report in 1958, the year of Khrushchev's Memorandum. And in both countries there followed a period of feverish activity in education but America did not need to alter radically the shape of its education system. Much larger amounts of money were injected into the system from federal sources through the National Defense Act of 1958, and the curriculum became a matter of intense debate and experiment as the Americans struggled to escape the banalities of 'life adjustment education' (described by Kenneth Richmond as the Mickey Mouse curriculum).[29] However, the pattern of schools, colleges, and universities remained intact and was further developed in such a way that even larger proportions of the population could go forward into the upper reaches of the education system before they were cooled out. Indeed, what America had was a system which, with all its deficiencies (and there were many), allowed for a form of selection which was far less frustrating than the systems in Britain and France and even the Soviet Union.

Yet the Americans had the same problem as the Russians:

much larger numbers than in France and Britain were pushing for post-secondary education in one form or another, because of the opportunities they believed were to be had through education in an economy as advanced as that of the United States. Once the bulge of veterans after the war had been through higher education, there was a lull, but then in the mid 1950s there was another expansion in higher education enrolments – by some 43 per cent for the public institutions and 25 per cent for the private as the high school graduates sought places. It is at this point we need to consider again the pre-war developments in American education.

Primary education was already universal by means of the public elementary schools. The junior high school, which we saw emerging earlier to take pressure off the senior high school became ever more widespread and the senior high school became truly an institution of mass education. However it is what happened to the students after the senior high school which permitted the Americans to ease the pressure created by heightened aspirations. The community college, which had made its first appearance earlier, went into a period of very rapid expansion: 360 of them were established between 1958 and 1968. Typically, in New York, two-year enrolments increased from 6 per cent of the total public enrolments in 1960 to 50 per cent in 1970.[30] This was one way in which frustration could be avoided, where 69 per cent of the eighteen-year olds were 'expected by their parents to go to college (which) demonstrates that a college education was widely regarded as sine qua non of personal success'.[31]

But this sort of development could be built only if the foundation of it were a system of comprehensive schools. Had children been in separate schools from the age of eleven or maybe even fourteen, then those in the schools of lower prestige would not have been motivated to go on – which was the case in Britain. So then the total structure of American education, Ralph Turner's contest system of education, the building blocks of which were being shaped before the war, had fallen into place. Students could move through the system easily and, apparently, remove themselves from it at the point most appropriate for them. (As we will see later, these appearances masked all sorts of difficulties.) Turner also pointed out, when comparing European and American models, that children in France and Britain had to be sponsored at a relatively early age into the upper reaches of education because after primary education, which ended at eleven, differentiated education followed, and only one narrow branch of it was truly secondary.

If the British and French economies were not to continue to be hampered by the under-promotion of able children and if the social frustration of premature rejection were to be avoided, then the British and French school structures would have to change, in part at least, and there is no doubt that when they did change they were influenced by the American (and perhaps even the Russian) example of the comprehensive school. There was also the much publicized introduction of comprehensive secondary education in Sweden, with which British and French educationists and administrators were acquainted. Nevertheless, the idea of comprehensive education was not completely novel in either country. Multi-lateral schools had been considered in England and Wales by the Spens Commission, and some authorities, after the 1944 Education Act managed to introduce them, in special circumstances – despite the opposition of the Ministry of Education, the antipathy of the grammar schools, and the ignorance of the population at large. In France too the *école unique* movement had been interested originally in common secondary schools. Some were actually established during Zay's period of office – as recommended by the Langevin-Wallon Report.

With hindsight we can see that such a move was probably unavoidable but how each country went comprehensive does underline the different historical and cultural conditions in each of them and the different approaches each has traditionally taken.

One of the interesting aspects of the development of British education is the importance of local experiments and initiatives, and the reluctance of central government to become involved in innovation. Even those important thrusts in the progress of education which can be attributed to Parliament, e.g. the 1902 and 1944 Acts, were really only codifications of changes which had taken place already in certain localities. They could even be regarded as pieces of conservative legislation in that they prevented certain other kinds of change. The 1944 Act held back the development of comprehensive education because so many politicians at both the central and the local levels thought that the Act had taken matters far enough. However, local authorities right back to the time of the first of them, the school boards, had to cater for the economic requirements of their localities – they introduced the higher-grade schools. The first county and county boroughs developed technical education to satisfy the same needs, and also because demands were made on them by the changing aspirations of the pupils in the schools. Later, the central and the junior technical schools were the work of the local education authorities.

The same is true with the introduction of comprehensive schools: certain local authorities faced with the economic realities of local industrial and commercial expansion and change, and with the shifts in social composition brought about by rapid structural mobility, recognized the deficiencies of the tripartite system and acted to dismantle it. London County Council had plans for comprehensive schools even before 1944 and Middlesex, which included much of greater London, produced early plans for comprehensive education. However, their intentions were frustrated by the Ministry of Education (in the persons of socialist ministers) where the protection of the grammar schools was seen as essential. The conditions laid down as to size and locality were so restrictive that such schools came in only very slowly. Yet come in they did – in Anglesey, the first authority to abandon the eleven-plus; in Coventry; in the West riding of Yorkshire; and, of course, in London. Scotland too, with its system separate from England and with its long tradition of common education, abandoned tripartism and embraced comprehensive education.

Despite slurs that the children in these schools were 'ungraded, untested, and unperturbed',[32] gradually the picture of the schools which emerged was encouraging, even though with few exceptions they had to compete with local grammar schools. As frustration built up as a result of the tripartite system and its emphasis on early selection, pressure groups began to form and more local authorities began to consider the possibility of comprehensives in their planning. Usually these were authorities controlled by the Labour party but not always (and neither were all Labour authorities interested in changing the system). Probably the most influential move was made by a Conservative authority, Leicestershire, in 1957. Brian Simon is worth quoting here:

> As the Director of Education for Leicestershire wrote, he had once accepted without demur the tripartite system 'backed as it was by the Norwood Report and by the Ministry of Education's pamphlet, *The New Secondary Education,* but it was now clear that the practice of selection was no longer tenable. With public disapprobation of the bi-partite system continuing to gain momentum, local authorities he concluded 'will be relentlessly driven to adopt the large scale comprehensive school' unless some satisfactory alternative was devised.[33]

The Leicestershire plan involved the gradual move, area by area, to a two-tier system which required little new building because the secondary modern schools became comprehensive 'high' schools taking all children at age eleven, and the grammar schools became 'upper' schools to which all children could go, if they wished, at fourteen. (After the raising of the school leaving age all children went on to upper schools.) This gave education in Leicestershire an American look and although this was justified by all sorts of sound 'educational' arguments, it was really accidental. Legally it was easier to do it this way because it avoided 'destroying' the grammar schools, a rock on which other schemes had foundered. Also it was cheap. Leicestershire was the first county in England to be able to avoid using the eleven-plus in some of its regions. This is one reason why many other authorities became interested in the plan and sent deputations to see how it worked.

The Labour Party had not adopted comprehensive education as part of its manifesto until 1951 when it was about to leave office, and even then its attitudes were ambiguous. However it felt it was on safer ground as criticism of early selection mounted and as reports such as Crowther (1959) drew attention to the economic consequences of differentiated secondary education. Moreover, there was a shift in the way the party publicized its policy. In the 1960s it began to stress the economic advantages of comprehensive education rather than social justice and:

> this style of presentation was very much favoured by the new leader, Harold Wilson, who, in his now famous 'Science and Socialism' speech to the 1963 Conference, laid great stress on the point that the Party opposed a segregated, élitist secondary system, not only because it was unjust and socially divisive, but also because, by failing to capture talent at the point of entry to secondary education, it held back Britain's technological development and operated against our success in economic affairs. There can be no doubt that this line of approach was to prove electorally popular.[34]

So it was that when Labour gained office in 1964, it was fully committed to the introduction of comprehensive education, its task being made easier by the increasing number of such schools (262 in 1965). However, it drew back from legislation and tried to operate the traditional approach to education policy, i.e. persuasion and consensus. The result was Circular 10/65 which asked the LEAs to submit plans for reorganization on comprehensive lines within a year. Unfortunately, the circular allowed for six different patterns of reorganization, not all of which were truly comprehensive. Even if some of these were seen merely as interim arrangements, this policy was dangerous because it gave those LEAs which still opposed comprehensive education the opportunity to delay proceedings. Circular 10/66 the next year did try to put financial pressure on the authorities to speed up their planning and many of them did. By the time Labour left office there were 1,145 comprehensive schools. They actually outnumbered the grammar schools. On the other hand large areas of the country were still not reorganized and the new Conservative Secretary for Education, Margaret Thatcher, revoked 10/65 and 10/66. Nevertheless, because plans were so far ahead in some authorities the number of comprehensives continued to expand, though not without interference from the government. The return of Labour to power later meant that the issue was forced once more but the government passed legislation only after it had been successfully challenged in the courts by a local authority, Tameside, in 1976. Even so, by then most children were in comprehensive schools of one kind or another.

Though the first comprehensive school, Windermere, had been set up as early as 1945, forty years later not all children were in comprehensive schools and pockets of the old system still exist today. Futhermore, there are several different patterns of schooling: all age; 11 to 16; Leicestershire type; and middle-school type. And this is all due to the division in the control of education between the local and the central authority. Nevertheless, almost willy-nilly, the comprehensive school has come to dominate British education, and looking back over the way this has happened we can see that the arguments which have usually prevailed have been concerned with economic interests and aspirations. Moreover, no matter how long this type of school has taken to develop, and no matter which variant has been adopted locally, the result is that, despite the existence of the independent sector, the structure allows for later selection and to that extent is more in keeping with the proclaimed ideology of the country.

In France, the removal of the vertical divisions in secondary education and their replacement by horizontal ones – the key factor in delaying selection – was accomplished in a much shorter period, i.e. the sixteen years between 1959 and 1975, but not without difficulty. The relative speed of the process has been due to the strength of the central authority because once decisions were taken they could be implemented more expeditiously than in England and Wales where, as we saw, the initiative was left at first with the local authorities. The French had another advantage: they had a blueprint to follow – the Langevin-Wallon plan. Though it was rejected at the time it is worth looking at in some detail because it was so influential later.

Compulsory education would last from age six to age eighteen, but pre-school would be available in the *école maternelle.* At six children would enter the primary school which would provide a common education until they were eleven, at which point they would all enter the second cycle *(d'orientation),* a course of four years. There would be a core curriculum but also specialization related to varying abilities and aptitudes with more options in the later stages. This would be followed by the *cycle de détermination* which would carry everyone through to eighteen, but it would be divided into three sectors: *pratique, professionnelle, and théorique,* with only the third leading to the baccalaureate. The merits of the whole package as a solution to the dilemma facing the education systems of advanced industrialized countries should be obvious: selection is delayed but the requirements of the economy can be catered for. However, in 1947, the plan was seen as too radical, especially as it appeared that orientation could override parental wishes. A compromise bill (Delbos) when put to the Chamber of Deputies in 1949 was thrown out, the *agrégés* describing it as a threat to French culture and the Parents Associations as undermining their rights. Apart from the experimental *classes nouvelles,* very little was done to change education in the 1940s despite the growing inadequacy in the changing conditions. Other bills also failed – Berthoin in 1955 and Billères in 1957, the latter going down in a welter of confusion.[35]

One important reason for this inability to reform education was the constitution of the Fourth Republic and the succession of weak coalition governments to which it gave rise. They 'did not always give a minister sufficient time to work out and propose effective measures'.[36] In these circumstances pressure groups of one kind or another both inside and outside the Chamber could torpedo proposals particularly if they were not well presented. The secondary teachers, for example, were partly responsible for the failure of the Billères proposals, because they felt threatened by them but in particular by the one which would have linked primary and secondary education by means of a middle school *(école moyenne).*

When the first reform came in 1959 it was tempered by what had happened to Billères, even though it took the form of a decree with Berthoin, its author, taking advantage of the fact that de Gaulle had accepted the premiership only on condition that he were given a set of special powers for six months: this arrangement had only a few days to run when the decree became law on 6 January. Berthoin drew attention to the changing economic conditions and the social developments attendant upon them but was also careful to defend French cultural traditions. Hence the tentativeness of the reforms. The school leaving age was raised (but delayed till 1967), the *certificate d'études primaires* was suppressed (unless parents wished it) and instead of an *école moyenne* there would be a two-year cycle d'observation. However, this would take place in separate schools and only the very first term of the cycle would be common to all pupils, though attempts should be made to increase the similarity of the courses in the different schools. In effect the lycée remained untouched, though a lycée technique was created: all other forms of education after the age of eleven remained under the control of the primary sector but the various *cours complementaires* were now to take place in the new *collèges d'enseignement général.* Though not very much seemed to have been achieved, the first step had been taken: a sort of comprehensive school had been set up – the CEG; an opportunity was given to the primary school teachers, the instituteurs, to move within the secondary sphere by becoming *professeurs d'enseignement général des collèges* (PEGC).

Though de Gaulle was never popular with the majority of French people and despite the dangers to democracy which were concomitant to his virtual dictatorship, greater cohesion was possible in government: from the early 1960s the economic recovery of France moved on apace. Perception of what was required if the economic miracle was to continue and if France were to recover her position in Europe were changing. J. Capelle referred to how thinking on education was begining to alter when he wrote:

> There remains to be elaborated, in detail and in concrete terms, a set of measures which will determine the final educational structures . . . . Fortunately, by their work the various committees of the Planning Commission have been able to propound an infrastructure by means of which the educational system can take on a new dimension and assume its new task. Moreover, the reports of the Rueff-Armand, Boullocke and Chenot Commissions have, in spite of the circumspection with which they have been received, contributed to a dialogue between hitherto isolated bodies of opinion, and to the preparation of a convergence of views among informed people.[37]

The result of the changing perceptions was that the Berthoin reforms could be extended. This occurred in 1963 when the *collège d'enseignement secondaire* was introduced by Fouchet. By extending the *cycle d'observation* to four years and putting it wholly in this new school he created lower-secondary comprehensive education in France, because all children in the age group were to be educated there. Unfortunately the schools were streamed: there were three *filières.* Modern I would provide a lycée type education, Modern II would continue the work of the CEG, and Transitional III would deal with the rest of the children. So the advance was marred by this piece of reactionary thinking. However, it was fear of the teachers which had caused this because each *filière* was to be taught by a different group: *agrégés* and *certifiés,* PEGC and *instituteurs* respectively.

Despite the fact that the Fouchet reforms were still viewed by some groups as too radical a change, they had to be adjusted further. Fontanet was planning the introduction of a modified form of mixed-ability grouping into the CES when he lost office on the death of Pompidou. It was then left to Haby to carry on the process of democratization. In 1975, he set up the *collèges* to replace the CES and any CEG which were still in existence. This is, in fact, as comprehensive a school as to be found anywhere because running through its four years the most important part of the curriculum is a common trunk. Some children may undertake certain vocational courses in the third and fourth years (even outside the college) but most of what children study is the same. So, though there is some orientation at the *cinquième* (third year of the course) the most important orientation is in the *troisième* (final year). This will take the pupils either into the lycées proper, now sixth-form colleges, and therefore towards the baccalaureate, or to the *lycées d'enseignement professionelle* (LEP), which were formerly technical schools, to prepare for a number of courses of varied lengths, difficulty and prestige, or to the *centre de formation d'apprentis.* None of this is very different from what was put forward originally by Langevin and Wallon.

Very few people in France or Britain could have imagined in 1945 that in thirty years time the lycée and the grammar school would have lost their pre-eminence. That, however, would have been calculating without the economic, social, and political pressures which the education systems of the two countries came under in those years. By different routes they both arrived at comprehensive education, at least up to the lower secondary stage. There are those who would argue that Britain and France have only sham forms of comprehensive education. To a degree this is true because streaming occurs in both of them, often openly, especially in Britain. However, very few schools either side of the Channel operate anything like the three *filières* of the Fouchet system. If we set aside for the moment the notion of social justice, then the shortcomings are not so important. Generally, parents (most of them) accept the relative justice of the school system and so one of the pressures for change has been reduced. It is more difficult for parents in Britain and in France to blame the actual structure of the school system if their children appear to 'fail'. Even so there is dissatisfaction with the quality of the teaching in the comprehensives and there is no doubt that the schools are affected in all sorts of ways by the particular social environment in which each one exists, but these are different questions.

Futhermore we have only to look at the expansion of opportunities which the schools have provided to see why the pressure to change the system, perhaps back, has been reduced. (To cite one outstanding case: parents in Solihull, a high-aspiring part of the Birmingham conurbation, opted to keep comprehensive schools when given the chance to return to the tripartite system.) In gross terms opportunities have increased extensively. In 1947 107,356 candidates entered for the school certificate and 26,322 for the higher school certificate. By 1977, 614,400 were entered for 'O' level in the general certificate of education (which had replaced the school certificate) and 252,700 for 'A' level. And these figures do not include those entered for the certificate of secondary education, nor the joint entries.[38] During roughly the same period the percentage of the relevant age group awarded the baccalaureat rose from 4.1 per cent in 1946 to 21 per cent in 1975.[39] There was obviously a large increase in the numbers entering university: in Britain from 50,246 in the year 1938-9 to 297,200 in the year 1980–81.[40] The numbers had doubled even before the time of the Robbins Committee which had been called 'because of the enormous increase in the number of secondary pupils achieving the minimum standard or better for university admission and the increasing awareness of the lack of coherent overall plan for the rapidly exploding higher education scene.'[41]

The Robbins Report of 1963 led to the creation of several new universities and to a doubling of the student intake by 1968. The same process was occurring in France. New universities were established in 1961 and 1965 and there was a four-fold increase in the student entry between 1950 and 1968, and that from a much larger base than in Britain. Further education (in England and Wales mainly that which is neither in school nor in university) also expanded – slowly at first, i.e. until the White Paper of 1956 (see above p. 123) and greater impetus was given to it by the Crowther Report. Between the White Paper and the Robbins Report full-time and sandwich course students rose from 76,000 to 184,000 and part-time day students from 469,000 to 613,000. Evening students rose to 1,854,800.[42] The number of institutions accommodating these students, whether regionally or locally, also increased. However, what is probably more important to the thesis of this book was the increasing prestige of many of the institutions in this sector, and of the awards which they made. Several regional colleges of technology were designated Colleges of Advanced Technology (CATS) and were then well on their way to becoming national institutions. Robbins recommended that they should become universities which most of them did by 1967. In the meantime other influential colleges were upgraded to become Polytechnics, 30 institutions being thus designated in 1974. Moreover, though these were still in the public sector (i.e. not working under the auspices of the University Grants Committee [UGC]), they had their degrees validated by the new Council for National Academic Awards, the creation of which 'finally ended the universities' monopoly of awarding degrees which had constituted an obstacle to the development of local authority higher education since the end of the Second World War'.[43] Consequently the awards in this sector, particularly of degrees, became more prestigious and by 1978 approaching a quarter of a million students were to be found in the polytechnics.

Comparisons between Britain and France in the further education sector are not easy to make because the categories are different (this does not matter, because we are concerned with the expansion of opportunity). Britain has no equivalent of the *grandes écoles.* These are more prestigious than universities in France and yet some of them are technological, the *école polytechnique* probably being the best known. Consequently, high-level technological education has never suffered the lack of confidence experienced in England and Wales. However, this led to considerable imbalance by the 1960s. Halls says that there were some 12,000 trained engineers that year but only 5,000 higher technicians and these positions should have been reversed.[44] So, in 1966, the *Instituts Universitaires de Technologie* (IUT) were established to provide two-year courses in preparation for industrial and commercial careers. The number of students in them increased steadily and they even took some of the pressure off university admissions because they provide another (and a clear-cut) route to qualifications which have good prospects in the labour market.

At lower levels, the French have made strenuous efforts to upgrade technical education, not only because of the requirements of the economy but also to reduce the pressure on entry to higher education. Thus, the apprenticeship centres of the immediate post-war years became part of the system proper in 1959 and were upgraded to colleges of technical education, *collèges d'enseignement technique.* In 1971 the Law of Orientation of Technological Education placed technical education on an equal footing with general education by introducing the *baccalauréat de technician* and also the *brevet de technician* as a lower qualification. Both of these have a more practical bent than the *baccalauréat technique* which was established much earlier. Furthermore the *collèges d'enseignement technique* have been further upgraded by being given the title of lycées (LEP) and they operate at the sixth-form level. They offer the possibility of several levels of qualification.

In the period before the oil crisis dealt such a severe blow to the confidence of economies such as the French and the British, we can see that education systems like theirs were much better placed to cope with the demands made upon them, though they were far from perfect. The removal of the eleven-plus and the *certificat d'études primaires* has meant that primary education can avoid the distorting effects of a premature selection examination and the more overt forms of streaming. Because all children move on to the next stage together there is no depressing sense of failure which was the lot of so many of them in the past. Furthermore, aspirations for their children of parents who think of themselves as upwardly mobile are not thwarted too soon. Consequently many more pupils are motivated to continue with their education and to acquire qualifications of all sorts and at many levels. This is not to say that there is no frustration of ambition, nor that these systems always provide the personnel actually required by their economies but we can say that they come nearer to the ideal than they did in the early 1950s. Without comprehensive education they could not have achieved even this limited success. However, the structure of the school system, though it is probably the most important factor in the equation, is not the only one with a bearing on the problem of selection in supposedly democratic systems and this can be illustrated by a consideration of the way in which the Soviet Union tried to reform its education system in the 1950s.

Though the Soviet Union is an advanced industrial society facing contradictions in her education system similar to those confronted by the other countries of this study, there is no doubt that her economy in certain details is less sophisticated than theirs. The labour-intensive aspect of her industry was pointed out earlier (p. 129) and reference was made (p. 112) to Littlejohn's point about the 'technical lag' in the Soviet Union. It could be that Stalin's determination to industrialize in such a mechanistic way has resulted in a certain amount of dysfunction. The result, it has been claimed, is that though the basic dilemma is the same (i.e. how to raise aspirations and select at the same time), the sort of dislocation experienced in the 1950s was different. This was due in part to the fact that the lower secondary stage of Russian education was already comprehensive, technically at least – certainly not everywhere but just as certainly in those areas (the cities of the highly industrialized west) where calls on the proclaimed ideology of equal opportunity were likely to be made and we saw Russian families doing this (p. 130).

But the problem was not confined to the cities. There was, and still is, a movement away from the land and into the towns and education makes this easier. People recognize this and it compounds the problem. So pressure built up for higher education in the 1950s and some way had to be found to reduce it, as there was no intention to expand higher education. A return to polytechnical education was one ideologically respectable way to achieve this, its origins being derived from 'holy writ', and this is what was attempted when the problem was first recognized, even before Khruschev came to power. It seemed important not to dismantle the school system:

> The best solution appeared to lie not in restricting access to the senior classes of the general school, but in giving a new slant to the curriculum, so that the country's youth might acquire some basic knowledge of production methods, useful skills and indeed a more positive attitude towards manual labour while still at school.[45]

So labour came back into the curriculum; vocational instruction was increased; links were made between school and work (farms and factories); and science and mathematics were made more practical and concrete. Predictably, this failed. In 1958, 75 per cent of schools were still using the unpolytechnicized curricula and VUZ orientation still dominated.[46]

Surprisingly, in view of this failure, Khrushchev decided to push on in the same direction, but with an important difference. He also decided to introduce changes into the structure of the school system. He had at first intended:

> that all children should start work after an eight-year education and that the schools for working and rural youth should be the principal channel for obtaining general schooling thereafter.[47]

However, the actual changes which took place were not as radical as this. The seven-year school was extended to eight years and given the title the 'incomplete, secondary and general, labour polytechnical school'. The means of acquiring upper secondary education were put forward in an interesting way so that the evening secondary general schools seemed to have been given preference over the secondary general schools proper. Moreover the pupils who attended this sector would now be receiving eleven years' education. The extension would help to accommodate the new trade training but it could also deter entrants. Some general schools were also to specialize. For example, in some, certain subjects were to be taught in a foreign language; in others, gifted children could receive extended instruction in music, ballet or art; and in yet others, in mathematics and science. Boarding schools and lengthened day schools were also encouraged. Polytechnicization of all these schools was to continue with the acquisition of manual trades being stressed.

We can see that the reforms were unlikely to achieve what Khrushchev wanted because lower secondary education, one of the factors in arousing aspirations, was not only still in place but strengthened. There were also other reasons why the reforms failed. One was the inertia of the system as it already existed. Though by 1962, two-thirds of the schools had extended their courses to eleven years, most of them had not rearranged their curriculum to any great extent.[48] Others found it difficult to extend from seven years to eight years. Indeed, in 1966, the total package reverted to ten years, but the eight-year school was kept and upper secondary education reduced to two years. In the same year came a decree which proclaimed that 'trade training' would occur 'when conditions existed for it'.[49] However, what was much more important was that attitudes had not changed.

Matthews says that the sociological surveys of the 1960s showed the continued widespread desire for early admission to the VUZ and that only a small proportion of students ever used the manual skills that they had acquired. [50] Polytechnicization was difficult to organize either in school or in the workshop and was regarded as a nuisance by both teachers and managers (though some collective farm managers must have welcomed it, or even regarded it as normal). It was also under-financed. However the most telling factor against it was that it was socially unacceptable.

> The more academically oriented pupils disliked having the manual lessons thrust upon them . . . the reactions of their parents must have been similar, few of whom could have welcomed the extensions of the school course . . . . Production work by itself did not change anyone's attitudes.[51]

Tinkering with the school structure and altering the emphasis of the curriculum in a ham-fisted way made very little difference to the situation. What was to be much more significant was the decanting of students from the school system proper and into the technical vocational courses. As we saw in a previous chapter, before the war, technical schools fell into two main groups – the secondary special institutions or *technikums* (SSUZy) and the lower-grade factory or works apprentice schools with about 1 million students in the former and half a million in the latter. The *technikums* were left as they were, but in 1940 the lower schools were almost completely absorbed by the State Labour Reserve Schools (SLR) set up by Stalin. Of these there were two levels, *uchilishcha* giving two-year courses in advanced skills and the factory and mining schools, the FZO. As the students in both schools were largely draftees their beginning was inauspicious, and though they did contribute to the survival of the Soviet economy both during and after the war, they were never popular, and never as efficient as they might have been. Their retention into the 1950s can be explained only by the acute shortage of manpower with low-level training – much of it very basic as the intake came largely from the peasantry. Even before Khrushchev's reforms, which transformed this sector, the *uchilishcha* had been improving in prestige because of its courses' more obvious usefulness and because in 1955 compulsory recruitment to them was abolished. Khrushchev disbanded the Administration of the State Labour Reserve and replaced it by the State Committee for Professional and Technical Education which was to control the new professional and technical *uchilishcha* (PTU) which absorbed the SLR and the remaining FZU. These new institutions were meant to take students from the new eight-year schools and they certainly proved more popular than the schools they replaced. Then in 1969 they became part of the secondary system proper and by 1975 they had half a million students. Moreover, the number of courses they offered increased and they even began to offer courses to ten-year as well as eight-year graduates. Furthermore, it was made possible (though unlikely) that PTU students could go on to VUZ. The intake, on the other hand, as might be expected, tends to come from the less favoured students.

The intake of the *technikums* is much abler because these institutions are intended to train technicians and semi-professional personnel of all kinds. Matthews says that:

> in some organizational respects which relate to the age and experience of their pupils, the SSUZy are like the general

> school: they bear a resemblance which is becoming increasingly marked, to the more advanced PTU. Yet in administrative matters they are run like higher education establishments and have long been subordinate to the same ministry.[52]

They do bear comparison with the upper reaches of the American Community Colleges and they offer courses at different levels to both eight- and ten-year graduates. They have been remarkable for their generally steady growth in numbers and in intake, with the latter reaching almost a million in 1978. Students can go to VUZ from them but it is likely to be a long process. In effect, what was happening to the Russian system was that it was becoming a more appropriate form of selection, though not as yet a very efficient one. Common lower-secondary education followed by forms, which in this period began to demonstrate a sophisticated type of differentiation, made it possible to continue to warm up early aspirations, and at the same time channel children towards routes which, it was thought, would satisfy the requirements of the economy. Polytechnical education might not have worked very well as a direct influence on this, but in a subtle way it did help to prepare pupils for the differentiation which was to take place later, and it was a forerunner of what was to come, as we will see in the next section.

What is striking about what happened to the education systems of these four countries in the period from the end of the Second World War to the time of the oil crisis is just how similar their underlying structures had become, once the combined pressures of economic needs and social aspirations had been brought to bear on them so forcefully. Superficially, individual components might have appeared different products of different cultural and historical traditions. The British college of further education, the American community college and the Russian *technikum* do not look alike at first sight, but taken along with other institutions and viewed as part of a process, they can be seen to be performing similar functions. However, it is the total process which is important.

If we take the initial stages of their education systems we can see that these had become similar by, or soon after, 1945.

Elementary education, in the nineteenth-century sense, had disappeared and had been transformed into universal primary education. Though this first stage of education proper could now become child-centred, even Rousseauian in its ethos, its real function had become to develop basic skills in preparation for secondary education, that being the stage which had real relevance both to the economic health of each country and to the growing desire for the qualifications which would increase the likelihood of entry into the more lucrative and prestigious parts of the ever more elaborate occupational structure.

Now, as we saw in the cases of France and Britain, making the first part of this second stage, i.e. lower-secondary education, a common experience for all children did prove very difficult. This was because traditional notions of who should have secondary education, which were based on outmoded class attitudes, still prevailed, even though they were inappropriate to the changing economic conditions. Nevertheless, comprehensive education was set up in both countries so that they matched more closely the systems of the USSR and the USA where comprehensive schools had been common much longer. We also saw that the compromise systems of secondary education found in France and Britain immediately after the war, that is the tripartite systems, could not survive. They were inadequate to both national and individual needs. Vertical divisions, in the form of separate schools, at the lower-secondary stage, no matter how appealing their nomenclature, cannot provide for the more subtle kind of selection which advanced industrial societies require. Such early separation of children into virtually watertight compartments proved to be too restrictive. Not enough of them remained in the system to acquire the advanced skills needed by the highly technological economy, and, moreover, too many ambitions were frustrated. In the end the traditional grammar school and the lycée, at least for most children under the age of fifteen, had to become institutions of the past. The Ralph Turner contest pattern of education, where the early obstacles to progress in the secondary sphere are easily negotiated, developed in France and Britain, just as it had in Russia and America. In France this lower-secondary stage is now quite distinct and takes place in a *collège*. In Britain, it is not so clear-cut because of local variations in schools. But whether children from the age of 11 to 14 are in the top end of middle schools, or junior high schools, or whatever other pattern, the chances are that, until they make choices about GCE or CSE – or now which level of GCSE – they are engaged in a form of lower-secondary education which is not so unlike the experiences of their equivalent age groups in France, Russia, and the USA. Any differentiation between children, apart from that to be found in one or two anachronistic enclaves, is internal to the individual school. Decisions are taken which will affect the futures of the children but these are masked. That early selection which bedevilled the tripartite systems, blighted the educational careers of children, and served the economies of France and Britain so poorly, has disappeared.

The more overtly crucial stage in the education systems of all four countries has now become the upper secondary school (or section of schools) because that is where the really important decisions are taken which will affect which part of the occupational structure students will enter later. However, though the essential task of these institutions in each country is the same, the level of flexibility displayed by each individual national system is different because of their different historical traditions.

The greatest flexibility is shown by the United States. This is not surprising as comprehensive education was introduced earlier by the Americans and affluence has enabled them to keep their children in education longer than anywhere else in the world. So, decisions taken at this stage in American schools are not irrevocable. Even so there is a high correlation between the electives chosen by American fifteen-year-olds and the kind of higher education they will receive later, or even if they will receive it at all. Moreover, though there is no examination like the GCE or the *attestat* at the end of the senior high schools continuous assessment is carried out and a students' average grade point will be important later. Furthermore, those students intent on entering more prestigious forms of higher education probably need to take the scholastic aptitude test or some equivalent. Nevertheless, most students are still together in the same schools even if some might find themselves in vocational courses for part of their time, or maybe even vocational centres for a proportion, in some instances all, of their work.

In the USSR, this is also the point at which differentiation begins but again there is flexibility. Compulsory education ends at the lower secondary stage, but the Russians still refer to it as incomplete secondary education. In fact about 60 per cent of fifteen- to seventeen-year-olds continue with secondary full-time education in the general school and even for those who do not, there are still opportunities because many take up part-time general education, which can give access to higher education, though the likelihood is limited. Fifteen is also the age when students can enter the PTU but even this is not the dead-end which lower prestige forms of technical education used to be, for again entry to the VUZ is still technically possible. Some students will also enter the *technikums* at this point, though places in these are now increasingly taken up by full ten-year (i.e. complete secondary) graduates. Though the institutions at this stage might appear different from American forms, this is only superficial – the function is the same: real differentiation occurs at this stage, but not in too frustrating a manner.

The situation for students in Britain also appears to be flexible because the final decision about what level of examination they should take, or whether they should take any at all, at sixteen is not reached until only a matter of months before the examination takes place. However, there is considerable variation between schools about how and when such decisions are taken, and for many pupils where they find themselves at the beginning of this stage is all-important, especially if the school is rigidly streamed. In fact, differentiation is occurring throughout this period, because, just as in the United States, the options chosen by students have implications for their occupational futures. What makes the British system so much less flexible than the American is the examination system because despite the fuzzy zone between CSE and GCE, for the majority of students the future is decided by which type of examination they are entered for and in what combination. GCSE has made no difference.

In France there is less flexibility than in the other countries. For a few students a decision has already been taken at the lower-secondary stage during which they might have embarked on technical courses which will give them only low-level qualifications. For the rest, where they go after the *collège* is all important. They can move on to the lycée proper which will take them on to one of the various forms of baccalaureat, or they can enter the LEP which usually leads to the *certificat d'aptitude professionelle* or the *brevet d'études professionelles,* but these do not preclude a later switch to a baccalaureate course, though this is difficult. Finally some will enter a *centre de formation d'apprentis.* There may be less changing course at the upper-secondary stage but there is still room for manoeuvre and certainly the system is more flexible than it was in the past and displays less overt unfairness.

Changing the shape of the school systems in these countries was not enough. Post-school educational opportunities have had to expand too, and again an indication of how this might be done appeared in the USA before the Second World War with the junior college. After 1945, along with the rapid expansion of the whole higher education sector, came the development of this alternative form of education which, as the community college, has eased pressure on the American system. It offers courses which are ends in themselves and can lead directly to employment and it offers others which can form part of a degree or lead on to university proper. In Britain the number of universities was increased, the polytechnics were developed as were the colleges of education, but probably just as important as any of these, the colleges of further education were increased both in numbers and in size. They have since the 1960s provided a wide range of courses varying from the low-level technical, through all types to virtually degree level. They also provide courses (e.g. GCE) through which access to university can be gained.

The Soviet Union has developed the *technikum* so that it now not only provides the middle range technical and professional courses which it always has, but also alternatives to higher education. University intakes have increased as have opportunities for part-time and correspondence courses at advanced and higher levels. In France too there has been a rapid increase in the numbers of students taking university courses, and even in the numbers in the *grandes écoles,* though these are still fiercely elitist. The *Instituts Universitaires de Technologie* have also been introduced and provide an alternative to higher education proper.

Again, what is remarkable about all this is just how similar the structure of education is in each country: selection is postponed until the age of fifteen through the device of common lower-secondary education. This is followed by a period of upper-secondary education, which, to borrow the French phraseology, is one of orientation when real differentiation begins to take place (though more subtly than in the past). Next comes post-school education which can either provide opportunities for employment, or deflect students away from higher education or alternatively can help them achieve higher education if they are determined enough. Opportunity appears to have been built in at every stage.

Indeed, to a great extent that is the substance of this chapter: the increase in educational opportunity, or at least the creation of systems, in Europe, which appear to offer some of the perceived educational equality of opportunity offered in the United States. As Natasan and Prost pointed out (see above p. 128) this suited the economies of the countries concerned because they needed to encourage larger proportions of their populations to develop the higher-level skills demanded by their advancing technologies and more elaborate forms of organization. The structures of the education systems, particularly in France and Britain, had to change to achieve this: they had to adopt the contest pattern of schooling where selection is postponed. This was one way of solving a dilemma which had its roots back in the nineteenth century when the need for mass systems of secondary education was first dimly perceived but when secondary education was understood only in elitist terms. However, the problem had not really been solved and even before the oil crisis when a downturn occurred in the world economy, all of these countries had to face the problem of cooling down some of the aspirations which they had aroused. Selection became the all-important question, but in one way or another it always had been.

The difference now was that selection could no longer be as blatant as it had been in the past. It had to operate in more sophisticated ways otherwise neither the exigencies of the economy nor the aspirations of parents could be satisfied. Furthermore, selection had to appear to be justified on educational grounds, and not to be merely a matter of parental choice. In fact, as we shall see, parental choice is still crucial but the appearances have to be that the routes taken by children after common lower secondary education are the 'right' ones for them as adjudged by the schools – in most cases.

Part 3

Selection now

7

Selection: educational or social?

Education systems in highly industrialized countries face a constant and probably insoluble problem. They have to provide at least a semblance of equality of educational opportunity and they also have to ensure that occupations of varying levels of responsibility and skill are catered for. In other words they have to act as sorting houses. They are vast selection mechanisms.

In Chapter 3 we saw that, in the second half of the nineteenth century, where a person slotted into the social or occupational hierarchy depended only to a small degree on education, because though it was recognized that education was necessary to the provision of the skills society needed, the kind of education anyone received depended on the choice made by his parents. Whether to send a child to school, or which school to send him (or increasingly, her) to, was what mattered. Selection was parental. The three great reports of the 1860s on education in Britain showed that the schools which existed reflected the social structure of the time. That structure was relatively simple, and fitted the occupational pattern so that a person's class, his likely status and his access to power were all at similar levels. Schools made little difference (once the parents had made a choice). They merely confirmed the social patterns of the time. This was also true to a greater or lesser extent for France and Russia and even the United States. However, these essentially divisive systems were becoming inadequate because of industrialization.

What we have seen happening since then has so changed the situation that education now plays a much more important part in deciding the kind of occupation a person might engage in, and to that extent it reflects the alterations in the systems of social stratification to be found in these countries. The deep-lying structures may not have changed very much – there are still wide differences between the richest and most powerful on the one hand and the unskilled, possibly immigrant and black, worker, on the other. However, there are undeniably more gradations in society. Power is not displayed as nakedly as formerly. Status no longer attaches so easily or precisely to class and to level of power. This latter point means that these three factors are often confused in the minds of most people to the extent where the importance of social class is even denied. It is such perceptions of class situation which make it imperative, in societies which claim to be open and democratic, to offer through education a measure of equality of opportunity. For governments (or even ruling classes, castes, or élites) not to do so is to risk alienating large sections of society. In the countries dealt with here, the proclaimed political ideologies are such that there must not be too much difference between the myth and the reality. When selection takes place in them, it must appear legitimate.

So, in such circumstances, selection cannot remain solely parental. It must be linked in some way (even spuriously is better than nothing) with talent or skill or knowledge – and preferably all three – and so schools have come to play an important part in this. They claim that they can develop skills and impart knowledge, and much more significantly, examine and therefore grant credentials. Futhermore, they have acquired the right to do (or perhaps the duty of doing) this over a period of time when it seemed not only proper that they should, but also expedient. The skills and knowledge required by highly developed means of production, for the running of increasingly complex organizations, and for managing the elaborate interrelationships found in a sophisticated consumer society, seemed to become much more difficult to acquire without education. Governments had no option but to expand education at all levels. Again this happened during a period when perceptions of the relationships between different parts of the class structure were changing, when political arrangements were becoming (even if only superficially) more open, and the means of mass communication were being developed in a way which made people more knowledgeable about each other.

What I have tried to show is how, as industrialization has moved on so education systems have become mass organizations offering in theory, and to some extent in practice, something approaching equality of opportunity – or at least equality of access to real education if only up to the point where the crucial differentiations and, therefore, selection for jobs, begin to occur. Futhermore, the systems are, by and large, accepted by their populations despite their inadequacies. Since access to their most important institutions, the secondary schools, has been made open, the greatest inequities of the sponsored system have disappeared, largely because overt forms of selection at about the age of eleven no longer exist in any of these countries. However, what these education systems offer appears more egalitarian than is the real case because when they differentiate between children, (supposedly because their economies demand occupation structures which are to some extent stratified), those differentiations still correlate quite strongly with social class.

This is so even in the Soviet Union where real effort has been made to provide something like equal opportunity. Indeed we saw earlier how there was an attempt to deliberately shift the balance in order to proletarianize education (see above p. 93). More recently (1959) this was tried again, by giving preference to applicants for VUZ places who had already worked. However, even making work experience compulsory had very little effect. Differentiation, of course, begins earlier – ostensibly at the end of the eighth year of education, when children face a choice: either to enter the ninth grade of the general school in order to have 'complete' secondary education; or to go into a *technikum;* or into a vocational school (PTU); or to begin work (and maybe to embark at the same time on an evening or a correspondence course). Murray Yanowitch says that a social selection process is at work here.

> Perhaps its most obvious aspect is that the high ranking occupational groups ('specialist', those holding jobs which require a higher or specialized secondary education) typically send a distinctly larger proportion of their children to the ninth grade of the general secondary school than do workers and non-specialist employees. This, it will be recalled is the path of the greatest promise of eventual

entry into higher education. Thus some 70 per cent or more of specialists' children, went on to the ninth grade, while the corresponding figure for the children of workers and lower-level non-manual employees was closer to 40 to 50 per cent. When the data permit us to distinguish subgroups within the 'specialists' and 'workers' categories, the influence of parental occupational status seems even greater. Among children reared in intelligentsia families (following Soviet usage for the moment, we treat 'intelligentsia' and 'specialists' as equivalent categories) on the other hand, the proportion taking this path (i.e. into the PTU) at the age of 15 to 16 was altogether insignificant (3 per cent in Leningrad among children of higher-level specialists).[1]

Yanowitch is dealing with figures produced in the late 1960s and early 1970s but what he has to say is borne out by Mervyn Matthews with figures for the late 1970s and he also draws attention to the fact that many of the *technikums* are not highly regarded by the upper social groups:

> The relative unattractiveness of the SSUZy *(technikums)* inevitably affected the social composition of their pupils. Intakes into the Leningrad SSUZy at that time (1978) were given as 65 per cent 'workers' and 5.5 per cent 'peasants' leaving nearly a third to come from 'employee' or white-collar groups. This breakdown was distinctly more 'proletarian' than that at the local VUZy, where 52 per cent of the entrants were of employee origins. We may doubt whether many of the employees who sent their children to the SSUZy were VUZ-trained specialists anyway; and the weight of this group may have been increased by the relatively high concentrations in a few of the best institutions.[2]

George Avis, on the other hand, claims that because improvements have been made in the PTUs (e.g. by introducing a measure of general education into them making them a possible if remote pathway to higher education) and because of improved vocational guidance throughout the education system, the balance may have shifted towards the children of manual workers, but he adds:

> Middle-class representation in some areas has not changed since the late 1960s, but it has suffered some decline overall. Despite this, the non-manual worker group, especially the highly qualified specialists and intellectuals, retains its traditional relative superiority in access to higher education.[3]

So, a socialist country which claims to have provided equality of opportunity, falls far short of its own ideal. What about the United States, the prime exemplar of capitalism and therefore of market forces? Is equality of opportunity any nearer being achieved there than in the Soviet Union? This is an interesting juxtaposition because, in the sort of ideologies which Americans proclaim, they are not so very far from the Russians on this question, America being the land of opportunity. If we look at the state which is sometimes seen as being the model for America in the second half of the twentieth century, i.e. California, we find that:

> Public subsidies for higher education tend to go disproportionately to students from relatively high-income families . . . almost 40 per cent of the student population receives no subsidy whatsoever, while a relatively small group receives very substantial subsidies.[4]

It is no surprise to discover that this is replicated throughout the USA. The most complete study of the problem is by Bowles and Gintis in *Schooling in Capitalist America.* They claim that economic success (i.e. gaining entry into an occupation with both high monetary rewards and social status) is closely related to the number of years schooling acquired and that this relationship is not explained by differences in ability as measured by IQ tests.[5] They produce figures to show that the effect of socio-economic background on economic success is strong even for individuals with equal education and IQ.[6] As in the USSR, a child from a socially advantaged family is more likely to stay at school longer, enter prestigious tracks, and then go on to those forms of higher education with stricter entry qualifications. Even in the community colleges, which, as we saw, were developed to ease the pressure on higher education from the late 1950s onwards, there is a bias in favour of those already at an economic advantage. Karabel says that:

> compared with students in transfer (to universities) programmes, vocational students are markedly lower in family income, fathers' education, and fathers' occupation. While almost half of community college students in the transfer curriculum are from white-collar families, only one-quarter of the students in vocational programmes are from such backgrounds. Students enrolled in technical programmes fall in between vocational and transfer students along various measures of socio-economic status. Black students show themselves to be considerably more likely than white students to enroll in community college vocational programmes. The relatively low social origins of vocational and technical students are likely to be reflected in their adult occupations.[7]

Writing elsewhere, Karabel maintains that what movement there has been towards meritocracy (i.e. where talent is rewarded) still favours the affluent. This was in *Social Forces* in March 1975.[8] In the same journal ten years later Krauze and Slomczynski say that 'the observed distribution of the labour force is and has been far from the meritocratic ideal'.[9] This is true also for France, of which Jane Marceau writes that:

> in 1962 Raymond Aron remarked that the representation of different social classes in the universities was the reverse image of their representation in the nation and the INSEE and BUS figures used by Bourdieu and Passeron showed clearly the truth of this.[10]

In fact, there has been a steady increase in the percentage of the relevant age group going into the universities in France since the 1950s. Baudelot *et al.* say that the increase between 1959 and 1976 was from 6 per cent to 16.4 per cent. Their figures also show that the children of agricultural workers increased their chances of entering university from 0.7 per cent to 2.1 per cent and workers (including domestic servants) from 0.5 per cent to 4.3 per cent. However, the chances of the children of top executives and members of the liberal professions rose from 37.3 per cent to 71.8 per cent. At the same time children from middle management homes improved their chances from 20 per cent to 31.9 per cent.[11]

Baudelot could find little evidence for the democratization of the *grandes écoles* either.[12] Looking at the tier below the universities, i.e. the IUT and the STS (*Sections de Technique Superieur*), the children of workers were better represented. What this indicates is that the same process is occurring in France which we saw in the Soviet Union in the case of the *technikums* and in the United States in the case of the Community Colleges, even though the qualifications to be had in the IUT are more prestigious than those of their counterparts. So then, in France a form of social selection is going on in education, and as for the great powers, it begins in the schools. Whether, at the age of fifteen, a child enters a lycée, or a *lycée d'enseignement professional,* or a *centre de formation apprentis,* depends as much on his or her social origins as on anything else. Any improvement in the chances of economic success for the humbler sections of French society are more than overshadowed by the far greater improvement in the chances of the middle or upper classes.

As late as 1968, the Report of the Public School Commission produced figures which indicated how powerful were the public schools in Britain. Though they catered for only 2.6 per cent of fourteen-year olds, their former pupils took 15.6 per cent of all the university places and 35.1 per cent of those at Oxford and Cambridge. The report also showed how former public school pupils were very strongly represented in positions of power: e.g. 90.9 per cent of Conservative cabinet members and even 43 per cent of Labour cabinet members. This situation has not changed to any great extent.[13] The schools continue to be as successful, even if this is now masked somewhat by the increasing numbers of youngsters with qualifications which take them on into higher education of one kind or another. But this is only the tip of the iceberg. If we look at the pupils staying on at school until 16 or later we find that 70 per cent of the children of the service class do so, 32.6 per cent of the intermediate class, and 26.8 per cent of the working class. The percentages of those obtaining 1 or more 'A' levels are 26.9, 6.9, and 2.8 respectively.[14] These figures from Halsey, Heath and Ridge's *Origins and Destinations* are now somewhat dated, but the proportions of each group going into higher education are still substantially the same, and if the wide categories used by Halsey are broken down further with more carefully defined sub-groups then the inequalities are more glaring. Indeed the same situation pertains in this country as in France: the differing levels of prestige attaching to different forms of post-compulsory education mirror the gradations to be found in society.

All of which seems to leave us with a paradox: the patterns of educational provision have become more elaborate in order to cater for the requirements of increasingly sophisticated economies and the complex societies which go with them. At the same time the old privileges associated with class differences seem to be still there, and to be confirmed by the very systems developed to offer equality of opportunity. However, systems which do not offer to the lower classes some chance of obtaining jobs with better remuneration and status will not satisfy the economic requirements of the country concerned either, as we saw in the case of tripartism as it operated in France and Britain immediately after the Second World War. Perhaps the difficulty here arises out of the phrase 'equality of opportunity'. What the systems must offer, for the sake of the economy, is opportunity, but not necessarily *equality* of opportunity. The trouble is, of course, that offering to all people an education which will provide economic opportunities might also change their perceptions of both themselves and the rest of society, and this might then make them dissatisfied. This was recognized as a danger to the privileged classes even in the late eighteenth century. 'Eusebius' writing in the *Gentleman's Magazine* in 1797 said:

> The man, whose mind is not illumined by one ray of science, can discharge his duty in the most sordid employment without the smallest views of raising himself to a higher station . . . . While those who have imbibed the pernicious doctrines of seditious writers, will be the first to excite rebellions.[15]

The system of elementary education introduced by men like Kay-Shuttleworth as forms of social control, in order to forestall the dangerous alternative of the working classes educating themselves politically though the Chartist Halls, succeeded only relatively briefly: it became in a limited way both means of opportunity and also one of the influences bringing about changed perceptions of the social order. The process, as we have seen, may have been long and painful, but it did happen, and led to further change. However, what we are dealing with here is how people *perceive* themselves and those around them and most people are not very interested with global notions of equality of opportunity. Goldthorpe says that they are rarely concerned with what those in social echelons remote from themselves might be doing, but they are influenced by the actions of those close to them socially.[16]

Now if we remember the changes in the structure of society which occurred as a result of industrialization, we can see that because the stratification systems are much more complex, then people are possibly more insulated from each other because of the greater number of intervening categories, but this does not matter too much as long as there is the possibility of moving up or down in the system. If we look at a particular set of changes we can see this. The INSEE study of mobility in the late 1950s and early 1960s found that there was not a great deal of movement, even though the period was one of rapid industrial expansion. Commenting on this, Jane Marceau says:

> The overriding impression is not of social mobility at all, but of considerable social immobility. In nearly every category there was a greater tendency for sons to enter their fathers' profession than any other. The major exceptions to this were the farm workers' sons, who were nearly three times more likely to become workers in industry than to remain in agriculture in the sons' generation, and the sons of patrons of industry and commerce. This was clearly due to fundamental changes in the industry in the first case and to the heterogeneity (social and professional) of the category in the second. *However, there was, of course, some movement in all categories* . . . the tendency for sons of all categories, with the exception of that of senior executives and the liberal professions, was to enter the ranks of the working class, the *classe ouvrière*, when they changed class. Not only was that the most frequent receiving category, but it was virtually always more frequent than all the other categories put together. Secondly,

> movements were very short; where sons did not enter their fathers' professional category and where they did not become workers, they were likely to be found most in the categories adjacent to that of their father. Thus, for example, the greatest proportions of sons of employees were found to be employees (the same), workers (below), or middle-grade personnel (*cadres moyens*) in the category above.[17]

This is quoted at length because it is quite instructive. The movement into the working class is not surprising given the tardy but rapid development of French industry and the untypically large size of the French primary sector. What is important, is, as Marceau admits, that there is movement in *all* classes. However, there is also the *possibility* of movement *upwards*, and if education offers an opportunity to do this, so much the better. This did, in fact, happen, because this was also the period when the structure of French education began to change dramatically to accommodate both the economic requirements of the country and the changing aspirations of a society, where upward mobility was possible even if not extensive. A crucial factor here was that access to secondary education began to open up – this is what gave (or seemed to give) opportunities which had not been there before. This does not however preclude the sociologists uncovering the underlying wide inequalities, and the politicians pointing them out when it suits them. Most people, however, even in the country with (possibly) the highest level of political awareness in Europe, are most concerned with what is happening to their neighbours. And their neighbours were sending their children to secondary schools.

How people understand their own situation in such circumstances is just as important as where they are located in the structure. However, it is probable that these two factors influence each other. How you view the world depends where you stand, but if you can change your position as a result of what you see, you may very well decide to do so. Some people have a clearer view than others, and are not likely to change their advantageous position willingly. Bourdieu writes:

> The law of the educational market may be read in the statistics which establish that, from the moment of entering

> into secondary education right up to the *grandes écoles,* the hierarchy of the educational establishments and even, within these establishments, the hierarchy of the sections and of the fields of study arranged according to their prestige and to the educational value they impart to their public, correspond exactly to the hierarchy of the institutions according to the social structure of their public, on account of the fact that those classes and sections of a class which are richest in cultural capital become more and more over-represented as there is an increase in the rarity and hence in the educational value and social yield of academic qualifications.[18]

However, Bourdieu also shows that the distribution of cultural capital is not the same as, though it is closely related to, economic capital. Teachers, for instance, have a greater measure of the former than the latter (on his figures). This therefore allows the education system some measure of autonomy and gives educational credentials a currency in the job market, though this has little effect on those so economically powerful that they do not need qualifications. Even so, a circle is set up and this is why Bourdieu and Passeron can say that education is so important to the reproduction of the class system.[19]

As a reproduction system, however, education is not perfect (the circle need not be vicious). Even Bourdieu concedes that the economically very powerful need not play the educational game; teachers, at any level, might not wish to benefit economically from their cultural capital; and at the bottom end of the social scale are those who choose not to play it. Commenting on Paul Willis's *Learning to Labour,* Henry Giroux writes:

> Not only do the lads reject the alleged superiority of mental labor, they also reject its underlying ideology that respect and obedience will be exchanged for knowledge and success. The lads oppose this ideology because the counter-logic embodied in the families, workplaces, and street life that make up *their* culture points to a different and more convincing reality. Thus, one major contribution that has emerged from resistance studies is the insight that the mechanisms of reproduction are never complete and are always faced with partially realized elements of opposition.[20]

However, that very resistance keeps them in their place, because by it they reject the tools and knowledge which might transform them into something other than they are.

This is not the case with most people: generally, they accept their education systems, and regard them as useful both to the individual person's well-being and to each person's economic opportunities. They might not, as implied by the argument above, understand all the mechanisms of the system very well, nor recognize the deeper, subtler consequences of them, but they are fairly certain that the systems can be made to work for their benefit. Now, if we accept the Bourdieu/Passeron thesis that education reproduces the class system – and we must accept it, in part at least, given the sort of unequal outcomes which we observed resulted from all the systems under discussion – then, the dysfunctions in the reproduction process (as exemplified by the higher executives, the teachers, and 'the lads') and the rather narrow possibility of upward mobility which we saw in the INSEE statistics, can only be partial explanations of why the systems appear acceptable.

Access to secondary education is another part of the explanation, especially as it broke the monopoly which the middle and upper classes had in this area. This does not deny the importance to the very rich of a group of public schools in Britain, nor of a handful of private schools in the United States, nor of some of the confessional schools in France, nor yet the clandestine schools for the children of the élite in Russia. However, perhaps with the exception of Britain, such schools are too few in number to fill even all the élite positions and certainly not those just below the top level, and so can be ignored by most aspiring parents. Such schools do not have to be attended in order to gain access to some measure of power, as was once the case. The state systems of open-access schools can be used (with some element of risk) and children can make their way through much of the system before differentiation takes place. If parents do complain, it is no longer about the structure of the system as it was in France and Britain in the 1950s. It is about the teaching, or the drawbacks of a particular social mix in an individual school. The structure, therefore, is regarded as one which offers fairness, by and large. This puts the schools in a very strong position: they have become the engines of selection.

8

The legitimation of selection

Why do we accept the schools as engines of selection? Why do we accept their judgments? In answering this question we might go further towards resolving the paradox raised earlier. One factor which has a long history is the traditional authority and respect given to the secondary school teacher. This goes back to the time when the graduate was in holy orders. It may have been diluted by the amalgamation of the upper parts of the old elementary education with the élitist schools during the first half of the present century but it must also be remembered that the French *instituteurs* were highly regarded by the general populace and were described as the backbone of the Third Republic. The elementary school teacher in Victorian Britain might have been regarded with disdain by his supposed social betters but he or she was respected by the vast majority. The situation in the United States has always been problematic in this respect but especially so in the twentieth century when so many American parents had had a college education at least as good as that of the teachers of their children. They are not overawed by teachers. However, the traditional authority of the teacher is still important and as parents have much direct influence on schools in the USA, are they not more likely to accept decisions taken by the schools? In the Soviet Union, the state deliberately cultivates the prestige of teachers and so their authority is accepted and they are highly regarded.

A third element is much more important and lies in the nature of education itself, and particularly in the pupil–teacher relationship, simply because teachers are adults and pupils children. From their very first day in school, children learn to accept the judgments of teachers. Admittedly, the atmosphere of today's schools is less authoritarian than ever before, but permissiveness has never really had much of a foothold, as the accounts of the classrooms observed by Bennett[1] and by Galton *et al.*[2] have shown in Britain, or those observed by Silberman[3] in the USA and these are the two countries most likely to exemplify such characteristics. Indeed, there are many fairly recent comments on schools in the United States and Britain which claim that teachers are still too authoritarian. The writings of John Holt are premised on this as are those of Postman and Weingartner.[4] In Britain Chanan and Gilchrist[5] make similar statements and so does Christian Join-Lambert[6] on France. There is no reason to believe that they, the Russians, will return to 'joyous bedlam' nor yet the libertarian approaches of A.S. Neill.

Moreover, the work done on the self-concept also gives force to this argument – going right back to the work of Rosenthal and Jacobsen, it has become clearer that teachers' opinions about children have a profound effect on what children think of themselves and each other. This was brought out very strongly in a piece of research carried out in Leicestershire during the 1970s. It showed that children graded each other according to the judgments which they heard and saw the teacher make about each individual in the class.[7] This research was concerned with children in primary schools. If anything, the opinions of teachers in secondary schools are even more important because by then it is not only the authority of the teacher as teacher which is being exercised but also the subject matter itself and in this the teacher is regarded as an expert. Teaching as a profession may not have the prestige of medicine or law but placed on what has been referred to as 'the continuum of professionalism' it is nearer to them than it is to the other extreme – and the older the children taught the more highly regarded is the teacher. So this effect is being felt particularly strongly just when the differentiation made between the children by the school has its most far-reaching effect.

That teachers' decisions might be harnessed in some way to how they perceive their pupils in terms of social class hardly ever occurs to pupils, who see the relationship in purely personal terms. Nor does it occur to their parents, who look at it in professional terms. Yet teachers constantly make decisions about children which are influenced by presumptions which they make about them and their social background: this was made clear by J.W.B. Douglas.[8] It also underlies what Baudelot and Establet say about French education.[9] Teachers probably feel that in most cases their prejudices are justified because of those pupils who reject the authority of the school, e.g. the 'lads' whom we met earlier. Such children may cause difficulties for their teachers but they are not typical, even though they generate a large amount of adverse comment. They are a small minority. The majority of pupils are not disruptive, and even though many acquire the knack of living through school without allowing it to impinge upon them too much, they accept what the teachers say about them, often without even realizing that the teachers opinions are prejudiced. By the time they reach the stage where they begin to follow different tracks, then most of them are well socialized into accepting the advice, or even the directions of their teachers. Some parents may argue about the decisions but most do not.

Anyway, the teachers have the academic yardstick to which they can refer: this is their metier; herein lies their expertise; this is why they have to be listened to. If we consider those academic examinations through which pupils gain access into higher education (and for which the majority of pupils will never enter) then we find their influence being felt long before a decision has to be taken on whether pupils should compete in them. They shape the work of secondary education, and influence the configurations of even those parts of the curriculum which 'appear' least academic. The longest standing is the baccalaureate in France and it still has huge prestige because it is not really a school examination but the first of the university examinations, and possession of it confers a place in higher education as of right. In Russia there is the certificate of maturity, or the *attestat zrelosti*, without which there is no access to higher education. In Britain there is the general certificate of education at 'A' level, possession of which does not guarantee entry to higher education; the level of the grades obtained also matters. Even in the United States, which boasts its lack of examinations, there is the scholastic aptitude test and the American college testing program – neither of these is essential for higher education but increasingly they are employed by universities and always have been by prestigious institutions. Now, particularly in the first three countries, and to a lesser extent in America, these examinations are what the schools teach towards and from the moment the children enter the secondary schools, this is what the parents hope they will achieve. Thus, this is the area of the teachers' real strength – even when the teachers are in fact advising on something quite different as in (say) vocational guidance. Since they are the hallmark of academic excellence a closer look at examinations and testing in all these countries would be useful at this point, because at their worst they give rise to credentialism (or the diploma disease).

Examinations are still the main influence on the curriculum. Traditionally these test what the best students do well, and it is therefore difficult to deconstruct their academic nature. Attempts *have* been made – by polytechnicization, by Nuffield science, by declaring that they should be '*empirique*', by using grade point average instead, etc., but in the end, it is the traditional, written, unseen examinations which predominate – because they are so easy to teach to. But there is another important aspect of them: they can be standardized more readily than many other forms of examination and therefore have the added cachet of fairness, which is important in systems of education which are essentially competitive.

In Britain, the all-important examination is preceded, usually two years earlier, by the new GCSE which combines the old GCE and CSE though they still exist within the new examination. This earlier examination is also used as a leaving certificate and so is important in the job market. Britain is the only one of the four countries which retains such an important public examination at this level. The French no longer have a Part I to the baccalaureat, they depend on internal assessment and orientation to direct children either into the various forms of upper secondary education, or into work. However, in marginal cases they use outside representatives. Moreover, results gained in mathematics in the *troisième* seem to be the crucial factor in orientation.[10] In the Soviet Union, examinations still play a part at this stage: 'examinations taken in grade VIII largely determine the kind of school attended after the age of 15'.[11] Only in the United States is there no vestige of an examination at this stage. Guidance and counselling are used to direct the students. However, that guidance often relies on the scores obtained in key subjects and these scores in turn depend on often extensive testing. So there is still a shadow of selection by examination operating at the point of transfer from lower to upper secondary education in America. (There is something much more substantial in all the others.) Though American education may appear examination-free, in reality formal testing is going on all the time, even more than in Europe – hence the earlier statement that the teachers' power is of an academic kind even when involved in guidance. So often the advice given to students is based on what is known about their academic ability, and that is based on examinations and testing and marks. Furthermore, this goes on throughout secondary schools in all the countries concerned.

In Britain at present there is much talk on profiling, i.e. trying to form a total picture of each pupil as an individual: emotional, social, intellectual, and so on. In fact, it is all too often the case that the only profile which exists in any usable form is the academic one, and often only lip service is paid to any other kind of record. Though serious attempts are made to use profiles to help low attainers – as in the low attainers programme set up by the DES in several local authorities – the problem remains of how the profiles are used later. Hargreaves draws attention to the danger of using them for selection when originally they were intended as motivators.[12] Given the emphasis on examinations at the top end of the ability range, as a means of selection, it is difficult to see how innovation in profiling such as the Oxford Certificate of Educational Attainment and that used in the City and Guilds 365, can do other than slot into the system. The selective function is too strong: it distorts every innovation.

One of the changes which the new GCSE is intended to introduce into British schools, by way of a new style of examination, is problem solving rather than stuffing with information to be regurgitated afterwards. This is commendable, and it is to be hoped it succeeds. Past records of such attempts, however, show few causes for optimism. When CSE was introduced, it too stressed such an element. Unfortunately, the making of grade 1 equivalent to an 'O' level pass meant that the credentialist bias of the then new examination (which was introduced to give those 'without parchments', to use a French expression, something to aim at) came to dominate, as it did GCE. Future-oriented pupils and teachers looked for ways of gaining passes – the regurgitation process crept back in. The same sort of difficulties faced the Russians with the reintroduction of the polytechnical ideal in the 1950s and 1960s. To live up to such an ideal is bound to be problematic when that system is also used as a means of certification which can lead to higher education or to jobs. The pride of French education is philosophy for *all* in the lycée, but to find baccalaureat entrants using Castex and Surer as a kind of catechism of philosophy comes as a shock: pointless regurgitation, par excellence. A glance at textbooks used right through the American system indicates that regurgitation is important: many of them contain tests which require simple memorization of the content.

However, neither the pupil nor the teacher should be castigated for looking for the shortest route to good certificates, but the effects are very serious, because they are *mis-educative.* At its crudest, credentialism seems to operate in underdeveloped countries. Brooke and Oxenham say:

> Equating education with diplomas generates an obsession with academic success. Because this has to be measured, attention seizes upon the mechanics of assessment, to the detriment of the process of education.[13]

In the same book Ronald Dore writes:

> Within the schools there are strong impressions that anxiety about selection, in the form of examination marks, or school grades, are almost as destructive of educational values in Britain, Japan, or the USA as they are in Ghana, Mexico, or Sri Lanka.[14]

And credentialism has become worse in recent years. The country which best exemplifies this is France because the array of qualifications and examinations offered there fits the structure of upper secondary and higher education more logically than anywhere else. Many of them are modifications of what went before. As the upper reaches of education have become more complex so has the system of licences (in the French sense), diplomas, *certificats* and *brevets*: this illustrates clearly how education systems develop to suit the needs of the economies in which they are set because French qualifications are very closely suited to the slots in the occupational structure. The easiest way to illustrate how the certification system is graduated is to use the (London) French Embassy's own representation of this (Figure 1).

How this all works is made perfectly clear to children and their parents so that everyone knows the level of every qualification from the prestigious diplomas of the *grandes écoles* down to the humble *certificat d'aptitude professionnelle*. However, the point to be made here is that, though pupils and parents are consulted, the most powerful influence on the direction taken by the individual child is how the teachers judge his academic ability, and that is mostly through examinations.

Little needs to be said at this point about the Russian system of awards because it is very similar, though less complex, than that of France. Each institution awards the relevant diploma. So, whether the child enters the world of work with a general school-leaving certificate, or a diploma from a vocational school, a *technikum* or a university, everyone knows the value of the qualification.

If the French and Russian systems work in a clear way, the reverse is true in Britain but this is changing and the teacher is in just as powerful a position because of credentialism. The continued existence of the prestigious examination at sixteen is one important cause of difference between Britain and France. 'O' level has a wide currency and is used by employers extensively, and by colleges of further education for selection for their more prestigious courses: it is the cornerstone of credentialism in Britain. The combining of it with its junior partner, CSE, has made little difference. But, just as CSE was introduced to give some sort of certificate to the non-'O'-level takers, so was the Certificate of Extended Education introduced for those who wished to stay on into the sixth form but were not sure of obtaining results at 'A' level. This was not, in fact, widely used anyway but it looks as though the Certificate of Pre-Vocational Education which is now also available, and is more clearly linked to the job market, could well be more popular. Some schools also offer courses leading to the qualifications of

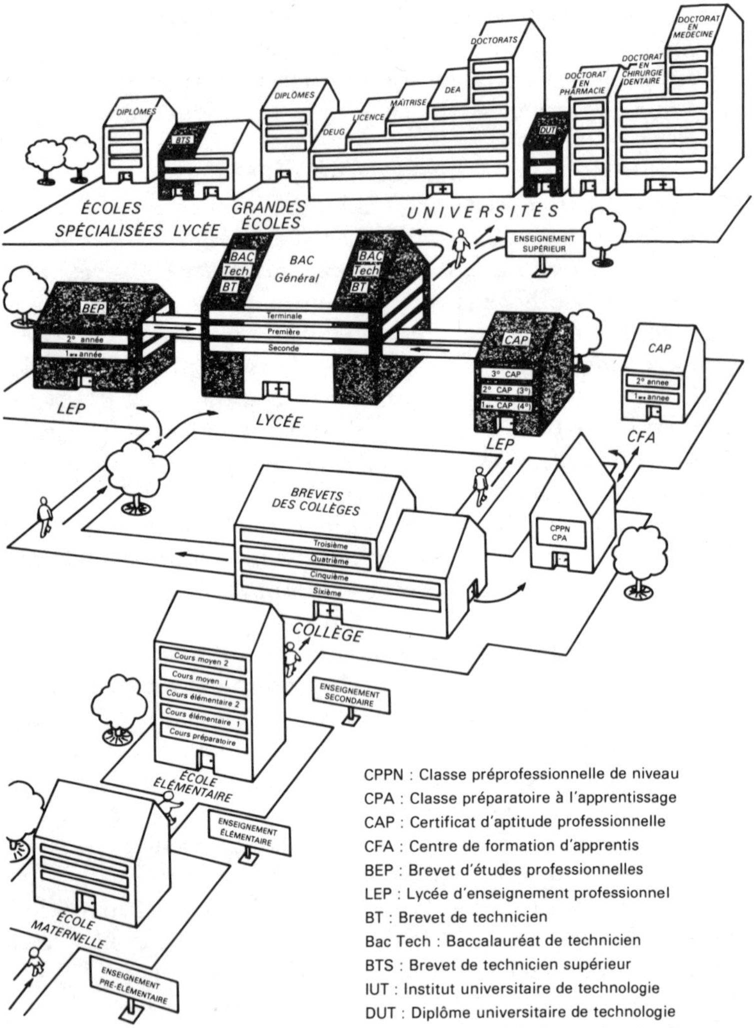

CPPN : Classe préprofessionnelle de niveau
CPA : Classe préparatoire à l'apprentissage
CAP : Certificat d'aptitude professionnelle
CFA : Centre de formation d'apprentis
BEP : Brevet d'études professionnelles
LEP : Lycée d'enseignement professionnel
BT : Brevet de technicien
Bac Tech : Baccalauréat de technicien
BTS : Brevet de technicien supérieur
IUT : Institut universitaire de technologie
DUT : Diplôme universitaire de technologie
UER : Unité d'enseignement et de recherche
PCEM : Premier cycle des études médicales
DEUG : Diplôme d'études universitaires générales
DESS : Diplôme d'études supérieures spécialisées
DEA : Diplôme d'études approfondes

FIG. 1. (Supplied by the French Embassy, London, July 1984).

the City and Guilds of the London Institute and the Royal Society of Arts, but these are much more likely to be taken in further education colleges (though even there they could be superseded by CPVE). It is with the further education colleges that the confusion really begins:

> the list of courses available nationally, provided in the *Directory of Further Education*, extends to several thousand and is further complicated by the variety of part-time and full-time modes of study as well as by course duration.[15]

However some qualifications, besides those mentioned above, have national currency: the Ordinary and Higher National Certificates are important as are the awards of the Business and the Technician Education Councils, and the certificate of further education examinations are important in all of those. However, many pupils still leave school with very little, and having no employment they are absorbed into the Youth Training Scheme which until recently offered them very little in the way of qualification. Into all of this has been thrown the Technical and Vocational Initiative, funded heavily in its pilot scheme by the Manpower Services Commission. It has stimulated courses in schools and colleges at different levels and does not preclude the taking of established examinations such as 'O' level, 'A' level, City and Guilds and some new ones. It is now to be extended to all schools but no one knows yet to what effect.

So the current situation is very confusing. However, a process has already begun which could mean that something like the French or Russian patterns could emerge in Britain. Michael Farley has pointed out that:

> YTS and CPVE are only the beginning of establishing satisfactory vocational preparation arrangements capable of meeting the needs of all young people in the 1980s and 1990s as they make the transition to adult and working life. But the potential should be embraced and moulded towards a tertiary concept of comprehensive, unified, and continuing education and training provision for the entire age group.[16]

That development has now gone further but unfortunately credentialism is becoming more firmly established within it. The government White Papers of 1984 and 1985[17] indicated a willingness to move in this direction and they culminated in the De Ville Report of 1986 in which the chairman, in his preface, said that, 'what is now called for is much more effective integration of education, training and work experience both in the process of learning and *in the certification of achievement*'[18] (polytechnical education?). The report recommended that a national council for vocational qualifications should be set up to introduce the required coherence, and to integrate, through a process of accreditation, the work of all the disparate examining bodies by establishing a national vocational qualification. This should have four levels (with a possible fifth or professional level) into which all the various certificates, diplomas and so on could lock – and this should include those to be awarded by the newly established YTS Certification Board (offering certificates at two levels) and the GCSE boards. The report also recommended that built into this system should be opportunity to move through the levels in a way reminiscent of the opportunities offered to Soviet PTU students for progression – even to higher education. Though how this is possible when the lower levels are already referred to as non-advanced further education, with the prophetic acronym NAFE, is difficult to see. The report's recommendations were all accepted by the White Paper of 1986 which said:

> The National Council will be appointed and operational by the Autumn of 1986. It should seek to agree and promulgate design criteria for the National Vocational Qualification early in 1987. It should complete its first accreditations not later than the summer of that year. The government looks to the National Council to have the first four levels of the new framework fully in place by 1991.[19]

As already observed, formal examinations seem not to play such an important role in American education. However, testing is important, and the results of it appear in American forms of certification. These seem to make sense, if looked at on a nationwide basis. For instance, the high school graduation certificate (or more probably the grades which go to make it up) is obviously important. It would appear to have national currency. However, David Turner says that:

> if high-school graduation certificates are to be considered graded, with vocational schools courses being regarded as second-rate, then the children who enter vocational tracks at an nearly age will thereby be excluded from higher education. On the other hand, if vocational courses are thought to have equal status with the traditionally academic courses, able students will be directed into vocational courses where they can graduate with better grades. Such a development will not help those for whom the vocational courses were originally intended, those not intending to go on into higher education.[20]

What such a certificate might mean depends on the location of the institution. However, it is important to have it and its quality can decide the sort of higher education which can be obtained. More high-school graduates go on to higher education in the USA than anywhere else in the world and so it is the degree that matters, hence the numbers entering the race for it. A decline in the number of university entrants was expected in the late 1970s, and there were some fluctuations. However, generally, the numbers have continued to increase. H.L. Smith maintains that if graduates do not obtain the kind of job which used to be considered commensurate with a university education, the economic value of a degree is still considerable, and has probably not fallen. He continues:

> A decade ago, Dresch (1975) called attention to the declining ability of the marginal college student and concluded that such diminished abilities were not compatible with a reasonable return on investment in a college education. He was correct in concluding that the marginal student is more marginal now than ever; he was wrong in assuming that fewer people would attend colleges as a result. Individuals go to college for a host of reasons other than its economic value, and forces stimulating high enrolment should persist for many years to come.[21]

The popularity of the community college is also indicative of the desire for qualifications whether they be in the form of associate degrees or in the certificates in the myriad of trades and skills which they make available. We also have to remember that in

America there are a large number of private institutions offering certificates in a very wide variety of skills: numbers do not seem to be diminishing. There are now numerous forms of certification in the USA, and though there may be very few examinations in courses which offer certificates, most of them include sets of marks based on regular testing of candidates.

As can be seen from the above discussion, the proliferation of qualifications and the examinations which accompany them is true for all these countries. The impetus which was felt at an earlier stage in Britain and France (at the beginning of this century) towards codification and unification of qualifications has played itself out. The reason is that it occurred when the all-important development in education was toward bringing the various parts into closer relationship with each other. This was a time when aspirations first began to grow noticeably. It was also expedient to tap those aspirations. Growing economies needed to encourage children to become more highly educated – the school certificate came in at this stage. But what has happened since the Second World War, and probably in an obscure fashion before that, is that those mass systems of education have had to develop internal flexibility in order to provide for the growing complexity of the occupation structure. Political necessity has obliged them to confer common schooling to the age of fifteen, but after that what we see is differentiation but of a more precise kind than at any time in the past. Every form of differentiation either leads to a particular qualification or soon will. The French and Russian systems already do. The British and the American are approaching it. Undeniably all systems, through the way they give access to jobs are now geared to the needs of the economies in which they exist. Whether they do this efficiently or not is another matter.

Teachers, even if unintentionally, play an important part in this process because not only do they help children to form opinions of themselves and their suitability for particular roles, they also decide for which examinations children will enter or along which tracks they will proceed. Rarely, in modern systems do they appear to do this arbitrarily. They make appeals to academic standards in order to justify not so much their decisions as their advice, or they claim to know as part of their professional competence what is best for the individual child.

Primary and lower-secondary education in all four countries prepare children for the 'guidance' which will be given the nearer they come to upper-secondary education where tracks are less easy to switch. Therefore, guidance should be considered next but perhaps it should be done in the light of a discussion of what has been called the new vocationalism. Not only has this given force to the argument that schools should be more closely tied to the economy, but it also strengthens the influence of the advice given in the schools.

Probably the most important single influence, in the West, on this swing back to vocationalism, has been youth unemployment because it has enabled bodies such as the Manpower Services Commission in Britain, or the National Employment Pact in France, to emphasize the need to make the routes from school to work more clear-cut, and to get wide support for this because of the fears which unemployment generates. But really this has merely accelerated a process which was already in motion anyway. The case of the Soviet Union illustrates this because there, where there are ways of avoiding unemployment (for instance through very widespread overmanning), the process has also gone on. This is not to deny the force of youth unemployment. The point is that it has been a catalyst rather than a root cause.

The best introduction to what is meant by vocationalism is an article by W. Norton Grubb which appeared in *Comparative Education Review* in 1983, in which he said that:

> in . . . advanced countries . . . there has been a tendency to consider specific skill training, especially secondary-level vocational education, to be the principal manifestation of vocationalism. This conception is too narrow: every level of schooling, including the university has become suffused with vocational goals, differentiated along vocational lines and judged by vocational criteria.[22]

Following on from the above argument, the relevance of this statement is obvious. He goes on to give some of the reasons why vocationalism has become so strong in recent years:

> In the past twenty years, the vocational education systems of many advanced countries have been promoted as a solution to many problems, especially as rising youth

> unemployment has challenged the schools to be more 'relevant'. Vocational education has also been seen as the answer to two different enrolment problems: the tendency of some students (especially lower-class students) to drop out of schools without occupational skills – a problem that vocational education promises to resolve by providing a more interesting and job-relevant curriculum – and the tendency for too many secondary school leavers to continue in higher education – a tendency that vocational education claims to remedy by providing real skills and upgrading the dignity of manual labor.[23]

All these factors can be seen manifesting themselves in Britain, France, the USA, and the USSR, both within schools and in the changing background to education. When Grubb gives details of how vocationalism functions, again we find what he has to say borne out. He cites, for example, the development of levels of higher education below that of university and he mentions 'short-cycle' courses in community colleges in America and the university institutes of technology in France. He also puts the British polytechnics in this category and whilst this may be true for their short courses, it is not so for the fully fledged degree courses some of which offer qualifications as prestigious as those of the universities. He could also have included the further education colleges and the *technikums* in this category.

Grubb refers to such courses as 'post-secondary analogues to secondary vocational programs [which] illustrate several manifestations of vocationalism: the tendency to differentiate all levels of education upon occupational lines'.[24] This is evident from what we said in Chapter 6 where we saw how the pressure for higher education places combined with the perceived changes in the economic requirements of all four countries led them to cultivate these alternatives to the universities. The United States led the way and provides the best example of how vocationalism, whilst catering, apparently, for the occupational needs of a community, can also deflect aspirants away from the most prestigious institutions. David Nasaw writes:

> The California Master Plan, which would become the model for so many other states, protected the selectivity of the four-year universities and colleges by state law. All but

> the top 12.5 per cent (by grade average) of the state's high school graduates were barred from the four-year state universities. All but the top 33 per cent were barred from the four-year state colleges. But . . . the same law that kept the lower two-thirds of each high-school class out of the four-year institution guaranteed them a place in the two-year community colleges. Here was the magic formula for maintaining selectivity within mass institutions. State systems of higher education could remain selective and 'open-access' simultaneously.[25]

We also know how important the community colleges are to vocational education. The IUT in France, the polytechnic and the further education college in Britain perform, inter alia, the same functions. The *technikum* does too. The editors of *Soviet Education* say that 'easing pressure for admission to higher education and shaping pupils' career aspirations to coincide with the real possibilities of the job market become especially important as secondary schooling attains mass enrolment.'[26] High levels of enrolment lead to higher aspirations. Students are deflected from universities into *technikums* or are given alternative prospects while still at school. So secondary schools play their part in this too and therefore it is important to look at the modifications which have taken place in them also.

Perhaps the best example of the changes are those we have seen in France, where, though the movement towards comprehensive education was very rapid, so was the development of vocational forms of the upper secondary education. In the *lycée d'enseignement général* the objective is the baccalaureat. It has five main branches:

A Arts/philosophy
B Economics and social sciences
C Mathematics and physics
D Mathematics and natural sciences
E Mathematics and technology

C is the most prestigious in the old academic sense but notice how even at this general level, 'relevance' is apparent. Also D1 is more so – it specializes in agricultural sciences.

In the *lycée technique* the *baccalauréat de technician* is the objective. It has eleven forms in the F series based on industrial sciences, four forms in the G series based on economics and one additional form, H, for computer science. No comment is necessary. The other forms of secondary education, the *lycée d'enseignement professional*, the *centre de formation d'apprentis*, and the *classe préparatoire a l'apprentissage* are even more obviously vocational, as we have already observed.

In the West then, France provides the clearest example of how vocationalism and differentiation operate together, but the USSR is also a good example of the same factors working in tandem. This should not surprise us. Grubb comments: 'Given the antagonism between differentiation and egalitarian pressures, it is interesting to note that Eastern European countries – where individualist and egalitarian ideologies are weakest – also have the most explicitly differentiated schooling systems.'[27] From the mid 1970s onwards, the importance of vocational education was stressed increasingly: articles appeared in Soviet education and sociology journals emphasizing the need to enhance the prestige of the vocational schools: 'The low prestige of vocational technical education institutions is due to the erroneous, but still prevalent attitude among teachers in our schools that these institutions are second-class.'[28] The benefits of upgrading vocational education seemed so obvious. In his report to the General Meeting of the Academy of Pedagogical Sciences in 1976, the president of the academy, Prokofiev said:

> As we know, the majority of the population work in material production and the younger generation for the most part is sent into the material production sphere. For this reason, it is very important to orient vocational guidance specifically towards production. The school cannot assume the function of a specialized vocational institution but the interests of youth upbringing require in-depth theoretical education combined with purposeful labour training.[29]

The old unpopular vehicles of technical education (e.g. the state labour reserve schools) were transformed and absorbed into the new and more acceptable professional technical *uchilischa* or

PTU, which by 1975 had become secondary schools proper in order to make them even more attractive. Furthermore, as Prokofiev's speech implied, strenuous efforts were made to persuade pupils to enter them rather than to continue in the general schools, or to apply for courses in the *technikums*. The general school itself is not unaffected by vocationalism because, though the return of polytechnicization in the 1950s and 1960s was largely a failure, in the form in which it was conceived, it has more than left its mark (officially the schools are still polytechnic and general schools). Not only does work experience form part of the programme but also an attempt is made to 'inform' the courses with polytechnical attitudes.

This trend is to continue: the draft guidelines for the Reform of the General and Vocational School – and the change of title is significant – published in 1984 says there is to be a 50 per cent increase in the intake of the PTUs. Furthermore, the intention is that at some future date all the various forms of upper secondary education will be merged – hence the change of title.[30] These reforms are now under way, though how quickly they are being implemented is not always clear. They have been followed by a set of draft guidelines for Higher Education (VUZ) and Secondary Specialized Education (*Technikumy*) in 1986 which aim, inter alia, to make graduates of both sorts of institution better prepared for work in 'modern automated and efficient production'.[31]

In Britain, the swing towards vocationalism began more than twenty years ago, but this is apparent only with hindsight. Even so a glance at its history is instructive. It can be discerned even in the Industrial Training Act of 1964, but there was great dissatisfaction with this piece of legislation. The Employment and Training Act 1973 to which it gave rise, superseded it. The second Act created the Manpower Services Commission which was set up in 1974, at first to deal with the training of adults. Increasingly, however, it came to deal with young people, especially as youth employment deteriorated, as the depression, put in motion by the oil crisis, set in. In the light of a government statement (1976) entitled *Unified Vocational Preparation* a pilot scheme given the same name was begun to deal with the education and training of those who left school without qualification. It was extended and then subsumed under the Youth

Opportunities Programme which was proposed by the MSC in 1977 and set up soon afterwards. YOP was intended to offer young people the opportunity to acquire occupational skills and knowledge and the opportunity to use them in context (work experience). Following the publication of a document, *Vocational Preparation* by the Further Education Curriculum Review and Development Unit (FEU), the MSC published a consultative document, *A New Training Initiative*, in 1981, one part of which resulted in the Youth Training Scheme to replace YOP. It began its work in 1983. Its clientele are unemployed school leavers to whom it offers skill training and work experience, though it differs in organization from its predecessor. However, what is really interesting is that the MSC which began its life on the educational periphery has now been thrust centre-stage. When, out of the blue, Margaret Thatcher announced the Technical and Vocational Initiative in Education, in the House of Commons in November 1982, she asked the chairman of the MSC and the Secretaries of State for Education to develop this as a pilot scheme. In the event, the initiative fell into the hands of the MSC and even though it takes place in schools and colleges, the Department of Education and Science is less and less in control of the scheme. So, the MSC, from dealing with unemployed youth became responsible for an important vocational development. (Cynics have commented that the MSC was asked to organize TVEI because YTS had been so successful in disguising the extent of youth unemployment, but anyway such an initiative is in keeping with the Thatcher government's instrumental view of education.)

The local education authorities invited to take part in the initiative were asked to submit coherent packages of technical training and work experience which could be directed towards certain types of occupation but could also be linked with existing qualifications and which could make an appeal to the whole ability range (by using a modular form). Though these would be additional and specifically TVEI courses the initiative could be dovetailed with existing courses, and yet be distinct (a necessity for MSC funding). Courses could straddle schools and colleges, and many were set up that way. The initiative has now been officially declared extended to *all* secondary schools. But this is not the only way in which the MSC has extended its influence if not its authority into the schools. The CPVE, which is a good example of creeping vocationalism, will also come under its ambit, as will most of the work of the FE colleges because the MSC will control the National Council for Vocational Qualifications which, as we know, will oversee all vocational qualifications.

Furthermore, the emphasis in the schools is beginning to change partly because of the influence of TVEI but also because of the new approaches required by GCSE. There is also a greater awareness of the need to link schools with the world of work, and since Callaghan initiated the 'great debate', the need to encourage pupils to look towards work in industry, which is ironic since most will not find jobs. Organizations like the School Curriculum Industry Project (SCIP) set up in 1977 have become gradually more influential and school–industry liaison officers (SILOs), financed by the Department of Trade and Industry, have been appointed in greater numbers so that by 1985, three-quarters of all LEAs had one.[32] The Youth Training Scheme not only has a reverse effect back into the schools from which its clients come, it also now has to be considered as part of the education system proper. Its predecessor, YOP, might have been introduced as a desperate measure to deal with youth unemployment, but the setting up of the YTS certification board makes the scheme an integral part of the bureaucracy of credentialism, just like the schools. It could be that many of those who are judged by the schools as having lower ability (or simply as being less well motivated) will find themselves taking courses such as the City Guilds 365, now Pre-16 B.Tec, whilst at school, perhaps along with a modicum of TVEI modules, and some measure of work experience, and then going on to YTS when they leave school. Thus, despite influential statements such as that in the De Ville report, where divisions between the academic and the vocational are declared to be spurious,[33] such children find themselves locked into vocational courses (at an early stage) which take them into low-paid employment, or unemployment. The more able also are encouraged to see their courses in vocational terms and this is so for sixth formers who now have the opportunity to enhance their qualifications by taking TVEI modules in prestigious courses such as information technology and by work experience, (e.g. work shadowing – of senior grades). Higher education, since the UGC cuts, also has a stronger vocational ethos, just as Norton Grubb said it would and just as the Advisory Council for Applied Research said it should.

Since the beginning of the century, vocationalism has been stronger in the USA than in any of the other countries. Christopher Hurn says that:

> at least three distinctive features of the American system deserve special emphasis in this regard: its decentralization, its egalitarian orientation, and its justification of educational enterprise as primarily instrumental in utilitarian terms.[34]

Furthermore he shows that it increased its importance in the American High School from 1915 to 1949, but then he goes on to claim that this trend not only slowed down but was partly reversed:

> e.g. the percentage students enrolled in 'business education' courses (typing, shorthand, book-keeping etc.) declined from 46.1 per cent in 1949 to 34.3 per cent in 1973, and the percentage enrolled in 'vocational trade and industrial education' declined from 5.4 per cent to 2.6 per cent. Enrolments in mathematics courses, in natural sciences, in foreign languages and in art increased over the same period. What makes these trends somewhat less than clear-cut, however, is the slight increase in the percentage enrolled in 'industrial arts' and home economics. Unfortunately we do not have data on what percentage of students in these latter subjects are primarily in a vocational programme and what percentage primarily in an academic programme but choose these subjects as electives.[35]

It could be said there is no 'new' vocationalism in the United States. However, before turning to those American institutions where vocationalism has been extended, it should be pointed out for the sake of comparison that the other three systems had a large amount of ground to make up before they could compare with the levels of vocationalism in American schools. Hurn himself says that, within the three-track system (college preparatory, general, and vocational), between 25 per cent and 30 per cent of all students are currently enrolled in vocational programmes and between 30 per cent and 50 per cent in college preparatory programmes. These unfortunately are only estimates based on surveys of selected high schools. The percentage of students in the vocational programmes of different schools can vary between 5 per cent and 50 per cent, often depending on geographical location. Consequently, there are very large numbers of high-school students engaged in vocational education.

It is at the next stage of education that vocationalism has expanded very rapidly since the war – most markedly in the community colleges, but also in the four-year colleges and universities.

> Increasingly, community colleges . . . are now oriented less towards the four-year institutions . . . and more toward a wide variety of educational activities in demand by the local population. This has meant the expansion of adult, non-degree educational programmes, of vocational and career training of quite specific character (in dental hygiene, automobile mechanics, computer programming, book-keeping etc.), the provision of remedial reading, writing, and mathematics courses, as well as the standard liberal arts and science courses leading to an Associate of Arts Degree and transfer to a four-year college . . . throughout the country the community colleges have been shifting towards terminal non-degree and vocational programmes.[36]

Furthermore there are at least 7,000 private institutions which offer courses similar to those of the community colleges and qualifications in very narrowly defined skills. Added to this, many of those students who do transfer to the senior institutions, take vocational courses there because the trend in the four-year institutions is the same as in the two-year, if less pronounced. Since 1915 natural science degrees have dropped by a third and humanities by two thirds, whereas social sciences doubled their share. Business and commerce degrees went from 0.7 per cent to 18.7 per cent of the total. This trend is also stressed by Grubb. Front runners now are business studies

(18.7 per cent), education, (13.7 per cent) and social sciences (11.8 per cent). To the rear are mathematics (2.5 per cent), 'letters' (4.4 per cent) and foreign languages (1.3 per cent).

Hurn's interpretation of these figures is interesting, especially when contrasted with some of the claims made here, but we can return to this question later. What is undoubtedly true is that vocationalism has become an even more important feature of American education than formerly and is emphasized even more than in France, Britain, and Russia. On the other hand, despite the superficial differences, which are largely matters of degree, the trend is the same in all countries. The United States also has a scheme like YTS set up by the Job Training Partnership Act of 1982 which aims to train the economically disadvantaged. There are also local schemes such as the Boston Compact, 'designed to raise the employability of inner-city youth'.[37] But the Europeans have something else to learn from the American experience: Hurn maintains that vocationalism of a direct kind (i.e. which teaches actual skills used in industry) in the schools seems to have failed. On the other hand, the 'professional' skills of higher education still have a pay-off. The lesson is that pupils should be very wary of the advice given in schools.

This brings us back to where the chapter began, i.e. the way in which schools, through the teachers, act on the pupils in such a way as to direct them towards particular occupations. It was claimed that this direction begins as soon as the child enters school. Indeed, Baudelot and Establet claim that it divides children[38] – that is its function. So what was said earlier should be borne in mind because it reflects an all-pervasive, even insidious, influence on children at all times. However, we will now concentrate on the more formal overt forms of guidance given to pupils. This is not to say that such guidance is any more powerful than the subconscious sort (and there is some evidence to show it is not) but it is an attempt to illustrate how this, as a formal mechanism, working within deliberately structured systems, complements the effects of the schools operating as engines of selection.

It is interesting to note here that Elizabeth Halsall makes the point that:

> just as in the USA school counsellors began to be appointed to high schools in small numbers after the schools had developed into common schools taking in pupils of all levels of ability, so in Great Britian, the establishment of the comprehensive school has also been followed by the appointment of counsellors.[39]

So we would expect vocational guidance to begin in America earlier than in the others: it began at about the turn of the century. As laid down by Frank Parsons in 1908, the three aims of vocational guidance were to help people understand themselves as individuals, to encourage them to understand the economic system, and to help them to decide how they fitted into that system.[40] The purpose then, at this initial stage was vocational but with developmental overtones, and this is interesting in the light of the way the whole guidance and counselling field developed in America. A glance at its history might be profitable.

Parsons worked in Boston and it was there and in the other big cities that the service developed, in the form of organized departments attached to school systems. By the end of the First World War, the National Education Association was interested enough to report on this new facet of education and suggested a developmental approach rather than a directive one, so the notion of the counsellor had begun to take shape. This was just as well because during the inter-war years, as we know, the business of intelligence and aptitude testing also developed rapidly, especially in the cities and even led in some instances to ruthless tracking by ability, with future occupations in mind (see above, p. 87). However, some teacher–counsellors, though rarely engaging in individual counselling, did try to see their task in wider curricular terms. Fortunately, further developments in testing (e.g. such as personality tests and inventories) in the 1940s led to the notion of the client-centred approach which culminated in the work of Carl Rogers in the 1960s. Since then counsellors have become an integral part of American education and as a group have acquired several of the attributes of a profession. The job of the counsellors according to the American School Counselor Association and described in the *American Encyclopedia of Education* is as follows:

> (1) helping to plan and develop the guidance program and the school curriculum in relation to the needs of the students; (2) counselling students to improve their self-understanding, self-acceptance, personal decision making, and personal problem solving; (3) co-ordinating the schools' program of pupil appraisal and information, including interpreting such information to teachers and parents; (4) collecting and disseminating information to students and parents regarding educational and vocational opportunities; (5) co-ordinating the use of the school and community services; (6) helping with educational planning and placement of students within a school or in transition between schools; (7) serving as a consultant to parents and to the administrative and teaching staff; (8) conducting local research related to pupil needs and to the effectiveness of the guidance program; and (9) communicating and interpreting the guidance program to the public.[41]

These duties are given in full because not only are they of interest but to have taken out of context those with greater relevance to this thesis would have an unfair effect on the rest. Attention is drawn to (2), (3), (4), and (6). Set in the total pattern and interpreted according to a Parsonian view of social stratification they seem entirely praiseworthy but put into a Bourdieu/Passeron context, and bearing in mind what Bowles and Gintis say about American schooling, they could in fact become sinister. J.E. Rosenbaum, writing in the *Sociology of Education*, recounted his own research and reviewed several other pieces concerned with tracking and guidance. He found that students misperceive their tracks (so much for the guidance) and underestimate their tracks' relationship with future outcomes and he says that:

> in particular, interviews and observations indicated that guidance counsellors gave college and non-college track students different kinds and amounts of information about the track system and its implications for post-secondary education, so that non-college track students were more likely to misunderstand tracking and its implications.[42]

A piece of research by Roslyn Aulin Mickelson also shows how personality traits are differently interpreted according to the social class of the children:

> This perspective suggests that independence, leadership, intrinsic motivation, and assertiveness tended to be rewarded and reinforced when exhibited in middle-class children, but negatively reinforced when displayed in working-class adolescents.[43]

She also describes how the facilities in the school of middle-class whites were vastly superior to those in the school of mixed races.

The American literature of the late 1970s and early 1980s was full of such articles. It should also be borne in mind that the entry in the encyclopedia was for 1971 when a certain optimism still reigned in schools in all advanced countries. By 1981, when the depression was being felt, some schools in Michigan actually closed briefly when the local electorate refused an extra millage to keep them open. In such circumstances it is often the counsellors who are the first group to be cut. In one large senior high school in Michigan, the workload of the counsellors had so increased as a result that they seemed able to concern themselves with little other than the grade point averages of many of the senior students. Are the guidance counsellors merely easing and facilitating the selection process for which the schools carry such a large measure of responsibility?

In higher education, the counselling continues. Burton Clark, in 1960 claimed that, besides their task of providing the vocational skills needed locally, the community colleges were also important parts of the cooling-out process of American education:

> In the junior college, the student does not so clearly fail, unless he himself wishes to define it that way, but rather transfers to terminal work. He may then interpret the second choice as more appropriate to his particular talent and be less frustrated that his intention did not work out. The terminal student can be made to appear not so radically different from the transfer student, e.g. an 'engineering aide' instead of 'engineer' and hence he goes to something with a status of its own. This reflects less unfavourably on a person's capacities. The junior college

> also provides a staff which is more oriented toward counselling the latent terminal student than would be the case in the state university.[44]

Elsewhere in the same book he shows how the students were tested, tracked, and counselled into accepting what the college decided was best.[45] Twenty years later he looked again at the colleges. He had not changed his mind about them but he also defended their twin functions (see R. Yarrington: *Questioning the Community College*, Jossey-Bass, 1980). Counselling services in American universities proper are much more highly developed and sophisticated than their European opposite numbers. Many have 'placement' centres: the name is significant.

This discussion of guidance counselling in the United States, though only scratching the surface, is more extended than originally intended because America again provides a highly developed model of a particular educational service, and one with attributes which the other systems seem to wish to emulate. Because of exigencies such as space, and the general view taken here of education, the treatment of counselling in the USA could seem partial. Many schools and colleges in the United States have excellent counselling departments with bona fide intentions and they try to live up to the ASCA ideals – though often they are in localities already well served with educational facilities. There are also guidance and counselling courses in American universities which try to impart the highest ideals to the school counsellors they train. Those I spoke to at Eastern Michigan University in 1981 were a good example of this, though they too at times did seem sceptical about the benefits of counselling.

Let us turn now to America's great rival, which so many people seem to think is so different from her. As far as vocational guidance is concerned this was once the case. Placement and information bureaux for young people had existed at the time of the NEP but were disbanded by Stalin in 1933. They re-opened in 1960. This marked a change in direction for Soviet education. Earlier we saw how the surge in aspirations, particularly for higher education had not only put the system under considerable pressure but was also causing serious problems for the still labour-intensive economy. Matthews uses figures from a Russian study of ten-year school-leavers in the Cheremushki district of Moscow in 1973 to indicate this. He says that:

> the figures from this . . . show that, despite all that had been done by way of school reform, only about 16 per cent of respondents actually wished to go out and work, which, to judge from the (achievement) figures, was greatly at variance with the requirements of the labour market. The study further showed that of 83.8 per cent who planned to continue their education, the overwhelming majority (nearly 70 per cent) wished to go into VUZy, and about 10 per cent aimed at secondary special institutions (*technikums*).[46]

This situation is what led to the restructuring of education and the bolstering of vocational education, but restructuring alone could not go far in changing the attitudes of parents and children. Jonathan Steele, writing in the *Guardian* in August 1981, said that a study made in Novosibirsk showed that 60 per cent of workers' children wanted white-collar jobs. No one wanted a job in agriculture. So the problem is a long-standing one: hence the reintroduction of vocational guidance.

Yet in one sense the problem had always been there. The work experience which formed part of the programme of the unified labour schools in early Soviet days had been intended to show the dignity of work and to stress its moral value in accordance with the principles of both Marx and Lenin. However, this did not achieve the desired effect. Stressing and extending skill learning through the re-establishment of the polytechnic principle at the time of Khrushchev did not have much effect either, though this was because of the inept way in which it was carried out. Nevertheless, the polytechnic ideal is still the cornerstone of Soviet efforts to orient children towards the points of need in the occupation structure and it always figures in Russian writings about vocational guidance – and these have increased extensively in recent years. Though the style of language used is different from that used in America, similarities can be found, especially as some emphasis is put on a person's own choice based on how the individual perceives society:

> Occupational orientation – the choice of a concrete occupational speciality and an appropriate educational

> institution, is an indication of societal orientation. . . . In other words, the choice of a future societal standing, of a certain line of work, precedes the choice of a concrete occupational speciality. A study conducted in six areas of the USSR in 1973 and 1974 showed that a decision to acquire the societal standing of a specialist was made before a concrete occupational speciality was chosen.[47]

So the Russians are now using a number of devices to orient children in directions mutually beneficial to them and to the state. At an international conference on vocational guidance at Ashiya University in 1978, the Soviet delegation gave an account of the forms of guidance used at that time. Kuznetzov was at pains to show how Russians try to make sure that those who go on to higher education are not mere degree-seekers but are oriented professionally by simulation exercises and guidance. However, what went on lower down the system was more relevant. Zhiltsov reported that there was now a Research Institute of Labour and Professional Guidance to develop diagnostic approaches to the interests and intentions of pupils and also ways in which to direct these in the interests of society – data was being collected about what teenagers think of jobs.

Moreover, each town and district now had a Commission for Professional Guidance to encourage links between schools and industry. This was happening through *kombinats* and attempts were being made to involve parents in three-way discussions with schools and local enterprises. Rooms were being set aside in schools for guidance. Zhiltsov also listed the various channels of propaganda which could be used to encourage children to make realistic choices: open days, talks to children by professionals and workers, material in the press and other news media, activities in the pioneer palaces, and olympiada. At about the same time, A. Marinick, minister of education for the Ukraine, said that youth should be educated to make sensible choices of vocations. He claimed that polytechnical education prepares for this, but the family, the school, and local enterprises should be involved and he gave examples of where this was already happening in the Ukraine. The Kharkov tractor factory and the Black Sea shipyards had links with schools. He made special mention of the Ivano-Frankovo secondary school and the Carparthian furniture combine because of the efforts of the engineers to teach the pupils both theory and practice, and of production workers to act as pioneer leaders. However, though he referred to the need to avoid giving guidance to children in large groups, he did seem to be over-concerned with production figures in local enterprises where pupils were engaged in labour of one kind or another.[48]

These sorts of activity could soon deteriorate into the meaningless links between schools and factories and farms which marked the polytechnical education of the 1960s. No one outside the Soviet Union really knows how successful the emphasis on vocational guidance has been. The PTUs do seem to be more popular and George Avis offers some evidence which shows that it may have been a little too successful with boys. They seem to have taken the opportunities of gaining technical qualifications with a quick pay-off. Girls have not done this. They are more determined to go into higher education. Unfortunately, as entrants to the universities they do not opt for the sciences as readily as boys. The consequence is that there are shortfalls in applications for some sciences in some institutions – the universities will also have to engage in vocational guidance.[49] Peter Rooney agrees the PTUs have become more attractive. Labour training connected with them is more practical and productive and vocational guidance is largely towards them. However, he suggests that the guidance is often ineffectual because the schools play only a minor role, as teachers are not very committed to it. He says that children's career plans are much more likely to be affected by parents.[50]

Tinkering with institutions will not solve the problems which are inherent in industrial societies. Moreover, in an article in the *Times Educational Supplement* in 1986, Janet Price says that Russian children still do not want to work in factories, that they are going into the PTUs only reluctantly, and that the response from the factories is rather like it was in the 1960s. She reports a teachers' union official as saying:

> Go into any enterprise and the director, chief engineer, and chairman of the trade union committee – who all unanimously approved the school reform – are not only

neglecting to create new workplaces for pupils, but couldn't care less that they are not being paid wages.[51]

However, the attempt at guidance is being made, and just as in America, it is meant to massage the students into the institutions and occupations which suit the economy, but the Russians are not very good at it yet.

What is true for Russia is also true for France, where, until the introduction of mass lower-secondary education, priority was not given to vocational guidance: it existed but in a weak form. From the time the French began to take seriously the link between economic development and the way the education system functioned, this became a serious matter. The French approach to it, on the other hand, is a traditional one, or at least goes back a long way – perhaps to the notion of *les compagnons de l'université* and certainly as far as Jean Zay whose experiments so influenced Langevin and Wallon. *Les compagnons*, Zay and the others, might have been egalitarians, but they themselves were also products of French academic traditions. They believed in high standards which is why *les compagnons* claimed that 'everyone must be taught but the best must be drawn from the crowd, etc.' The way they would be drawn was by 'orientation'. Zay tried it in the first year of his experimental schools and Langevin and Wallon recommended it, though in a more extended form, i.e. for four years – as it now actually appears in the *collège unique*. Beullac, when minister of education, said in an interview with *Le Monde de l'Education* in 1981, that orientation 'must be the result of a collaboration between first and foremost the children concerned, the parents who are responsible for them, and the school.'[52]

The form which it takes has evolved since 1959, when the first changes were introduced in secondary education, but the *collège d'enseignement général*, introduced at that time was little more than a secondary modern school. It was the introduction of the *collège d'enseignement secondaire*, a multi-lateral, which made it more likely. From 1963, the first two years of secondary education, came to be seen as a *cycle d'observation* and the second pair as a *cycle d'orientation*. But this change was still little more than a sham because the continuation of streaming (*trois filières*) meant that whether a child went on to a long or a short course of upper secondary education (either academic or technical) or to work, really depended upon the judgment of the teachers, and only occasionally a guidance specialist. That judgment might have been based technically on continuous assessment rather than on an examination but the die had been cast at the beginning of secondary education when the child entered a particular *filière*. However, when, after a protracted struggle mixed ability came in with the *collèges uniques*, orientation developed further and became a continuous process. Patricia Broadfoot writes:

> Thus part of Haby's reform included a proposal for orientation to be based on group recommendation – in which the vagaries of individual teachers (and hence the exposure of individual teachers to excessive pressures) would be guarded against by orientation based on the *conseil d'orientation* which would discuss with the pupil and responsible personnel the recommendations of the *conseil des professeurs*. This procedure requires that throughout a pupil's high-school life vocational guidance is to be based on continuous observation by his teachers, recorded in a cumulative dossier. Regular meetings are to be held between the teachers, a guidance counsellor (*conseiller d'orientation*), a school doctor and psychologist, and representatives of the parents. Such meetings are to be held every year, with two major ones taking place at the end of the second and last years at collège, when decisions must be made on the basis of the dossier as to the type of studies the pupil will subsequently undertake.[53]

This, ideally, is how the system is supposed to work now. If parents disagree with the recommendation (about where the child should go next), they can appeal to yet another committee and even after that, resort finally to an externally assessed examination. But Broadfoot also says that

> many teachers resent the additional burden it places on them and their exposure to criticism, as well as their almost total lack of preparation and training for the task. Not surprisingly, the result has been that many dossiers are not filled in with more than rudimentary information and the *conseiller d'orientation* in a collège has neither the time nor

> the information to give a considered response to each child. The orientation is as often as not merely the recognition of a choice already made, often by default.[54]

She goes on to point out that, though the National Office for Information and Orientation (ONISEP) may interpret orientation as helping the pupil 'to know himself and to prepare well for his future school and professional career choice', critics of the system see it as less than benign and she quotes Herzlick: 'Thus for the most part, orientation functions as a mechanism of successive exclusions to the detriment of less favoured groups.'[55]

Moreover, there are academic hurdles – especially when marks in mathematics in the *troisième* are considered, for these seem to have become particularly significant for the direction which orientation takes. It is in fact a form of social selection, a cooling out process because

> orientation . . . is likely to provide a new and increasingly rigorous basis for the identification of an élite since orientation towards vocational education is six times more frequent among the working class.[56]

An enormous amount of money has been invested in vocational guidance, if only to set up the various echelons of ONISEP which operate at national, regional, and local levels, the latter consisting in each case of an office to which children and parents have open access. (Incidentally, each office has copies of all government regulations on orientation: everyone's rights are spelled out.) A guidance counsellor from that office will visit each school on a regular basis to give information and advice on careers and on the qualifications necessary for them. There is a room set aside in each collège for this. At each stage through the collège and lycée, each child receives a large, colourful, and well presented booklet which gives details of what is available at the next stage in the way of courses and qualifications. Other documents from ONISEP show the total pattern of qualifications, the prerequisities for them, and the sort of occupations to which they might lead. It must be that in many individual cases orientation functions as described by ONISEP, but for the majority it gives only the appearance of fairness. However, this is more important than the reality, which is that, through orientation, selection is legitimated. Many teachers, some trade unions, and certain political groups are critical of it. Some parents are disillusioned with it; most of them probably are not.

What happens in Britain has the same effect, but vocational and career guidance are less well organized. This is probably due to the ad hoc way in which it has developed in Britain. On the other hand the Juvenile Employment Service was set up relatively early, in 1909. It was part of the structure created by the Labour Exchanges Act and this gives a clue to the philosophy behind it; it was what Inge Bates has called 'talent-matching'.[57] Through it employers could find young workers, and young workers could find jobs. Most children made little use of the service and those who did were likely to come from the elementary schools. Careers education, however, began in the secondary schools in the late 1920s with interested teachers giving advice in a not very structured way. By 1939 many secondary schools had a teacher responsible for careers as did many senior sections of elementary schools.

It was not until the 1960s that a noticeable interest in vocational guidance and career education began to emerge. Because economic conditions were good, the emphasis, as expressed in DES and Schools' Council documents, or as it emanated from the Vocational Research Unit at Leeds, was along developmental lines, and very much influenced by American theory and practice. Descriptions of such an approach can make its influence seem benign. For example:

> The process of vocational development is essentially that of developing and implementing a self-concept: it is a compromise process in which the self-concept is a product of the interaction of inherited aptitudes, neural and endocrine make-up, opportunity to play various roles, and evaluations of the extent to which the results of role playing meet the approval of superiors and fellows.[58]

However, bearing in mind what has been said about the influence of teachers on the self-concepts of children, and the schools' control of the roles children are permitted to play, then such a process could easily become part of an insidious form of selection. It is no coincidence that careers education and vocational guidance were given additional impetus as the comprehensive schools were becoming more firmly established and selection at eleven occurred less and less. Furthermore, at about the same time the examination system was expanding. More pupils were entered for the GCE and CSE courses (as an alternative for the less able). This gave increased power to the teachers. Moreover, careers education and vocational guidance became much more prominent and they began to occur earlier in the secondary-school life of the children. This was because they were becoming closely associated with the selection mechanisms operating in the schools. They now help to justify the teachers' decisions about which examination streams children should enter (and these are difficult to alter when both children and parents had been consulted on the decisions). Conversely, which stream children enter affects the kind of guidance they receive.

The quality of guidance a pupil receives depends upon the school and the authority in which that school is situated. However, what now seems to be the most common pattern is for some introductory work to be done on careers when children are in the third year (i.e. about the age of fourteen so that they can link their fourth-year option choices to whatever they may see as their career patterns, assuming they have any at this early stage. Then in the fourth and fifth years there is usually a timetable slot (albeit a narrow one) for careers education, conducted by the careers teacher(s) – perhaps in partnership with officers from the Careers Advisory Service of the local authority.

A similar process often occurs in the sixth form. There will also be opportunities for parents to discuss courses with the teachers and the officers at several points throughout these years. Again, depending on the authority, pupils may be given the chance to attend conferences and exhibitions and go on work experience projects. Often, outside speakers on various occupations are invited into the schools. However, most schools do much more than merely impart information about occupations and the qualifications required for them. Careers education rarely operates in isolation. It has become part of the pastoral system of schools, and so is linked with social and moral education, or with education in personal relationships. It may be part of any active tutorial work done in the schools. Moreover, Watts and Law observe:

> Careers education has also become linked with other trends in schools. One of these has been the concern with strengthening school–industry links. . . . The roots of this lie not in the notions of influencing individual career development but in political and economic education: the central concern is that all school pupils – regardless of where and when they are to work themselves – should be taught to understand the place of industry in our society. Nonetheless, the experience-based methods used by the more innovative school–industry projects – notably the School Curriculum Industry Project, with its emphasis on work experience, work simulation, and the use of adults other than teachers in the classroom . . . – have been symbiotic with parallel developments in careers education and guidance. . . . Such methods have also been encouraged by other developments, such as TVEI and CPVE. These trends have all been clearly linked to the effects on schools of the fracturing and deferring of entry into employment which growing youth unemployment and policy responses to it – notably the YTS – have caused.[59]

Watts has further developed this last point in a recent article where he says that career education for those who leave school at sixteen leads to placement on a training scheme rather than to a job and this takes the pressure off the schools in the dilemma they face when dealing with the less able.[60] Those who remain at school or go on to further education present fewer problems and for them the same sort of guidance continues as before.

An optimistic view of careers education and vocational guidance in Britain, especially as it is linked with other aspects of schooling – the curriculum, personal and social development, profiling, and records of achievement – would see it as operating to the benefit of the individual child, as in the statement of the American School Counsellor Association. However, looked at in the light of the Watts and Law statement and given the total impact of schooling on the child's self-concept discussed at the beginning of this chapter, they then can be seen as part of the process of slotting children into the occupational structure. Self-awareness, having a realistic view of the possibilities and so on, simply mean that the child knows where it is put and why it is right and proper that s/he should be put there. Linking careers education with other work of the schools simply makes selection all the more insidious. Watts should have the last word:

> The 'matching' approach which has long characterized much career guidance practice has required that broad categories of jobs be described in ways which make it possible to match individual attributes to them. It has accordingly been drawn towards the bureaucratized sector of the labour market, where jobs are formalized in groups, with formal entry channels defined in terms of educational qualifications. In doing so, it has performed an important task in oiling the operations of the employment bureaucracies and relating them to the operations of the correspondingly bureaucratic educational structures.[61]

This view sums up the point of this chapter. Even infant and primary schools prepare children for the decisions which are to be made about them later. They socialize children into accepting that the certification processes which occur in secondary, further, and higher education, are legitimate and should lead to particular kinds of jobs. Recent developments in the world of work and the responses they have provoked in the schools – e.g. the strengthening of vocational education – have tied the education systems of these four countries even closer to their occupation structures. Because early selection (sponsored) has disappeared, guidance and counselling oil the wheels of selection, which now appears as self-selection – but self-selection according to how a person has been judged by the schools.

The structuring of education systems in response to industrialization and social change has been going on for at least two hundred years, but the most recent developments have established a shape (i.e. pre-primary, primary and lower-secondary in common, followed by a series of differentiating alternatives) which make guidance and counselling very necessary. If the schools are engines of selection, then the lubrication which permits them to run smoothly is guidance and counselling. The decisions of the schools may be biased in favour of the middle strata of society, but those decisions are accepted by most people as legitimate.

Epilogue

I had already completed this book when a piece of research into comprehensive education in part of Wales was published.[1] It was seized upon immediately by a section of the British press as a means of condemning the comprehensive school: one large headline consisted simply of the word 'Failed!'[2] This reaction came because many people believe that in the best interests of Britain – economic, social, political, and even spiritual – the grammar schools, and with them the tripartite system should be restored. However, one of the authors of the research responded to the outbursts in the newspapers by saying:

> Simply, we argued that the schools failed because they were merely 'grammar schools for all' and therefore 'pseudo-comprehensive' . . . it is important to state again what we believe the authentic comprehensive school should be like. This school must aim for the academic and social development of all its pupils. It must be consistent, cohesive, and giving of identity in an uncertain world, with a body of knowledge all children have in common. It must therefore be universal, giving the same experience to all children. It must also, however, be selective in its organization, giving different children and different ability ranges a selectively different experience . . . the comprehensive school is to be both universal and selective.[3]

This is what we have now in Britain, France, the United States, and the Soviet Union. The systems do not work very efficiently. There are bad schools in all of them; there are bad sections of schools in all of them. However, the development of something like the comprehensive school as defined by Reynolds is possible in each of these countries, and many schools come closer to that ideal than they are often given credit for. I know this from my own experiences – at first teaching in them, and then more recently visiting them – not only throughout the Midlands in England but also in Michigan in the USA, in Aix-en-Provence in France, and in Moscow and Leningrad in the Soviet Union.

Going back to the tripartite system in Britain and France (the Americans and the Russians are not likely to be so daft) might improve aspects of selection but those who advocate such a move must look again at what was said about that system in the 1950s. They should examine the figures produced in the Crowther Report,[4] which showed how extensively talent was wasted. They should note how ridiculously inefficient and blatantly unfair were the methods of selection. They should look, too, at how vociferously parents criticized the system when it 'failed' their children and condemned them to the secondary modern schools, which were very rarely the institutions they were supposed to be and in most cases unlike those which appear in the research of Reynolds *et al.*

Should they claim that in Germany a tripartite system works efficiently, then it would have to be pointed out to them that Germany has had one hundred and fifty years of successful technical education which has conferred prestigious qualifications – accepted by *all* classes. Moreover, the problem of too-early selection is recognized in Germany and some *lander* have tried to introduce comprehensive education to counter it. Should they cite the case of Japan, then it would have to be pointed out that the basic building-block of Japanese education is common schooling – it is only ferocious competition engendered by aspiring parents that distorts it. Do they want to put their children under such pressure? Do they want the worst consequences of what the French used to call '*bourrage*' (stuffing) in education? Even the Japanese are afraid that the products of such schooling lack the creativity which, with all their faults, the British and American systems manage to foster – sometimes. To re-establish the grammar schools would be to return to Turner's sponsored mobility model of education and that would be flying in the face of all the evidence of how anachronistic it was even when it operated. It would be to deny how advantageous to modern societies comprehensive education is. That means not only to the societies discussed here, but most others, Germany being the exception which proves the rule.

Education, anyway, is not the problem. Education systems have responded to the changes brought about in societies by advancing industrialization. They might have done so too slowly and even too late on occasions, but they have changed, and in ways which show that they have tried to solve some of the contradictions present in those societies: tripartism in Britain and France was an attempt to look both ways at once; polytechnical education in the Soviet Union was a similar attempt; as was the development in the United States of both testing and equivalents at the same time in the 1920s and 1930s. The ultimate paradox came when secondary education had to become both universal and selective, as Reynolds says.

Comprehensive education is not the only way to hold that contradiction in some sort of control but it is one of the more obvious methods and it does allow selection to take place in a more subtle way and over a longer period of time so that it *seems* to be in keeping with the nature of things – and therefore politically more acceptable. Just consider how elaborate our systems of education have become in the upper reaches, and look at the variety of qualifications available through them. Children can now be eased gently and over a considerable period of time, towards those final channels – they are now more like capillaries – which will carry them into the appropriate slots in society. The systems considered here actually do that more efficiently now than ever before. Anyone who would change this back to a clumsier system is either naive or ignorant of the history of education.

So the problem is not education. The problem is selection – or rather, why we need to select in the first place – and this goes right back to the division of labour, by which we are still mesmerized because it is so profitable, because it is so efficient, in the narrow sense. Moreover, competition to sell each other goods and services for the sake of profit, obliges everyone now, on a worldwide scale, to engage in the same sort of division of labour, no matter what the social consequences might be. If we look again at what has happened to occupations over the last two hundred years we can see that the early division of labour, the 'workshop' division of labour, despite its detrimental effect on factory workers helped to bring about changes in society which accelerated what we distinguished in Chapter 1 as the 'social' division of labour, which in turn gave rise to a new kind of workshop division of labour – one based on more sophisticated and science-based technologies. This, in turn, helped to create further elaboration of the social division of labour, and so on. This process has gone on throughout the past two centuries. Let us illustrate it from a fairly recent series of events as recounted by Braverman:

> For a short time in the 1940s and early 1950s, the data-processing occupations displayed the characteristics of a craft. This was during the period when tabulating equipment based on the punched card dominated the industry. Installations were small and the tabulating craftsmen worked on all the machines: the sorter, collator, tabulator, calculator etc. (Except the key punch machine; being a keyboard machine, this was immediately recognised as a job for 'girls'.) These machines were programmed by wiring a panel board for each machine, and this operation was learned as the worker gained a general familiarity with all the machines. Thus the equivalent of an apprenticeship was a period of learning the use of all the equipment, and the programming done at that time was simply the highest skill of an all-round trade.
>
> The development of a data-processing craft was abortive, however, since along with the computer a new division of labour was introduced and the destruction of the craft greatly hastened. Each aspect of the computer operation was graded to a different level of pay frozen into a hierarchy: systems managers, systems analysts, programmers, computer console operators, key punch operators, tape librarians, stock room attendants etc. It soon became a characteristic that entry into the higher jobs was at the higher level of the hierarchy, rather than through an all-round training. And the concentration of knowledge and control in a very small portion of the hierarchy became the key here, as with automatic machines in the factory, to control over the process.[5]

This kind of development has taken place and is taking place constantly. It does lower the level of skill required by some – it reduces them to 'hands', but it also creates a hierarchy, the upper parts of which are filled by those aspiring to status. The process influences the division of labour in both senses of that term and in effect shows that there should really be no distinction between them. The impetus towards the establishment of hierarchy is as important as the technology in creating the division of labour. But consider what this means for education.

Such a scenario, the total industrial, commercial and social setting of the above situation is unimaginable without mass education. On the other hand, because of the division of labour, the actual level of education (beyond the primary stage) required by the majority of people is not high – provided they are amenable to training.[6] However, for a very large minority the level required *is* high (though I think even this can be exaggerated). Now, an education system has to provide for both levels, besides some in between, and at the same time help to keep society cohesive, and in democracies, or proclaimed democracies, that means it has to offer a semblance of equality of opportunity.

The schools then become the places where those contradictions are resolved – in part at least – and that is why they have become so important to selection and the division of labour. But the schools can no longer perform this service in a ham-fisted way. They have to appear to be giving real education, i.e. helping each child to develop his or her full potential. In many cases this is what schools do. However, they are also preparing children for the decisions which will be taken later on which qualifications children will be entered for and therefore which occupations they will take up – which part of the hierarchy. Counselling and guidance are used to ease these decisions: they legitimate them – because teachers know best.

There is, of course, another way of looking at the whole difficulty and that is to consider the division of labour itself and then to find ways of either removing it or of mitigating its worst effects. Now, though the former would be preferable, perhaps, there seems to be little likelihood of achieving that in the near future, though attempts have been made, in various kinds of communes. Braverman obviously believes that the Russians could have organized alternatives after 1917 but he says they imitated the West instead.

The Chinese have also flirted with such notions. However, it is the other line which offers more hope that we can mitigate those worst effects though it probably means that we have to move in a piecemeal fashion (as education has so often) and live up to our own proclaimed ideologies by educating every child to take part in *all* aspects of life as an adult. On the other hand, that would make sense only if we had some measure of real democracy in *all* workplaces, and there are some indications that we might actually be moving in that direction. The division of labour in the co-operative experiment at Mondragon in Northern Spain does not have the divisive social repercussions found in more traditional forms of organization. There are even moves towards greater democracy in workplaces in the countries under discussion here.

It is possible that economic survival could be through this route – as Burns and Stalker showed had actually occurred in certain firms which adopted a more organic approach to management. They say that:

> the lead in joint decisions is frequently taken by seniors, but it is an essential presumption of the organic system that the lead, i.e. 'authority' is taken by whoever shows himself most informed and capable, i.e. the 'best authority'. The location of authority is settled by consensus.[7]

In such circumstances, everyone can become committed to the enterprise, but hierarchical chains of command which leave those at the bottom of the pile to be regarded simply as 'hands' cannot operate such an organic system. And those hands are people! Burns says of them:

> I am more than ever impressed with the extraordinary gap that exists between the perceptiveness, intellectual grasp, and technical competence of the people who work in industrial concerns, and the cumbrous, primitive, and belittling nature of the administrative structures by which they direct their efforts, and of the constraints they see fit to impose on their thinking and liberty of action.[8]

Here are the real consequences of the division of labour.

Notes

1 Industrialization and social change

1 A.E. Musson and E. Robinson (1969) *Science and Technology in the Industrial Revolution*, Manchester: Manchester University Press.
2 N. Hans (1951) *New Trends in Education in the Eighteenth Century*, London: Routledge & Kegan Paul.
3 G. Timmons (1986) 'Science, technology and education in the Industrial Revolution', *Endeavour*, new series, vol. 10, no. 2.
4 E.J. Hobsbawm (1977) *The Age of Revolution*, London: Sphere Books, pp. 43 and 44.
5 T. Bilton, K. Bonnett, P. Jones, M. Stanworth, K. Sheard, and A. Webster (1981) *Introductory Sociology*, London: Macmillan, pp. 446 and 447.
6 K. Kumar (1978) *Prophecy and Progress*, Harmondsworth: Penguin, p. 85.
7 Quoted by R.E. Schofield in *The Lunar Society of Birmingham*, 1963, Oxford: Oxford University Press, p. 350.
8 P.J. Corfield (1987) 'From rank to class: innovation in Georgian England', in *History Today*, vol. 37, Feb. 1987, pp. 36 and 37.
9 Ibid., p. 38.
10 H. Braverman (1974) *Labor and Monopoly Capital*, New York: Monthly Review Press, p. 8.
11 Bilton *et al.*, op. cit., pp. 61 and 62.
12 H.G. Gerth and C. Wright Mills (1946) *From Max Weber: Essays in Sociology*, London: Routledge & Kegan Paul, pp. 185–91.
13 J.H. Goldthorpe, C. Llewellyn, and C. Payne (1980) *Social Mobility and the Class Structure in Modern Britain*, Oxford: Clarendon Press, p. 6.
14 Ibid., p. 12.
15 F. Parkin (1972) *Class, Inequality and the Social Order*, London: Paladin, p. 46.

16 A. Giddens (1973) *The Class Structure of Advanced Societies*, London: Hutchinson, p. 122.
17 Braverman, op. cit., Chapter 15.
18 Goldthorpe, Llewellyn, and Payne, op. cit., p. 14.
19 P.M. Blau and O.D. Duncan (1967) *The American Occupational Structure*, New York: Wiley.
20 K. Davis and W. Moore (1945) 'Some principles of stratification', *American Sociological Review*, vol. 10.
21 Bilton *et al.*, op. cit., p. 182.
22 Ibid., p. 187.
23 C. Barnett (1986) *The Audit of War*, London: Macmillan, p. 192.

2 Education and society in the first half of the nineteenth century

1 Fourth Annual Report of the Poor Law Commissioners (1838), quoted in J. Hurt (1972) *Education in Evolution*, London: Paladin, p. 113.
2 The Taunton Commission.
3 S. Bowles (1976) 'Unequal education and the reproduction of the social division of labour', in R. Dale, G. Esland, and M. Macdonald (eds) *Schooling and Capitalism*, London: Routledge & Kegan Paul, p. 34.
4 W.D. Halls (1976) *Education, Culture and Politics in Modern France*, Oxford: Pergamon, pp. 5–6.
5 D. Bell-Leary (1971) 'Education and autocracy in Russia', in S.M. Rosen, *Education and Modernisation in the USSR*, London: Addison-Wesley, p. 24.
6 H.J. Habakkuk (1967) *American and British Technology in the Nineteenth Century*, Cambridge: Cambridge University Press, p. 215.
7 W.G. Hoffman (1958) *The Growth of Industrial Economies*, Manchester: Manchester University Press, p. 51.
8 Ibid., p. 51.
9 Habakkuk, op. cit., p. 203.

3 Developments in education in the second phase of industrialization: the beginnings of selection

1 P.R. Gregory and R.C. Stuart (1981) *Soviet Economic Structure and Performance*, New York: Harper & Row, p. 28.
2 E. Etzioni-Halévy (1981) *Social Change*, London: Routledge & Kegan Paul, p. 98.
3 M. Shipman (1971) *Education and Modernisation*, London: Faber & Faber, p. 142.
4 R.L. Heilbronner (1977) *The Economic Transformation of America*, San Diego CA: Harcourt Brace Jovanovich Inc., p. 93.

5 C. Singer, E.J. Holmyard, A.R. Hall, and T.L. Williams (1978) *A History of Technology*, vol. V, Oxford: Clarendon Press, p. 232.
6 D. Nelson reported in *Technology and Culture*, Vol. 21, January 1980, p. 69.
7 C. Singer, *et al.*, op. cit.
8 G. Dupeux (1978) *French Society 1789–1970*, translated by P. Wait, Oxford: Clarendon Press, p. 35.
9 B.E. Brown (1976) *The French Experience of Modernisation*, in C.E. Black (ed.), *Comparative Modernisation*, Free Press, (Macmillan).
10 C. Singer, *et al.*, op. cit., p. 805.
11 H.J. Habakkuk (1967) *American and British Technology in the Nineteenth Century*, Cambridge: Cambridge University Press, p. 193.
12 T. Veblen (1920) *The Engineers and the Price System*, quoted in D. Bell, *The Coming of the Post-Industrial Society*, London: Heinemann, (1974).
13 C. Singer, *et al.*, op. cit.
14 T. Kemp (1969) *Industrialisation in Europe*, London: Longman.
15 M. Shipman, op. cit., p. 41.
16 E. Etzioni-Halévy, op. cit.
17 G. Dupeux, op. cit., p. 159.
18 K. Kumar (1978) *Prophecy and Progress*, Harmondsworth: Penguin.
19 T. Kemp, op. cit, p. 76.
20 S. Bowles and H. Gintis (1976) *Schooling in Capitalist America*, London: Routledge & Kegan Paul, p. 183.
21 G. Dupeux, op. cit.
22 B. Simon and D. Rubinstein (1969) *The Evolution of the Comprehensive School*, London: Routledge & Kegan Paul, p. 5.
23 A. Prost (1968) *Histoire de L'Enseignment en France, 1800–1967*, Paris: Arnold Colin.
24 Ibid.
25 The most important aspect of elementary education as a form of social control.
26 F. Smith (1931) *A History of English Elementary Education, 1760–1902*, London: University of London Press, p. 260.
27 Funds from a tax on spirits to support police superannuation and to compensate publicans for loss of their licences was diverted from the publicans to technical education.
28 A. Prost, op. cit.
29 Ibid., p. 58.
30 F. Buisson (1887) 'Rapport a la Commission Mixte', in Prost, op. cit.
31 G. Dupeux, op. cit., p. 156.
32 C.F. Kaestle (1973) *The Evolution of the Urban School System*, Cambridge MA: Harvard University Press, p. 92.
33 D. Nasaw (1979) *Schooled to Order*, Oxford University Press, p. 83.

34 R. Freeman Butts (1978) *Public Education in the United States*, New York: Holt, Rinehart & Winston, p. 106–7.

35 M.B. Katz (1968) *The Irony of Early School Reform*, Cambridge MA: Harvard University Press, cited in R. Freeman Butts, op. cit.

36 S.B. Levine (1980) 'The rise of the American boarding school and the development of a national upper class', *Social Problems*, vol. 28., no. 1., Oct. 1980.

37 D. Nasaw, op. cit., pp. 118, 119.

38 R. Freeman Butts, op. cit.

39 Ibid.

40 The A.F.L. Report of 1915, quoted in R. Freeman Butts, op. cit., p. 216.

41 B. Meissner (1972) *Social Change in the Soviet Union*, translated by D.P. Kommers, Notre Dame IN: University of the Notre Dame Press, p. 17.

42 P. Gregory and R. Stuart, op. cit., p. 23.

43 B. Meissner, op. cit., p. 19.

44 N. Hans, (1963) *The Russian Tradition in Education*, London: Routledge & Kegan Paul.

45 O. Anweiler, 'Education policy and the social structure in the Soviet Union', in Meissner, op. cit.

46 W.E. Johnson (1969) *Russia's Educational Heritage*, London: Octagon Books, p. 137.

47 Ibid.

48 S.M. Rosen (1971) *Education and Modernisation in USSR*, London: Addison-Wesley, p. 25.

49 W.E. Johnson, op. cit., p. 196.

4 Industry and education in the first half of the twentieth century: selection by differentiation

1 G. Barraclough (1964) *An Introduction to Contemporary History*, Harmondsworth: Penguin, p. 26.

2 Ibid., p. 29.

3 K. Davis and W. Moore (1945) 'Some principles of stratification', *American Sociological Review*, vol. 10.

4 R.L. Heilbroner (1977) *The Economic Transformation of America*, San Diego CA: Harcourt Brace Jovanovich Inc., p. 146.

5 G. Marin and A. Mattei (1961) *The Motor Car*, Schwarz Editore (p. xvii of the introduction by R. Walkerley).

6 Ibid., p. 134.

7 390,000 cars and 118,000 commerical vehicles in 1929. H. Perkin *The Age of the Automobile*, London: Quartet Books, (1976) p. 111.

8 J. Dunning and C. Thomas (1961) *British Industry: Change and Development in the Twentieth Century*, London: Hutchinson, p. 22.
9 D.C. Marsh (1965) *The Changing Social Structure of England and Wales*, London: Routledge & Kegan Paul, p. 143.
10 A.M. Carr-Saunders and P.A. Wilson (1933) *The Professions*, Oxford: Clarendon Press, cited in the above.
11 D.C. Marsh, op. cit., p. 138.
12 K. Kumar (1978) *Prophecy and Progress*, Harmondsworth: Penguin, pp. 200–201.
13 Dunning and Thomas, op cit.
14 D.C. Marsh, op cit., p. 137.
15 Ibid.
16 T.S. Khachaturov (1973) 'The development of science and technology in the USSR', in B.R. Williams (ed.), *Science and Technology in Economic Growth*, London: MacMillan, p. 147.
17 P.R. Gregory and R.C. Stuart (1981) *Soviet Economic Structure and Performance*, New York: Harper & Row, p. 45.
18 Ibid., p. 85.
19 M. Dobb (1948) *Soviet Economic Development since 1917*, Routledge & Kegan Paul, revised edition 1966.
20 A.G. Mazour (1967) *Social Change in Bolshevik Russia*, London: Van Nostrand.
21 B. Meissner, op. cit., pp. 38–9.
22 Ibid., p. 42.
23 Ibid., p. 43.
24 Ibid.
25 H. Braverman (1974) *Labor and Monopoly Capital*, Monthly Review Press, p. 12.
26 E.J.R. Eaglesham (1967) *The Foundations of Twentieth-Century Education in England*, London: Routledge & Kegan Paul.
27 Ibid., p. 63.
28 Ibid., p. 69.
29 Quoted in G. Bernbaum (1967) *Social Change and the Schools, 1918–1944*, London: Routledge & Kegan Paul, p. 16.
30 Introduction to the Hadow Report 1926, HMSO.
31 E. Boutary (1899) *Le baccalauréat et l'enseignement secondaire*, Paris, p. 18, quoted by J.E. Talbot in *The Politics of Educational Reform in France, 1982–40*, Princeton NJ: Princeton University Press, 1969, p. 12.
32 Ibid., p. 39.
33 Ibid., p. 41.
34 Ibid., p. 57.
35 Ibid., p. 60.

36 Ibid., p. 99.
37 Prost, op. cit., p. 314.
38 Ibid., p. 414.
39 Talbott, op. cit., p. 176.
40 S. Hoffman (1963) 'Paradoxes of the French political community', in Hoffman *et al.*, *In Search of France*, p. 117.
41 H.G. Good and J.D. Teller (1969) *A History of American Education*, London: Macmillan, p. 453.
42 Ibid., p. 453.
43 Ibid., p. 459.
44 Ibid., p. 449.
45 B.R. Clark (1960) *The Open Door College*, New York: McGraw-Hill, p. 3.
46 R.H. Turner, *Sponsored and Context Mobility and the School System*, originally presented at the Fourth World Congress of Sociology, 1958, and in E. Hopper (ed.) (1971) *Readings in the Theory of Education Systems*, London: Hutchinson, pp. 71–90.
47 E.B. Gumbert and J.H. Spring (1974) *The Super School and the Superstate: American Education in the Twentieth Century, 1918–70*, Chichester: J. Wiley, p. 100.
48 Ibid., p. 108.
49 Bowles and Gintis, op. cit., p. 196.
50 L. Terman (1961) *The Measurement of Intelligence*, Houghton-Miffin, pp. 27–28, quoted in Bowles and Gintis, p. 197.
51 S.A. Rippa (1980) *Education in a Free Society*, David McKay, p. 289.
52 P. Bourdieu and J.C. Passeron (1977) *Reproduction in Education, Society and Culture*, L. Sage.
53 S. Rosen (1971) *Education and Modernisation in USSR*, London: Addison-Wesley, p. 39.
54 J. Pennar, I. Bakalo, and G.Z.F. Bereday (1971) *Modernisation and Diversity in Soviet Education*, New York: Praeger, p. 34.
55 V. George and N. Manning (1980) *Socialism, Social Welfare and the Soviet Union*, London: Routledge & Kegan Paul, p. 66.
56 L. Spolton (1967) *The Upper Secondary School*, Oxford: Pergamon, pp. 1–13.
57 George and Manning, op. cit., p. 69.
58 O. Anweiler (1972) 'Education policy and the social structure in the Soviet Union', in B. Meissner, op. cit., p. 180.
59 Ibid., p. 181.
60 Ibid., p. 182.
61 S. Fitzpatrick (1979) *Education and Social Mobility in the Soviet Union, 1921–34*, Cambridge: Cambridge University Press, p. 62.
62 VUZ: acronym for higher education institution.

63 Anweiler, op. cit., p. 185.
64 Ibid., pp. 185–6.
65 Fitzpatrick, op. cit., p. 237.
66 Ibid., p. 237.
67 Ibid.

5 Britain, France, the USA, and the USSR as advanced industrial societies

1 Daniel Bell (1974) *The Coming of the Post-Industrial Society*, Heinemann, p. 25.
2 Krishan Kumar (1978) *Prophecy and Progress*, Harmondsworth: Penguin.
3 Take-off point.
4 M.M. Postan (1967) *An Economic History of Western Europe 1945–1964*, London: Methuen.
5 A. Bergson (1978) *Productivity and the Social System – the USSR and the West*, Cambridge MA: Harvard University Press, p. 123.
6 Ibid., p. 122.
7 T. Khachaturov (1975) *The Economy of the Soviet Union*, translated by J. Sayer, Moscow: Progress Publishers, p. 25.
8 H. Kahn and A. Wiener (1967) 'The next thirty-three years: a framework for speculation', *Daedelus*, Summer 1967, cited in D. Bell, op. cit., pp. 461–2.
9 C. Barnett: *The Audit of War*, London: MacMillan, 1986, p. 157.
10 Ibid., p. 192.
11 Quoted by Barnett, p. 191.
12 All these figures are taken from Ross M. Robertson (1973) *History of the American Economy*, San Diego CA: Harcourt Brace Jovanovich Inc., third edition, p. 611.
13 J.C. Dewdney (1982) *USSR in Maps*, London: Hodder & Stoughton, p. 59.
14 R.M. Robertson, op. cit., p. 612.
15 J.C. Dewdney, op. cit., p. 58.
16 S. Pollard (1969) *The Development of the British Economy, 1914–1967*, E. Arnold, p. 421.
17 F. Caron (1979) *An Economic History of Modern France*, translated by B. Bray, London: Methuen, p. 236.
18 R.M. Robertson, op. cit., p. 603.
19 F. Caron, op. cit., p. 231.
20 S. Pollard, op. cit., p. 431.
21 D. Bell, op. cit., p. 215.
22 T. Khachaturov, op. cit., p. 118.

23 P.R. Gregory (1974) *Soviet Economic Structure and Performance*, New York: Harper & Row, p. 405.
24 J.C. Dewdney, op. cit., p. 68.
25 R. Hutchings (1971) *Soviet Economic Development*, Oxford: Blackwell, p. 81.
26 J.C. Dewdney, op. cit., p. 64.
27 P.R. Gregory, op. cit., p. 341.
28 R.M. Robertson, op. cit., p. 616.
29 Ibid., p. 616.
30 F. Caron, op. cit., p. 239.
31 T. Khachaturov, op. cit., pp. 235–6.
32 R. Hutchings, op. cit., Appendix.
33 P. Bourdieu and J.C. Passeron, op. cit.
34 J.H. Goldthorpe, C. Llewellen, and C. Payne, op. cit.
35 A.L. Stinchcombe (1983) *Economic Sociology*, London: Academic Press, pp. 108–9.
36 Ibid., p. 108.
37 J. Marceau (1977) *Class and Status in France*, Oxford: Clarendon Press, p. 23.
38 NIESR (1976) *The United Kingdom Economy*, London: Heinemann, pp. 41–2.
39 K. Kumar (1976) 'Industrialism and post-industrialism: reflections on a putative transition', in *Sociological Review*, vol. 24, no. 3.
40 Figures taken from Table 1.1, in R. Hyman and R. Price (eds), *The New Working Class*, London: MacMillan, 1983, p. 6.
41 D. Lane and F. O'Dell (1978) *The Soviet Industrial Worker*, Oxford: Martin Robertson, p. 13.
42 G. Littlejohn (1984) *A Sociology of the Soviet Union*, London: Macmillan, p. 233.
43 B. Meissner, op. cit., p. 131.
44 Braverman, op. cit., p. 10.
45 Ibid., p. 200.
46 US Government Report, *Work in America*, 1973, quoted by Braverman, op. cit., p. 34.
47 Ibid., p. 328.
48 Ibid., p. 34.
49 N. Abercromby and J. Urry (1983) *Capital, Labour and the Middle Classes*, London: Allen & Unwin.
50 E. Etzioni-Halévy (1981) *Social Change: The Advent and Maturation of Modern Society*, London: Routledge & Kegan Paul, pp. 103 and 104.
51 C.E. Black (ed.) (1975) *The Modernization of Japan and Russia*, New York: Free Press, p. 308.
52 L. Schapiro (1977) *The Government and Politics of the Soviet Union*, London: Hutchinson, pp. 37–8.

53 A. Marwick (1980) *Class Image and Reality in Britain, France and the USA since 1930*, London: Fontana, p. 241.
54 Ibid.
55 J. Ardagh (1977) *The New France: A Society in Transition, 1945–77*, Harmondsworth: Pelican, p. 22.
56 A. Marwick, op. cit., p. 252.
57 Ibid., p. 284.
58 Schapiro, op. cit., p. 52.
59 B. Meissner (1972) 'Social change in Bolshevik Russia', in *Social Change in the Soviet Union*, Notre Dame IN: University of Notre Dame Press, p. 63.
60 Schapiro, op. cit., p. 54.
61 Meissner, op. cit., p. 64.

6 Education for advanced industrial countries

1 J.S. Maclure (1965) *Educational Documents*, London: Methuen, p. 230.
2 W.H.G. Armytage (1970) *Four Hundred Years of English Education*, Cambridge: Cambridge University Press, p. 245.
3 J.S. Maclure, op. cit., p. 239.
4 White Paper on Technical Education, in J.S. Maclure, op. cit., pp. 239–40.
5 *15 to 18, a Report of the Central Advisory Council for Education*, the Crowther Report, HMSO, 1959, vol. 1, p. 472.
6 W. Taylor (1963) *The Secondary Modern School*, London: Faber & Faber, p. 29.
7 A. Shonfield, 'The apprenticeship scandal', *Observer*, 4 June, 1961.
8 K. Liepmann (1960) *Apprenticeship*, London: Routledge & Kegan Paul.
9 P. Drucker (1958) *Landmarks of Tomorrow*, London: Heinemann.
10 The Crowther Report, op. cit., p. 742.
11 D. Glass (ed.) (1954) *Social Mobility in Britain*, p. 160.
12 D. Rubinstein and B. Simon (1969) *The Evolution of the Comprehensive School*, London: Routledge & Kegan Paul, p. 59.
13 A.H. Halsey and L. Gardner (1953) 'Selection for secondary education', *British Journal of Sociology*, March 1953.
14 P.E. Vernon (ed.) (1957) *Secondary School Selection*, London: Methuen.
15 A. Yates and D.A. Pidgeon (1957) *Admission to Grammar Schools*, Feltham: Newnes Books.
16 J.J. Carré, P. Dubois, and E. Malinvaud (1976) *French Economic Growth*, translated by J.P. Hatfield, Oxford: Oxford University Press, p. 479.

17 Ibid., p. 479.
18 Ibid., p. 214.
19 Quoted in R. Gilpin (1968) *France in the Age of the Scientific State*, Princeton NJ: Princeton University Press, p. 39.
20 J.J. Cremieux-Brilhac (1965) *L'Education Nationale*, Paris: Presses Universitaires de France, p. 36.
21 Ibid., p. 38.
22 J. Natanson and A. Prost (1963) *La Revolution Scolaire*, Paris: Les Editions Duvrières, pp. 45–6.
23 'Memorandum by N.S. Khrushchev on strengthening the ties of the school with life, and further developing the system of public education', Soviet Booklet no. 42, October 1958, *Soviet News*, p. 3.
24 Ibid., p. 5.
25 L. Liegle (1975) *The Family's Role in Soviet Education*, translated by S. Hacker, New York: Springer, p. 7.
26 N. de Witt (1961) *Education and Professional Employment in the USSR*, National Science Foundation, p. 16.
27 W. Kenneth Richmond (1971) *The School Curriculum*, London: Methuen, pp. 50–51.
28 James B. Conant (1959) *The American High School Today*, New York: McGraw-Hill, p. 40.
29 W. Kenneth Richmond, op. cit., p. 47.
30 D. Nasaw (1979) *Schooled to Order*, Oxford: Oxford University Press, p. 214.
31 C. Jencks and D. Riesman (1962) *The Academic Revolution*, New York: McGraw-Hill, quoted in D. Nasaw, op. cit., p. 206.
32 Eric James in the *School-master*, April 1954, quoted in D. Rubinstein and B. Simon (1973) *The Evolution of the Comprehensive School*, London: Routledge & Kegan Paul, p. 76.
33 S. Mason (1970) *The Leicestershire Plan*, in Rubinstein and Simon, op. cit., p. 83.
34 M. Parkinson (1970) *The Labour Party and the Organisation of Secondary Education*, London: Routledge & Kegan Paul, p. 88.
35 W.R. Fraser (1963) *Educational Society in Modern France*, London: Routledge & Kegan Paul, p. 7.
36 D.L. Hanley, A.P. Kerr, and N.H. Waites (1984) *Contemporary France*, p. 288.
37 J. Capelle (1967) *Tomorrow's Education: the French Experience*, translated by W.D. Halls, Oxford: Pergamon, pp. 23–4.
38 P. Gosden (1983) *The Education System Since 1944*, Oxford: Martin Robertson, p. 75.
39 W.D. Halls (1976) *Education, Culture and Politics in France*, Oxford: Pergamon, p. 129.
40 Gosden, op. cit., p. 137.

41 Ibid., p. 150.
42 Ibid., p. 173.
43 Ibid., p. 177.
44 Halls, op. cit., p. 127.
45 M. Matthews (1982) *Education in the Soviet Union*, London: Allen & Unwin, p. 20.
46 Ibid., p. 23.
47 Ibid., p. 25.
48 Ibid., p. 31.
49 Ibid., p. 32.
50 Ibid., p. 32.
51 Ibid., p. 89.
52 M. Matthews (1983) 'Long-term trends in Soviet Education', in J.J. Tomiak, *Soviet Education in the 1980s*, Beckenham: Croom Helm, p. 2.

7 Selection: educational or social?

1 M. Yanowitch (1977) *Social and Economic Inequality in the Soviet Union*, Armonk NY: M.E. Sharpe Inc., p. 64.
2 M. Matthews (1982) *Education in the Soviet Union*, George Allen & Unwin, p 94.
3 G. Avis (1983) 'Access to Higher Education in the Soviet Union', in J.J. Tomiak, *Education in the Soviet Union in the Eighties*, p. 222.
4 W.L. Hansen and B.A. Weisbrod, *Benefits, Costs and Finance of Public Higher Education*, quoted in I. Berg (1970) *Education and Jobs: The Great Training Robbery*, New York: Praeger, p. 193.
5 S. Bowles and H. Gintis (1976) *Schooling in Capitalist America*, London: Routledge & Kegan Paul, p. 111.
6 Ibid., p. 142.
7 J. Karabel (1977) 'Community colleges and social stratification', in J. Karabel and A.H. Halsey, *Power and Ideology in Education*, Oxford: Oxford University Press, p. 241.
8 J. Karabel and A.W. Austin (1975) 'Social class, academic ability and college "Quality" ', *Social Forces*, vol. 53, no. 3, March 1975, p. 394.
9 T. Krauze and K.M. Slomczynski (1985) 'How far to meritocracy? Empirical tests of a controversial thesis', *Social Forces*, vol. 63, no. 3, March 1985, p. 639.
10 J. Marceau (1977) *Class and Status in France*, Oxford: Clarendon, p. 107.
11 C. Baudelot, R. Benoliel, H. Cukrowicz, and R. Establet (1981) *Les Etudiants, l'Emploi, la Crise*, Maspero, pp. 25–6.
12 Ibid., p. 46.

13 I. Reid (1986) *The Sociology of the School and Education*, London: Fontana, p. 145.
14 A.H. Halsey, A.F. Heath, and J.M. Ridge (1980) *Origins and Destinations*, Oxford: Clarendon, pp. 142–3.
15 J.M. Goldstrom (1972) *Elementary Education, 1780–1980*, Newton Abbott: David & Charles, pp. 22–3.
16 J.H. Goldthorpe (1969) *Social Inequality and Social Integration in Modern Britain.*
17 J. Marceau, op. cit., p. 84.
18 P. Bourdieu (1973) 'Cultural reproduction and social reproduction', in R. Brown, *Knowledge, Education, and Cultural Change*, London: Tavistock, p. 85.
19 As they do in *Reproduction in Education, Society and Culture*, Sage, (1977), op. cit.
20 H.A. Giroux (1983) 'Theories of reproduction and resistance in the new sociology of education: A critical analysis', *Harvard Educational Review*, vol. 53, no. 3, August, 1983, p. 283.

8 The legitimation of selection

1 N. Bennett (1976) *Teaching Styles and Pupils' Progress*, Shepton Mallet: Open Books.
2 M. Galton and B. Simon (1980) *Progress and Performance in the Primary Classroom*, London: Routledge & Kegan Paul.
3 C. Silberman (1970) *Crisis in the Classroom*, New York: Random House.
4 N. Postman and C. Weingartner (1971) *Teaching as a Subversive Activity*, Harmondsworth: Penguin.
5 G. Chanan and L. Gilchrist (1974) *What School is For*, London: Methuen.
6 C. Join-Lambert (1978) *Apprendre L'Ecole*, Paris: Calmann-Levy.
7 S. Spavin (1984) 'Expectancy effects in the primary classroom', unpublished M. Ed thesis, Leicester University.
8 J.W.B. Douglas (1964) *The Home and the School*, London: MacGibbon and Kee; (1968) *All Our Future*, Peter Davies.
9 C. Baudelot and R. Establet (1971) *L'Ecole Capitaliste en France*, Paris: Maspero.
10 D. Handley, A. Parr, and N. Waites (1984) *Contemporary France*, London: Routledge & Kegan Paul, p. 292.
11 J.J. Tomiak (1985) 'Equality and the new Soviet man', in B. Holmes (ed.), *Equality and Freedom in Education*, London: George Allen & Unwin.

12 A. Hargreaves (1985) 'Motivation versus selection: a dilemma for records of personal achievement', in P. Lang and M. Marland (eds), *New Directions in Pastoral Care*, Oxford: Blackwell, pp. 148–162.
13 N. Brooke and J. Oxenham (1984) 'The influence of certification and selection on teaching and learning', in J. Oxenham (ed.), *Education Versus Qualifications*, London: George Allen & Unwin, p. 147.
14 R. Dore and J. Oxenham, 'Educational reform and selection for employment', ibid., p. 13.
15 B. Goacher (1984) *Selection Post 16: the Role of Examination Results*, London: Methuen, p. 34.
16 M. Farley (1985) 'Trends and structural changes in English vocational education', in R. Dale (ed.), *Education, Training and Employment*, Oxford: Pergamon, p. 93.
17 *Training for Jobs*, Cmnd 9135, HMSO (1984); *The Education and Training of Young People*, Cmnd 9482, London: HMSO, (1985).
18 Preface, *A Review of Vocational Qualifications in England and Wales*, (Chairman, H.G. De Ville), MSC and DES, (1986).
19 *Working Together – Education and Training*, Cmnd 9823, London: HMSO, (1986), para 5.33.
20 D. Turner, 'Education in the USA', in B. Holmes, op. cit., p. 115.
21 H.L. Smith (1986) 'Overeducation and underemployment: an agnostic view', *Sociology of Education*, vol. 59, April 1986, p. 97.
22 W. Norton Grubb (1985) 'The convergence of educational systems and the role of vocationalism', *Comparative Education Review*, vol. 29, no. 4, Nov. 1985, p. 546.
23 Ibid., p. 527.
24 Ibid., p. 531.
25 D. Nasaw, 'Schooled to order', op. cit., p. 209.
26 Introduction, *Soviet Education*, vol. XIX, 1978.
27 W. Norton Grubb, op. cit., p. 546.
28 N. Ottenburg (1978) 'Changes in the occupational structure of the workforce and training requirements', *Soviet Education*, vol. XX, 1978, p. 67.
29 Translated in *Soviet Education*, vol. XIX, 1977.
30 *Soviet Education Study Bulletin* (1984) published by UK Study Group on Soviet Education, vol. 2, no. 1, Spring 1984, pp. 1–4.
31 Ibid., vol. 5, no. 1, Spring 1987, pp. 1–8.
32 I. Jamieson (1985) 'Corporate hegemony or pedagogic liberation', in R. Dale (ed.), *Education, Employment and Training*, Oxford: Pergamon, p. 34.
33 De Ville Report, op. cit., p. 37.

34 C.J. Hurn (1983) 'The vocationalism of American education', *European Journal of Education*, vol. 18, no. 1, p. 47.
35 Ibid., p. 52.
36 Ibid., p. 55.
37 *Competence and Competition* (1984) NEDC and MSC, p. 38.
38 C. Baudelot and R. Establet (1979) *L'Ecole Primaire Divisé*, Paris: Maspero.
39 E. Halsall (1973) *The Comprehensive School*, Oxford: Pergamon, p. 45.
40 J. Waidley (1981) Course Document used by the Guidance and Counselling Department of Eastern Michigan University.
41 'Guidance' in the *America Encyclopedia of Education*, (1971) p. 242.
42 J.E. Rosenbaum (1980) 'Track misperceptions and frustrated college plans', *Sociology of Education*, vol. 53, no. 2, p. 74.
43 R.A. Mickelson (1980) 'The secondary school's role in social stratification', *Journal of Education*, vol. 162, no. 4, Fall, 1980, p. 27.
44 Burton R. Clark (1960) *The Open Door College*, New York: McGraw-Hill, p. 164.
45 Ibid., pp. 71–6.
46 M. Matthews (1982) *Education in the Soviet Union*, London: George Allen & Unwin, pp. 57–8.
47 'The sociological problems of vocational education', *Soviet Education*, October 1984, pp. 34–5.
48 A. Marinick (1977) 'Labour training', *Soviet Education*, vol. XIX.
49 G. Avis (1983) 'Access to higher education in the Soviet Union', in J.J. Tomiak, *Soviet Education in the 1980's*, Beckenham: Croom Helm, p. 207.
50 P.J. Rooney (1986) 'Recent developments in vocational guidance in the USSR', M. Soc. Sc. Thesis, Digest in *Soviet Education Study Bulletin*, vol. 4, no. 1, 1986.
51 J. Price (1986) 'The young say "nyet" to factory jobs', *TES*, 21 March 1986.
52 P. Broadfoot (1984) 'From Public Examinations to Profile Assessment: The French Experience', in P. Broadfoot (ed.) *Selection, Certification, and Control*, Lewis: Falmer Press, p. 204.
53 Ibid., p. 205.
54 Ibid., p. 207.
55 Ibid., p. 207.
56 Ibid., p. 206.
57 Inge Bates (1985) *Schooling for the Dole*, London: MacMillan, p. 175.
58 D.E. Saper (1953) 'A theory of vocational development', *American Psychologist*, vol. 8, no. 4, 1953, quoted by Bates, op. cit., p. 178.

59 A.G. Watts and B. Law, 'Research needs in pastoral care – the vocational aspects', in Lang and Marland, op. cit., p. 143.
60 A.G. Watts (1987) 'Beyond employment? Schools and the future of work', in *BJES*, vol., XXXV, no. 1, Feb., 1987, p. 4.
61 Ibid., pp. 14–15.

Epilogue

1 D. Reynolds, M. Sullivan, and S. Murgatroyd (1987) *The Comprehensive Experiment*, Lewes: Falmer Press.
2 *Daily Mail*, 1 May 1987, article by R. Honeyford.
3 D. Reynolds in the *Guardian*, 12 May 1987.
4 *15 to 18*, The Crowther Report, vol. 2, (1960), London: HMSO. See sets of figures, pp. 118–25.
5 H. Braverman, op cit., p. 329.
6 See Ivan Berg, 'The great training robbery', op. cit.
7 T. Burns and G.M. Stalker (1966) *The Management of Innovation*, London: Tavistock, p. 122.
8 Ibid., introduction, p. xxii.

Name Index

Abercrombie, N. 114
Adams, F. 47
Albert, F. 80, 81
Anweiller, O. 54, 93–4, 96
Ardagh, J. 119
Arkwright, R. 7, 13
Aron, R. 162
Avis, G. 160, 197

Babbage, C. 113
Barlow, Lord 123
Barnard, H. 38
Barnett, C. 23, 100
Barraclough, G. 62, 68
Bates, I. 201
Bates, J. 41
Baudelot, C. 162–3, 171, 190
Bell, D. 99, 100, 111
Bennett, G. 64
Bennett, N. 70
Bérard, L. 80
Bergson, A. 99
Bessemer, Sir H. 31, 32
Beullac, C. 198
Bilton, T. 10, 16
Binet, A. 87
Black, C.E. 115
Blau, P.M. 22
Blum, L. 82
Bourdieu, P. 90, 110, 162, 166–8, 192
Boutary, E. 78
Bowles, S. 25, 88, 90, 116, 161, 192
Braverman, H. 15–16, 18, 21, 72, 113, 114–15, 209, 211
Brezhnev, L. 121
Brigham, C. 88
Broadfoot, P. 199–200
Brooke, N. 174
Bryce, Lord 41
Buddle, John 13
Buisson, F. 46, 50
Burns, T. 211
Burt, Sir C. 77
Butler, R.A. 77, 122

Callaghan, J. 187
Capelle, J. 139
Caron, F. 104
Carr-Saunders, A.M. 66
Cartwright, E. 13
Castex, T. 174
Chanan, G. 170
Churchill, W.S. 123
Clarendon, Lord 24–5, 40
Clark, B.R. 86, 193
Clark, C. 67

Conant, J.B. 131
Corfield, P.J. 14–15, 36
Cort, H. 13, 31
Cremieux-Brilhac, J.J. 127
Crompton, S. 13
Crowther, Lord *see subject index*

Dahl, R. 22
Davies, K. 22, 63, 192
Davy, Sir H. 13
De Gaulle, C. 126, 127, 138–9
De Ville, Lord 178, 187
de Witt, N. 130
Desrosières, 104
Devonshire, Lord 41
Dewdny, J.C. 106
Dewey, J. 51, 91
Dore, R. 174
Douglas, J.W.B. 171
Dresch, S.T. 179
Drucker, P. 124
Du Bois, W.E. 50
Duncan, O.D. 22
Dunning, J. 65
Dupeux, G. 32, 37
Durkheim, E. 35

Eaglesham, E.J.R. 73
Eisenhower, D. 119
Engels, F. 11, 91
Establet, R. 171, 190
Etzioni-Halévy, E. 31, 115
'Eusebius' 164

Farley, M. 177
Ferry, J. 38
Fitzpatrick, S. 96
Fontanet, J. 140
Fouchet, C. 139, 140, 141
Freeman Butts, R. 47–8

Galliéni, J.S. 98
Galton, M. 170
Gambetta, L.M. 46
Gardner, L. 126
Giddens, A. 20
Gilchrist, L. 170
Gintis, H. 88, 90, 116, 161, 192
Giroux, H. 167
Glass, D. 125
Goldthorpe, J.H. 17, 18, 110, 116, 165
Good, H.G. 84
Gorbachov, M. 121
Gregory, P.R. 69–70, 107
Grossmith, G. and W. 37
Guizot, F.P.G. 26
Gumbert, E.B. 87

Habbakuk, H.J. 28, 31, 33
Haby, R. 140, 199
Hadow, Sir W.H. 76–7, 79, 122, 126
Hall, A.R. 33
Halls, W.D. 143
Halsall, E. 190
Halsey, A.H. 92, 126, 163–4
Hans, N. 7, 54
Hargreaves, A. 173
Harris, W.T. 50
Heath, A.F. 163
Heilbroner, R.L. 64
Herriot, E. 79, 82
Herzlick, G. 200
Hobsbawm, E.J. 9, 14
Hoffman, S. 84
Hoggart, R. 101
Holmyard, E.J. 33
Holt, J. 170
Hurn, C. 188, 190
Huxley, J.S. 41

Ignatiev, N.P. 57, 90, 92

Jacobsen, L. 170
Join-Lambert, C. 170

Kahn, H. 99
Karabel, J. 162
Katz, M.B. 48
Kay-Shuttleworth, Sir J. 24, 39, 164
Kemp, T. 34
Khachaturov, T.S. 69, 105, 108
Krauze, T. 162
Kruschev, N. 106, 116, 120, 128–9, 130, 131, 145–7, 195
Kumar, K. 11, 14, 35, 36, 67, 99, 112–13
Kuznetzov, V.M. 196

Lamoureux, L. 81
Lane, D. 112
Langevin *see* subject index
Laski, H.J. 92
Law, B. 203
Lenin, V.I. 72, 120, 195
Liepmann, K. 124
Littlejohn, G. 112, 144
Llewellyn, C. 110
Lloyd-George, D. 75
Locke, J. 8
Lovett, W. 38
Lowe, R. 37, 40

McGuffy, W.H. 48
Maclure, J.S. 123
Malenkov, G.M. 120
Marceau, J. 112, 162, 165–6
Marinick, A. 196
Marsh, D.C. 66, 68
Marwick, A. 118, 119
Marx, K.: and Marxism 4, 16; on class 12, 17–18, 20, 21–2, 35, 113; on division of labour 11, 12, 15; Marxist ideology 71–2, 91, 195; on polytechnics 92; on USA 22
Matthews, M. 146, 147, 160, 194
Meissner, B. 54, 70–1, 113
Mickelson, R.A. 192
Monnet, J. 119
Moore, W. 22, 63, 192
Morant, R. 41, 73–6
Mosca, G. 22
Musson, A.E. 7

Napoleon 26, 28, 53
Napoleon III 31
Nasaw, D. 182
Natanson, J. 128, 129, 153
Neill, A.S. 170
Nelson, D. 32
Newcastle, Lord 24, 25
Norton-Grubb, W. 181–2, 184, 188, 189
Norwood *see subject index*
Nuffield, Lord 172

O'Connor, F. 37
O'Dell, F. 112
Oxenham, J. 174

Pareto, V. 22
Parkhurst, H. 91
Parkin, F. 20
Parsons, F. 191–2
Passeron, J.C. 90, 110, 162, 167–8, 192
Payne, C. 110
Pidgeon, D.A. 126
Playfair, Baron L. 41
Poincaré, J.H. 82
Pollard, S. 103
Pompidou, G. 140
Postan, M.M. 99
Postman, N. 170
Price, J. 197

Prokofiev, M.A. 184–5
Prost, A. 38, 45, 128, 129, 153

Reynolds, D. 206–8
Richmond, W.K. 131
Rickover, Admiral 130–1
Ridge, J.M. 163
Rippa, S.A. 89
Robbins, Lord 141–2
Robertson, R.M. 103, 108
Robinson, E. 7
Rogers, C. 191
Rooney, P. 197
Roosevelt, F.D. 119
Rosenbaum, J.E. 192
Rosenthal, R. 170
Rousseau, J. -J. 149
Rubinstein, D. 125
Runkle, J.D. 50

Shipman, M. 31
Shonfield, A. 124
Siemens, Sir W. 31
Silberman, C. 170
Simon, B. 125, 135
Simon, T. 87
Singer, C. 33
Singer, I.M. 29, 32
Slomczynski, K.M. 162
Smiles, S. 22
Smith, A. 11–12, 15, 32
Sorokin, P.A. 18
Spencer, H. 35
Spens *see subject index*
Spring, J.H. 87
Stalin, J. 68, 70–2, 95, 96, 120–1, 129, 130, 144, 147, 194
Stinchcombe, A.L. 111–12, 115
Stolypin, P. 30
Strumilin, S.G. 130
Stuart, R.C. 69–70
Surer, P. 174

Taft, W.H. 119
Talbot, J.E. 79, 80, 84
Tardieu, A. 82
Taunton, Lord 25, 40
Tawney, R.H. 76, 79
Taylor, F.W. 21, 65, 72, 113
Taylor, William 124
Teller, J.D. 84
Terman, L. 87, 88
Thatcher, M. 136, 186
Thomas, C. 65
Tolstoy, Count D.A. 91
Tomlinson, G. 122
Truman, H.S. 119
Tufnell, E.C. 39
Turner, D. 178
Turner, R. 86, 132–3, 149, 207

Urry, J. 114

Veblen, T. 34

Wallon *see* Langevin-Wallon *in subject index*
Watt, J. 13
Watts, A.G. 203–4
Webb, B. 91
Webb, S. 42, 73, 91
Weber, M. 16–20, 36, 116–17
Weingartner, C. 170
Whitney, E. 32
Whitworth, Sir J. 32
Wilkinson, E. 122
Williams, T.L. 33
Willis, P. 167
Wilson, H. 136
Witte, S. 30

Yanowitch, M. 159–60
Yarrington, R. 194
Yates, A. 126

Zay, J. 80, 81, 82–3, 84, 126, 133, 198
Zhiltsov, E.N. 196
Zoretti, L. 79
Zuckerman, Lord 123

Subject index

academies 8, 46, 48–9
accumulation, capital 12, 15, 17; *see also* consumer goods
administration: in advanced industrial society 109, 112; in nineteenth century 34–5, 36, 54–5; in twentieth century 64, 65, 66
advanced education *see* tertiary education
advanced industrial societies 98–121; education for 122–53; *see also* Britain; France; industrialization; Russia; United States
Advisory Council for Scientific Policy (Britain) 123
agriculture 112; decline 36, 70; reform 70, 101, 106, 120
air transport 98,100
Algiers Plan (France) 126
American system of manufacturing (ASM-USA) 32, 63
apparatchiki (Russia) 71
apprenticeship schools 45, 94, 140, 143, 147, 152, 163
art in schools 8, 9, 39, 42
Association Polytechnique (France) 45
atomic bomb 98–9
Attestat Zrelosti (Russia) 96
Austria 112
authority: rejected by pupils 167–8, 171, 193; *see also* teachers

Bablake school (Britain) 41, 74
baccalaureat (France) 43, 44, 78, 138, 140–1, 143, 151–2, 171, 174, 183, 184; *see also* examinations
Barlow Report (1946 – Britain) 123
Berthoin Bill (1955 – France) 138–9
Bessemer process 31, 32
Beverly elementary school (USA) 48
Billères Bill (1957 – France) 138
Binet–Simon test 87
Blacks in USA 47, 50, 90, 119
Boston high school (USA) 48
Boullocke Commission (France) 139
Britain 206–7, 208; as advanced industrial society

99–106, 108–9, 111–12, 115, 118; (education for 122–6, 131–7, 140–3, 149, 150, 151, 153); education and society in nineteenth century 24–5, 27–9; industrialization and social change 4, 7–8, 10–15, 19, 22, 23; selection in 163–4, 165, 167–8; (beginning of 30–43 *passim*, 50–3; by differentiation 63–8 *passim*, 73–8; legitimation of 169–75 *passim*, 177–91 *passim*, 201–3)
Bryce Report (1895 – Britain) 41

California Master Plan (USA) 182–3
Cambridge 53
capital: accumulation 12, 15, 17; cultural 167
capitalism 10–12, 15–16, 34; *see also* industrialization
careers advice *see* guidance in schools
Carnegie Corporation 131
cars *see* motor vehicles; transport
central schools (Britain) 134
certificates *see* examinations
charity schools 8
Chartism 24, 37
chemicals industry 33, 66, 102–3, 106–7
Chenot Commission (France) 139
City and Guilds of London 42
civil rights (USA) 119
civil service *see* administration
Civil War (USA) 25
class 126, 128; in advanced industrial society 110, 117–18; and education *see* elementary schools; in nineteenth century 12–17 *passim*, 20, 22, 35, 37, 55, 116; and teachers' perceptions of pupils 170–1, 193; in twentieth century 62–3, 68, 70–2, 75, 77, 78, 84, 85, 93–5, 157–68 *passim*; *see also* 'intermediate'; middle class; working class
'*classes nouvelles*' (France) 138
classical curriculum 40, 43, 48, 56, 80
clerical work *see* administration
coal industry 32, 33, 54, 70, 100, 102
Code of 1904 (France) 73
cold war 100
'collective' power 20–1
collège unique (France) 198–9
colleges *see* tertiary education
Colleges of Advanced Technology (Britain) 142
collèges d'enseignement (France) 128, 139, 143, 149, 198
colleges of further education (Britain) 148, 152, 183
Colt revolver 29
commercial education 74
Commission for Reorganization of Secondary Education Report (1918 – USA) 85
Committee of Ten (USA) 85, 89

common schools (USA) 47
communications 98; *see also* transport
Communist Party (Russia) 69, 70, 72, 128–9
community colleges (USA) 132, 148, 152, 161–2, 179, 183, 189, 193–4
compagnons de l'université nouvelle (France) 79–80, 81, 198
complexity of economy *see* advanced industrial societies
comprehensive education 38, 134–41 *passim*, 144, 149–51, 206–8; *see also* high schools (USA)
computers 109, 113–14, 209–11
concentration of production 107–9
Confédération Generale du Travail (France) 37, 80
confessional schools *see* religion
conglomerates 109
conseil see guidance in schools
Conservative Party (Britain) 135, 136, 163
consumer goods: acquisition of 17, 19, 22, 36, 54, 67, 68, 106, 117; mass-produced 31, 32, 33, 63, 67; *see also* life style
control *see* power
Cort process 13, 31
cotton *see* textiles
Council for National Academic Awards (Britain) 142
counselling *see* guidance
cours complementaires (France) 83, 126, 139
credentialism *see* examinations
credits (USA) 84
Crimean War 53–4
Crowther Report (1959 – Britain) 124–5, 135, 142, 207
CSE *see* examinations
cultural capital 167
curriculum *see* art; classical; modern; science
cycle d'observation (France) 139, 198

Dalton Plan 91
denominational schools *see* religion
deprivation *see* poor
de-skilling 113–15, 210
Deville Report (1986 – France) 178, 187
Devonshire Commission (1870–75, Britain) 41
differentiation, selection by 61–97
division of labour 64, 208–11; alternatives to 210–11; in nineteenth century 11–12, 15–16, 21, 34, 35
divorce 130
dritte personen see 'intermediate strata'
Dumas (Russia) 55

école maternelle (France) 137
école moyenne (France) 138
école polytechnique (France) 143
école pratique (France) 45, 82–3
école primaire supérieure (France) 82

école unique (France) 79–80, 81, 133
écoles, grandes (France) 142–3, 152, 163
economic function of schools 8; *see also* selection
economy: complex *see* advanced industrial; of scale 107–9; *see also* industrialization
education 23; in advanced industrial society 112, 115–18, 121, 122–53; and selection, beginning of 37–57; and society in nineteenth century 24–9; in twentieth century 72–86; *see also* comprehensive; primary; secondary; selection; teachers; tertiary education
Education Acts (Britain): (1870) 37; (1902) 73, 133; (1918) Fisher Act 75; (1944) 77, 122, 133–4
Educational Provisions Act (1907) (Britain) 52, 73, 74
egalitarianism *see* comprehensive education
electricity 65, 102, 103
Electrotechnical Institute (Russia) 56
elementary schools 126, 129; in nineteenth century 8, 9, 38–48 *passim*, 55–6, 164; in twentieth century 73, 74, 76, 78, 79, 81; *see also* primary schools
élites *see* ruling classes
Employment and Training Act (1973) (Britain) 185
endowed schools (Britain) 8, 41, 42
energy production and consumption 101–3, 106–7, 115
engineering 33–4, 65, 66, 104–5, 113
equality of access and opportunity, theoretical 159, 164; *see also* social mobility
equivalents (USA) 84
eugenics 88
evening classes 45, 74, 92
examinations/testing/certification 123, 126, 138–43, 150–2; in nineteenth century 43, 44, 53; in twentieth century 87–8, 89, 90, 96, 158, 161, 167; *see also* selection, legitimation

factory schools 45, 94, 147
family 130
France 206–7, 208; as advanced industrial society 99–100, 102–6 *passim*, 108–9, 111–12, 115, 118–19; (education for 126–8, 131–3, 137–43, 149–50, 151, 153); education and society in nineteenth century 26, 27, 28; industrialization and social change 1, 2, 7, 22; selection in 157, 162–8 *passim*; (beginning of 30–46 *passim*, 53; by differentiation 63–4, 68, 78–84; legitimation of 169–76 *passim*, 180–4 *passim*, 190, 198–201)
franchise, expansion of 37, 118
further education *see* tertiary

gas, natural 102, 103, 106–7
GCE/GCSE *see* examinations
Germany 7, 28, 29, 42, 50, 207–8
Ghana 174
Gilchrist–Thomas process 31
government: involvement 99, 101, 158; *see also* Five Year Plans; political service, employment in 35, 71, 111
grammar schools (Britain) 206; in nineteenth century 39, 41; in twentieth century 74, 75, 76, 77, 122, 123, 125–6, 133, 135, 140
grandes écoles (France) 142–3, 152, 163
Great Exhibition (1851 – Britain) 28–9
guidance in schools 53, 88–9, 210; and legitimation of selection 173, 181–203, 204
gymnasia (Russia) 56, 93

Hadow Report (1926 – Britain) 76–7, 79, 122, 126
Handbook of Suggestions (Britain) 73
Henry VIII School (Britain) 41
high schools (USA) 46, 48–9, 85, 86–7, 90, 131, 132, 178–9, 188
higher education *see* tertiary
higher grade schools (Britain) 39, 41, 74, 134
honour, concept of 17
housing 109–10
hydro-electric power 102

ideologies, political 22, 100, 129–30
illiteracy (USA) 131
immigrants (USA) 9
Industrial Training Act (1964) (Britain) 185
industrialization 208–11; and social change 7–23, 165; in twentieth century (1900–45) 64–70, 78, 84, 123, 127, 137, 144, 153; *see also* advanced industrial societies; chemicals; coal; energy; engineering; iron; motor vehicle; primary; tertiary; transport
industry, schools of (Britain) 8
inspectors, school (Britain) 123
Institute for Advancement of Technical Education (Britain) 42
Instituts Universitaires de Technologie (France) 143, 152
intelligence testing 126, 161
'intermediate strata' concept 17–18, 19, 35, 54, 71–2, 95; *see also* middle class
Invano–Frankovo school (Russia) 197
iron and steel industry: in nineteenth century 13, 31–4 *passim*, 54; in twentieth century (1900–45) 66, 70; in advanced industrial society 100, 101, 103–4
Italy 112

Japan 7, 105, 174, 207
Job Training Partnership Act (1982) (Britain) 190
junior colleges (USA) 86–7
junior high schools (USA) 86–7, 132, 150
junior technical schools (Britain) 75, 134
Juvenile Employment Service (Britain) 201

Kharkov Technological Institute (Russia) 56
komsomol (Russia) 93–5

labour *see* division of labour; occupations; unions
Labour Reserve Schools (Russia) 96
Labour Exchanges Act (Britain) 201
Labour Party (Britain) 118, 122, 134, 135–6, 163
Lancasterianism 47
Landucci Report (1956 – France) 127
Langevin–Wallon Report (1947 – France) 82, 126, 133, 137, 140, 198
large-scale production 34, 107–9
Le Havre apprenticeship school (France) 45
legitimation of selection 169–205; credentialism 171–80, 187, 191, 202; guidance and vocationalism 173, 181–203, 204; teachers' influence on child's self-concept 169–71, 175, 180, 190, 201, 203–4
Leicestershire Plan (Britain) 135, 137
life styles 16–17, 19–20, 67–8, 127; in advanced industrial society 99, 106, 109–10, 117; *see also* consumer goods
Lille group (France) 80
literacy, universal (Russia) 93
London Technical Education Board 42
Lunar Society 7
lycées (France) 43, 79–82 *passim*, 126–8, 140, 163, 174, 183–4

McCormick reaper 28
machines *see* engineering; motor; technological
Manpower Services Commission (Britain) 181, 185–6
market: capacity concept 16; *see also* consumer goods
Marxism *see* Marx *in name index*
mass production 31, 32, 33, 63, 67; *see also* consumer goods
Massachusetts Institute of Technology (USA) 50
medicine 98
mergers 107–9
metal-working industries 34, 66, 103–4; *see also* iron and steel
Mexico 174
middle class: in nineteenth century 15, 21, 35–6, 37, 44, 193; in twentieth century 68, 71, 84, 161, 163; *see also* class; 'intermediate strata'
middle schools (France) 138, 150
mining 13, 31, 33, 54; *see also* coal
modern school subjects introduced 8, 9, 40–4, 46, 80–2
Mondragon co-operative 211
monopoly 108
moral development aim of education 8; *see also* religion
motor vehicles 63–5, 70, 102, 105–6, 108; *see also* transport

narkompros (Russia) 94–5
National Association of Manufacturers (Britain) 50
National Defense Act (1958) (USA) 131
National Education Association (Britain) 51
National Education Association (USA) 191
National Employment Pact (France) 181
National Institute of Demographic Studies (France) 128
National Office for Information and Orientation (France) 200
National Society for Promotion of Industrial Education (Britain) 50–1
National Union of Teachers (Britain) 74
nationalization of industries 101
natural gas 102, 103, 106–7
New Economic Policy (NEP – Russia) 69, 70–1, 93, 120, 194
Newcastle Commission (1861 – Britain) 24, 25
Norwood Report (1943 – Britain) 76–7, 79, 124, 135
Nuffield science 172

occupations 51–2, 157; changing 66–7, 71–2, 78, 93, 101, 110, 116–17; professional increased 66, 111–12; and status 18–19, 21, 23
office work *see* administration
oil industry 67, 102, 106–7
oligopoly 108
Organic Statute (France) 80, 82
orientation 200
output increased *see* advanced industrial society
owners of means of production *see* ruling
Oxford 53

parental choice *see* selection, beginning of
parochial schools (USA) 85
peasant youth schools (Russia) 94
penicillin 98
Permanent Committee on Scientific Research (France) 127
political ideologies and systems 22, 30, 69, 70, 72, 100, 118–20, 122, 126, 128–30, 134–6, 163
polytechnics 42, 45, 92, 95–6, 174, 182, 195; in twentieth century 142–3, 144, 146; *see also* tertiary education
poor people 8; *see also* exploitation; working class
Popular Front (France) 82–3, 119
population loss (Russia) 129
populism 119
power: and class 20–1, 22, 37, 62, 157–8; industrial 107–9; *see also* energy
practical schools *see écoles pratiques;* technical and vocational education
prestige *see* status
primary industries 67, 111–12; *see also*

agriculture; industrialization; mining
primary schools: in nineteenth century 38, 39, 40, 44, 52, 57; in twentieth century: 1900–45 75, 76, 81–2, 83, 86, 87, 92–3, 95; from 1945 126, 128, 132, 133, 137, 139, 143, 149; *see also* elementary
private schools (Britain) *see* public schools
private schools (USA) 47, 48, 85, 168, 180, 189
productivity increased *see* advanced industrial society
professional schools (France) 45
professions, increased numbers of 66, 111–12; *see also* occupations
profiling 173
profit motive 10
progressive education (Russia) 90–1
proletariat *see* working class
property 16, 68
property-owning class *see* ruling
proprietary schools (Britain) 8
PTU *see uchilishcha*
public schools (Britain) 8, 41, 74, 75, 163, 168
pupil–teacher relationships *see* teachers

qualifications *see* examinations

racism *see* Blacks
radar 98, 100
radio 98
railways *see under* transport
Reform Act (1867) (Britain) 37
reformed schools (Britain) 8
religion and education 8, 56, 78, 79–80, 168
retail trade 33, 36
Revolutions (Russia) 55, 97
Robbins Committee (1963 – Britain) 141–2
rockets 98
Royal Society of Arts (Britain) 39, 42
Rueff-Armand Commission (France) 139
Rugby School (Britain) 41, 75
ruling/property-owning classes 71; in nineteenth century 15, 18, 20, 23, 44, 54, 55; *see also* class
Russia (later Soviet Union) 206–7, 208, 211; as advanced industrial society 99–107 *passim*, 110–13 *passim*, 115–16, 118, 120–1; (education for 123, 128–30, 131, 144–8, 150–1, 152); education and society in nineteenth century 26–7, 28–9; industrialization and social change 1, 2, 7, 22; selection in 157, 159–61, 168; (beginning of 30, 53–7; by differentiation 61, 63, 65, 68–73, 90–7; legitimation of 169–75 *passim*, 178, 180–5 *passim*, 190, 194–8)

SAT (USA) 53
School Curriculum Industry Project (Britain) 187, 203
School of Engineering (Russia) 56

school–industry liaison officers (SILOs – Britain) 187
science: in advanced industrial society 98–9, 109; in schools 8, 9, 39, 40, 42, 43, 91; *see also* technical; technological
'scientific management' *see* Taylorism
secondary industry *see* industrialization
secondary modern schools (Britain) 123, 124–5, 135
secondary schools 101; in nineteenth century 39–43 *passim*, 48, 52, 56; in twentieth century: 1900–45 73–87 *passim*, 90, 92–6; 1945–70s 122–53 *passim*; since 1970s 159–68 *passim*; and selection 172–7, 180–5 188–204 *passim*
selection: beginning of 30–57; by differentiation 61–97; educational or social 157–68; *see also* legitimation
self-concept of children *see* teachers, influence
serfdom abolished (Russia) 53, 54
services *see* tertiary industry
shipping 32, 34, 100
shops 33, 36
silicon chip 113
Singer Sewing Machine Factory 32
Smith-Hughes Act (1917) (Britain) 51
socialization of children *see* teachers, influence
society/social 123; change and industrialization 7–23; control 8, 38, 48; division of labour 11, 14, 21, 34, 35, 209; and education in nineteenth century 24–9; mobility 22, 36, 49, 61, 71, 84, 101, 110, 128, 144, 159, 165–6, 168; selection 157–68
socio-economic status *see* status
sonar 98
Soviet Union *see* Russia
space exploration 116, 130–1
Spain 211
Spens Report (1938) (Britain) 76–7, 79, 122, 126, 133
Sri Lanka 174
SSUZ *see technikum*
standard of living *see* life styles
Stanford-Binet scale 87
State Labour Reserve Schools (Russia) 147
status 157–8; in advanced industrial society 110, 114, 115, 117–18; in nineteenth century 15, 16–17, 19–20, 36–7, 116; in twentieth century 62, 64–5, 72, 84, 116; *see also* class, social mobility; teachers
steamships *see* shipping
stocks and shares 33, 109
stores, retail 33, 36
streaming in comprehensive schools 141
strikes 37
suffrage, expansion of 37, 118
Sunday schools (Britain) 8

Sweden 133
synthetics 66, 102–3

Taunton Report (1868 – Britain) 25, 40
Taylorism 21, 72, 113
teachers 167; influence on children 169–71, 175, 180, 190, 201, 203–4; *see also* guidance in schools
Technical Instruction Acts (1889) (Britain) 42
technical and vocational education: for advanced industrial society 173, 181–203, 204; in nineteenth century 41–2, 45, 49, 50, 56–7; in twentieth century: 1900–45 73, 74, 82, 85, 92, 94; 1945–70s 123, 125–6, 134, 140, 143, 145–8, 151–2; since 1970s 159–60, 162; *see also* science; technological
Technical and Vocational Initiative in Education (Britain) 186–7, 203
technikum (Russia) 94, 96, 147, 148, 151, 152, 159, 160, 183, 185
technological change: in advanced industrial society 104, 109, 113–14; in nineteenth century 10, 13–14, 15, 18, 31, 32, 33; in twentieth century (1900–45) 64, 65, 69; *see also* science; technical
telegraph and telephone 33, 98
Tennessee Valley Authority (USA) 102
tertiary education: in advanced industrial society 110, 111–12, 113, 171–2, 177–90 *passim*, 193–6, 198–9, 203; in nineteenth century 39, 42, 44, 45–6, 56; in twentieth century: 1900–45 79, 87, 89, 93, 95, 96; 1945–70s 128, 129, 132, 139, 141–3, 148–9, 152; since 1970s 161–4, 167
tertiary industry 33, 36, 67–8; *see also* administration
testing *see* examinations
textile industry 13, 31, 33, 34, 53, 66, 106
trade schools *see* technical
Trade Union Congress (Britain) 37
trade unions 37, 50, 53, 74, 93
transport 64, 68; in advanced industrial society 98, 100, 101, 102, 105–6, 111; railways 31–2, 33, 53–4, 102; shipping 32, 34, 100; *see also* motor vehicles
tripartite systems: return to 206–7; *see also* primary; secondary; tertiary
TVEI *see* Technical and Vocational Initiative

uchilishcha (PTU – Russia) 147, 148, 151, 159, 160, 178, 184–5, 197
underdeveloped countries, credentialism in 174
unemployment, youth 181
unified labour schools (Russia) 92–3
unions 37, 50, 53, 74, 93
United States 206–7, 208; as

advanced industrial society 99–111 *passim*, 114–16, 119; (education for 130–3, 148–53 *passim*); education and society in nineteenth century 25–9 *passim*; industrialization and social change 1, 2, 7–8, 22, 23; selection in 157, 161–2, 168; (beginning of 30–8 *passim*, 42, 46–50, 53; by differentiation 63, 65–6, 68, 70, 84–90; legitimation of 169–74 *passim*, 179–83 *passim*, 188–94, 203)
universities *see* tertiary education
University Grants Committee (Britain) 142, 188
upper classes *see* ruling classes
urban growth 10, 70
USSR *see* Russia
UVZ (Russia) 95, 145, 146, 148, 151, 159, 160, 185

vocationalism *see* guidance in schools; technical

wage labour 10–12
war and revolution 25, 53–5, 97; cold 100; First World 61–2, 64, 65, 75, 77, 78, 98, 123; Second World 99–100, 123, 128
War Communism (Russia) 69, 70
White Papers (Britain): on educational reconstruction (1943) 77, 123–4; on training (1984, 1985, 1986) 178
Winchester School (Britain) 74
work *see* labour; occupations; unions
working class 126; anti-school attitude 167–8, 171, 193; in nineteenth century 10–11, 14, 15, 21, 35, 45–6, 49, 53, 54; (education for 45–6, 49; *see also* elementary); in twentieth century 70–2, 77, 85, 93–5, 159, 163, 166, 167; *see also* class; social mobility
workshop division of labour 11–12, 15, 21, 34, 35, 209

Youth Opportunities Programme (Britain) 185–6, 187
Youth Training Scheme (Britain) 178, 186, 187, 203

zemstros (Russia) 55–6
Zuckermann Report (1955 – Britain) 123